Here & Gone

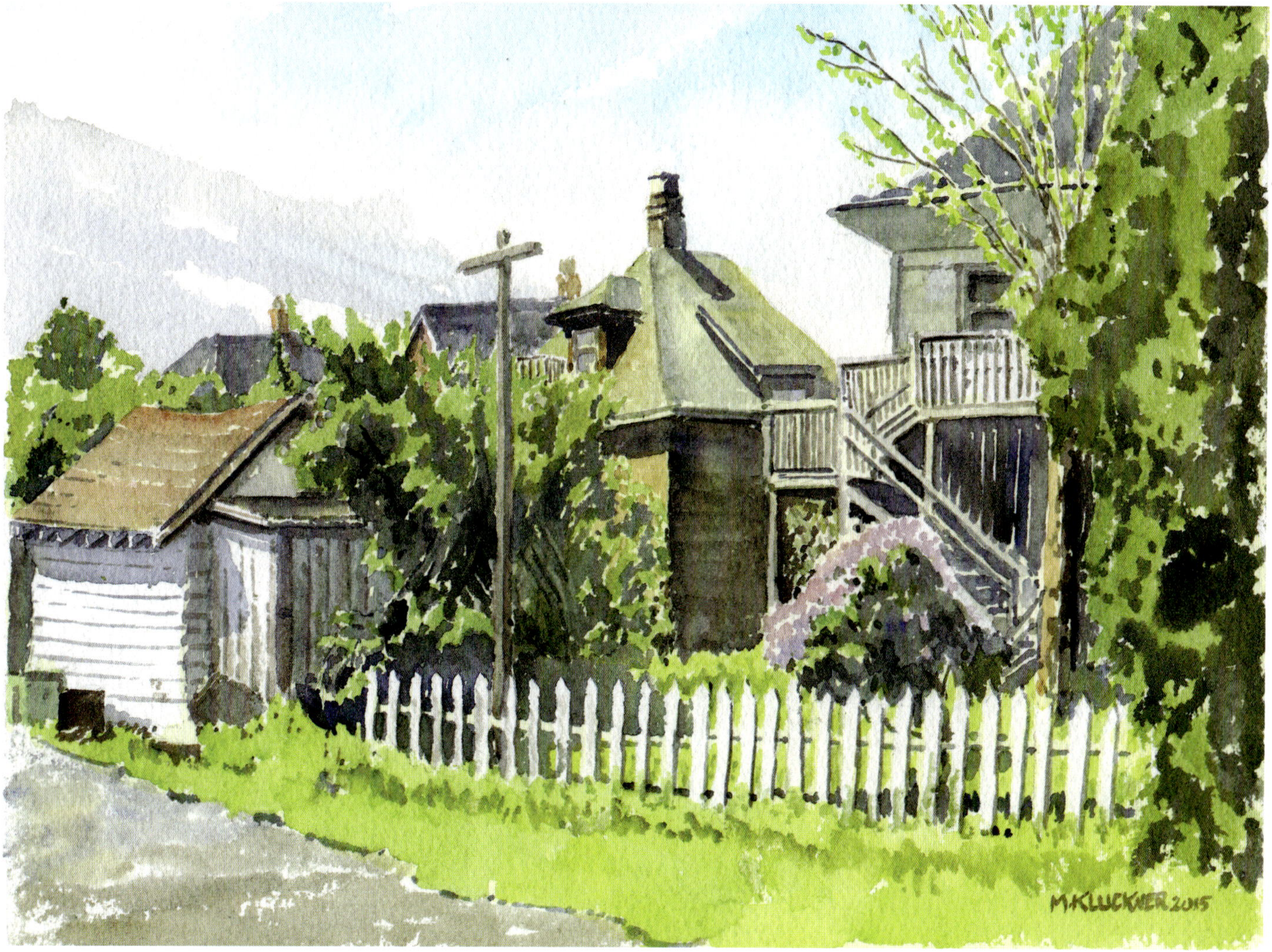

Artwork by Michael Kluckner

Midtown Press

Midtown Press
7375 Granville Street
Vancouver, BC V6P 4Y3
Canada

ISBN 978-1-988242-38-5 (Print)
ISBN 978-1-988242-40-8 (EPUB)
ISBN 978-1-988242-39-2 (PDF)

Legal deposit: 4th quarter 2020
Library and Archives Canada

This book has been typeset in ITC Cheltenham and Avenir Next LT Pro, and printed and bound by H&C Printing Center, China.

Editor: Louis Anctil
Layout: Michael Kluckner
Production: Denis Hunter Design

Library and Archives Canada Cataloguing in Publication

Title: Here & Gone / artwork by Michael Kluckner.
Other titles: Here and Gone
Names: Kluckner, Michael, artist, author.
Identifiers: Canadiana 20200281011 | ISBN 9781988242385 (softcover)

Subjects: LCSH: Kluckner, Michael–Travel. | LCSH: Vancouver (B.C.)–In art. | LCSH: British Columbia–Rural conditions–In art.

Classification: LCC ND249.K5836 A4 2020 | DDC 759.11–dc23

Kluckner, Michael, author, illustrator
Here & Gone / Michael Kluckner

Front cover: A view down the lane north of busy Hastings Street from Templeton Drive toward the glass forest in December 2019.

Back cover: A dude chilling on a park bench, reminiscent of Michael Dennis's "Reclining Figure" public art piece in Mount Pleasant's Guelph Park, which inspired artist Viktor Briestensky to install the famous "Dude Chilling Park" sign there in 2012.

Title page: Overgrown back lanes, low picket fences and tiny garages recall an earlier Vancouver, less crowded and full of "stuff" than the current one. This is the lane between Napier and Parker west of Victoria Drive in Grandview, as it was in 2015.

Here

Shortly before he died, an old friend told me that "if you live long enough, you'll find out you don't belong anywhere."*

He was implying that he had once "belonged" and that society had moved on, leaving him in a roadside ditch with many other seniors – unlike the elders of other cultures who, we are told, are valued for their memories and wisdom.

I look at my own life and ask, did I ever belong? Well, yes. I had a stable upbringing in Kerrisdale, that quintessentially middle-class Vancouver neighbourhood. I chose my parents well. But I always felt, or at least wanted to feel, like an outlier – critic, skeptic, no boss, freelance artist – which certainly has something to do with my coming of age around 1970, a time when being free usually meant being "wilfully poor."

What does that mean? Working just enough to survive in order to leave time to experiment, explore and create – in my case, to teach myself to draw and write. Kindred spirits were musicians, actors and journalists for the alternative press. We ate cheaply and wore old clothes – the whole bohemian thing – and if our jeans were ripped and distressed, it was because we had worn them, and only them, until they began to fall apart.

But you can't be wilfully poor in Vancouver anymore. Like New York City and San Francisco (where I lived in 1974), Vancouver has lost its cheap options. The plight of artists and the disappearance of studio and performance spaces have been much in the news in recent years. The cruel irony, of course, and a defining element of recent urban history, is that people who *choose* to be outliers are now vastly outnumbered by displaced people sleeping in the streets.

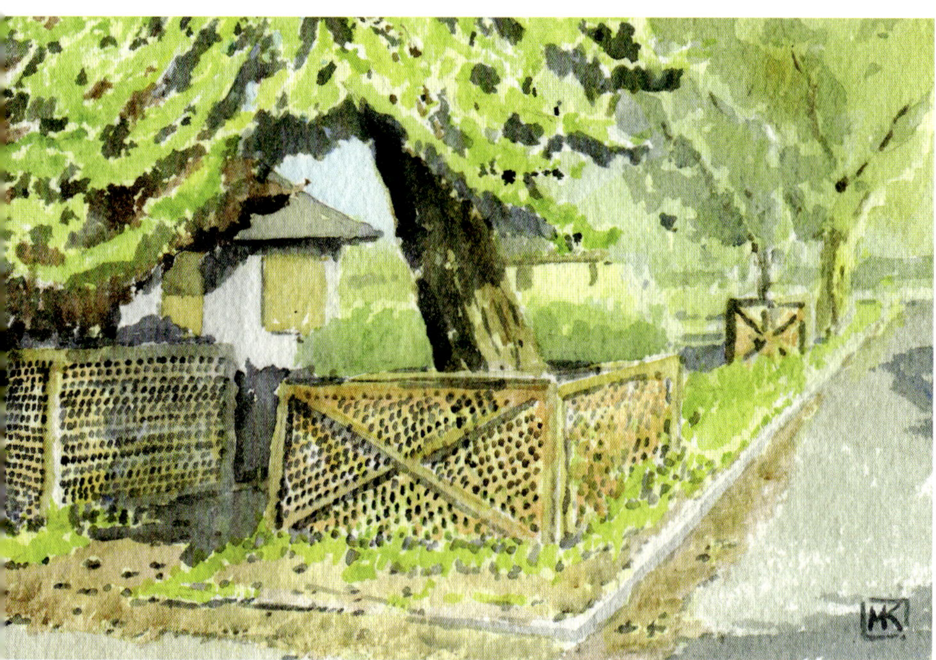

"The Orange Fence of Death" has become a familiar sight on almost every block in Vancouver, intended to protect trees from the carelessness of builders and their machinery as relatively affordable homes are demolished and, in most cases, replaced by costlier ones.

*The friend was Jan Tuytel (1926–2010), the sheep mentor character in my two farm books: *The Pullet Surprise* and *Wise Acres*. I also wrote about him and his wife Dyna in the 2012 edition of *Vanishing Vancouver*, page 178.

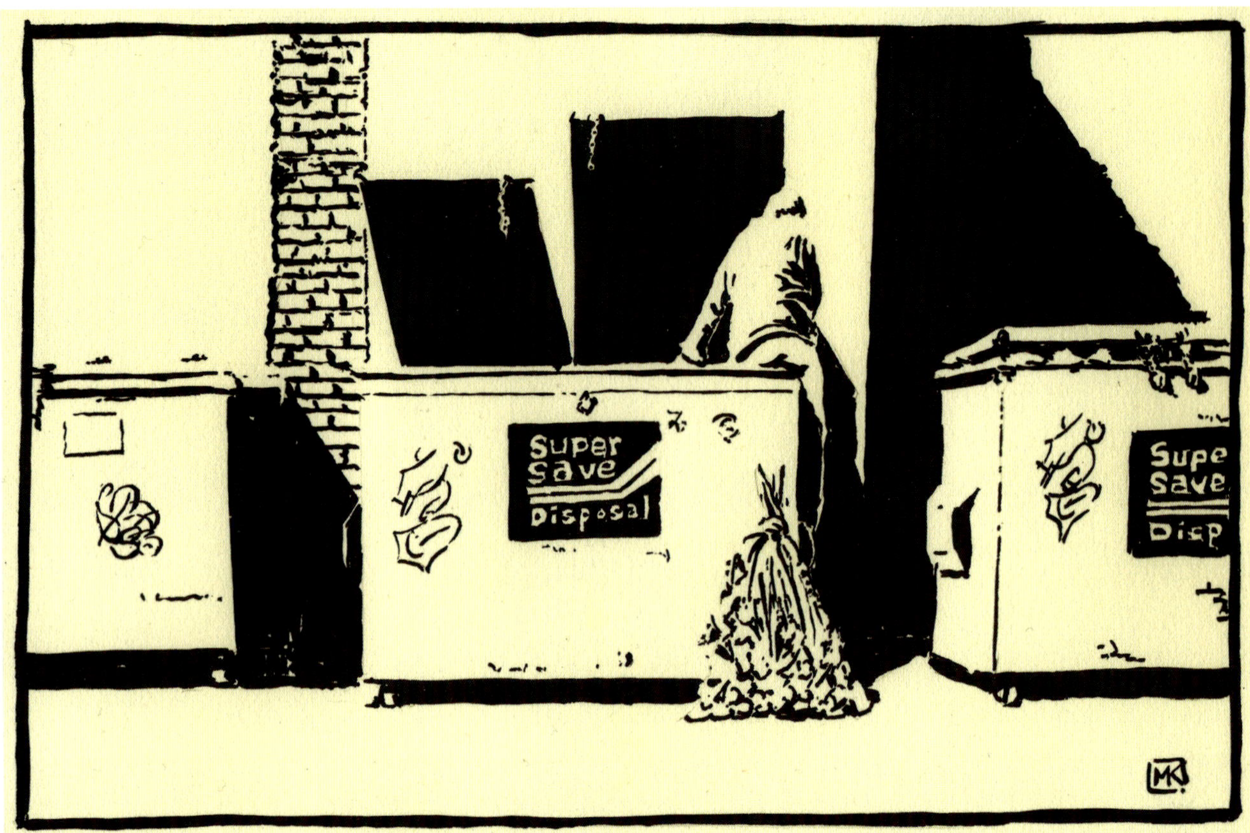

It's almost 40 years since I first began to see homeless people in Vancouver, sleeping under the Georgia Viaduct in that short sharp recession around 1982. A food bank started and has never closed. "Dumpster diver" became part of the local language. Twenty-five years ago, the drug problem exploded, rapidly becoming an epidemic far more lethal than the COVID-19 pandemic and highlighting the increasing divide between the established and the homeless poor, more than 40 percent of whom are Indigenous.

Do I still feel like I belong here? Sure. This book isn't intended as a swan song. Vancouver is still stimulating, home to our friends, with some beautiful neighbourhoods for those who are lucky enough to have settled here.

Why am I still painting and drawing the city after 35 years? I see myself as a witness, certainly not an activist anymore or a serious historian. But as I did with previous books – *Vanishing Vancouver* (1990 and 2012), *Vancouver Remembered* (2006 and 2011), and ones with a wider lens such as *Vanishing British Columbia* (2005) and *British Columbia in Watercolour* (1993) – I am still a moth drawn to a candle flame when I see a place about to disappear.

Reader be warned, though: there is no in-depth analysis in this book – it is not intended to address in any systematic way the issues of affordability, of "making room," of speculation and overseas capital and all of the other preoccupations Vancouver shares with other popular cities. It also doesn't focus on social justice issues, including the ongoing campaign in Vancouver for Indigenous reconciliation. It's just a set of pictures of curious places that were here, however tenuously at the time I came upon them, in which I can see my kind of "Vancouver poetry."

"Here" is here – some of which is now gone – and "Gone," beginning on page 35, is places I have travelled to, strung together loosely around the theme of change or the lack thereof. It begins with abandoned places in rural British Columbia and ends with timeless scenes in Europe and Japan.

— Michael Kluckner, Vancouver, 2020

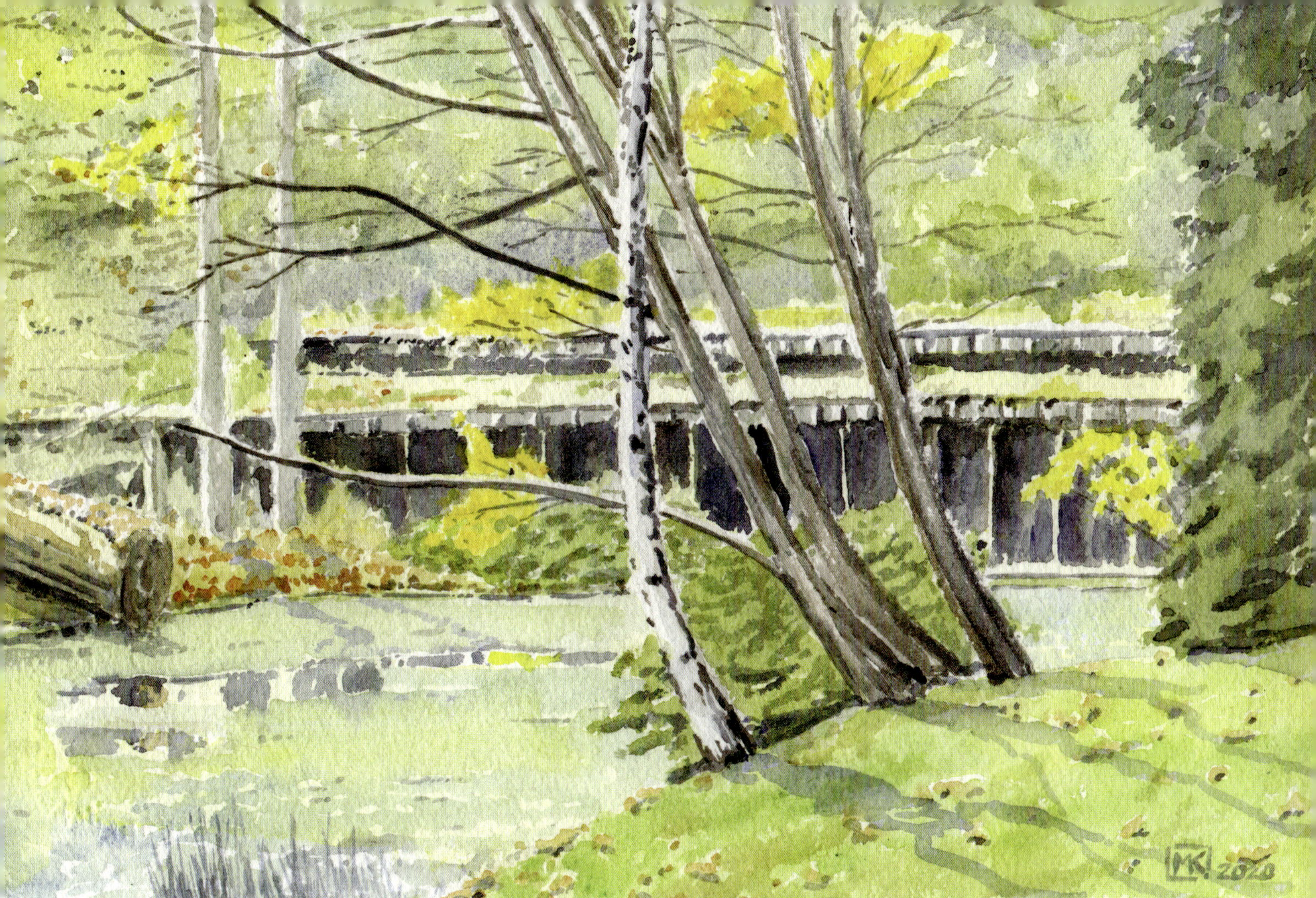

You come upon it like a Mayan temple lost in a jungle. In an untended corner of VanDusen Botanical Garden in Vancouver, on the edge of an algae-choked reflecting pond, a graceful low building emerges from a tangle of overgrown brush, its roof a mess of weeds and grasses long gone to seed.

The building called the Forest Education Centre is a modernist masterpiece lost in the forest. Built in 1976, it was originally known as MacMillan-Bloedel Place, named for its donor, the largest forest company in what was then the largest industry in British Columbia. Its unique educational displays, including a 50-seat theatre, were called "A Walk in the Forest."

Architect Paul Merrick, working then as chief designer for Thompson, Berwick & Přatt, set the pavilion into a small hill on the edge of a lake in the northwest corner of the garden. Its green roof was one of the first in the city, and its unique internal columns used some of the finest wood in BC. The late Henry Hawthorn, an architect and former chair of the VanDusen Botanical Garden Association, described it as "an architecture of abundance."

MacMillan-Bloedel turned the building over to the Park Board's stewardship in 1986. Although used for some years for staff and educational purposes, it was soon neglected, abandoned, and eventually all but forgotten. Clearly, it is in the wrong place – far from the entrance to the Garden, backing onto a residential lane in South Shaughnessy. A covenant negotiated with the owners of its toney neighbour – Shaughnessy Place – limited its use to educational purposes, leaving no possibility of a profitable one such as a wedding pavilion or café. It is now unusable due to mould, its only purpose being the storage of the decorations used each year by the Garden's wintertime Festival of Lights.

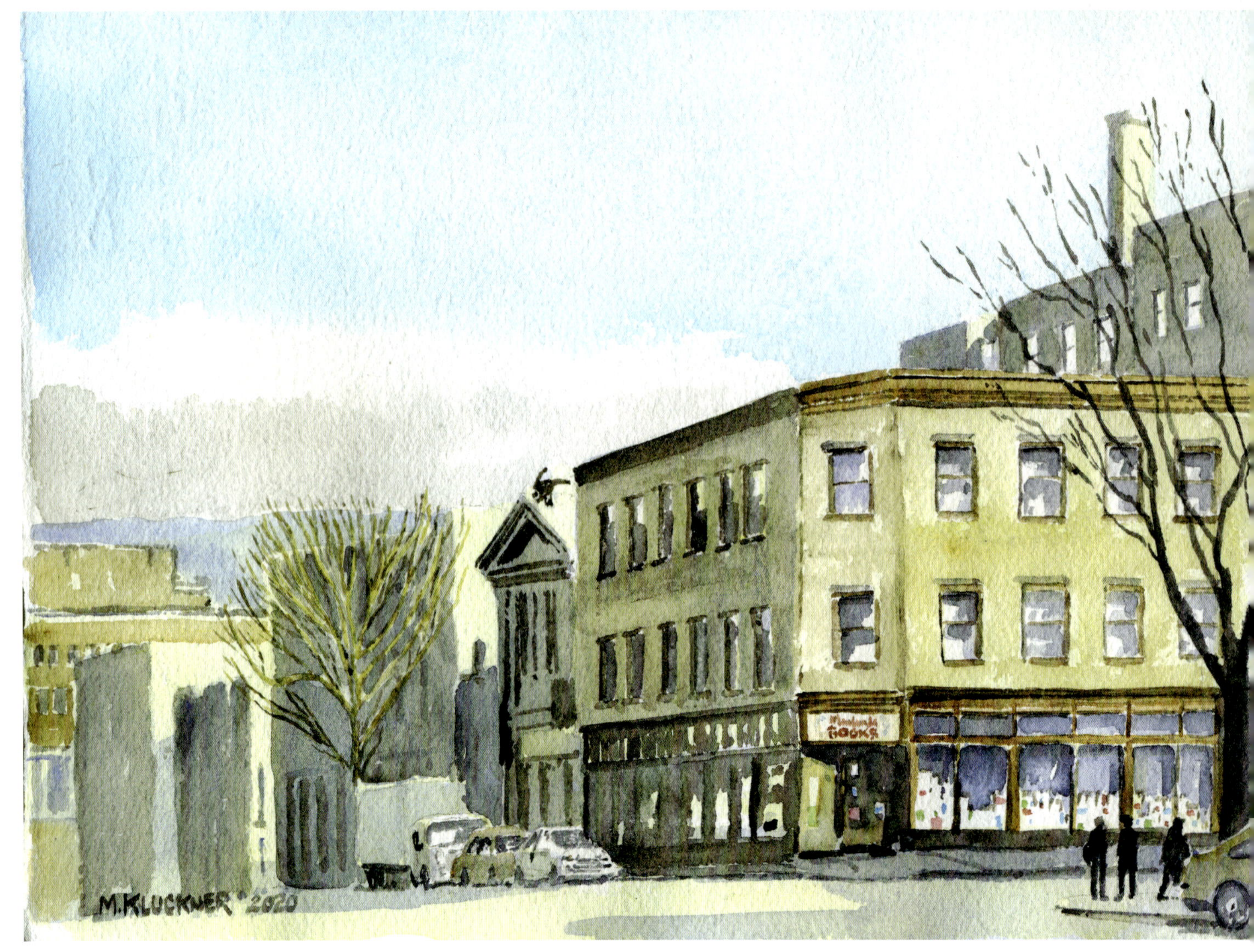

Through 2019 and 2020, shuttered storefronts and For Lease signs became another symptom of a sick city. A villain was quickly identified: the provincial government's assessment system, which used "highest and best use" for the valuation of a piece of land. A property containing, for example, a one-storey building was taxed on what *could* be built, which might be five or ten storeys, and the retail tenant ended up paying it all through triple-net leases. The City bureaucracy, eager to upzone whenever a developer walked through the door, was less eager to downzone streets that had neighbourhood shopping strips of independent businesses in small older buildings. Dunbar and West Point Grey were especially hard hit due to declining populations – satellite families living in large new houses for only a part of the year – and a demographic shift, notably to Asian Canadians who preferred to shop elsewhere, such as in the malls of Richmond. Added to that came the technological shift to online shopping, and a continued move to big-box stores for many whose incomes have stagnated while their expenses soar with the eagles. Add in the COVID-19 pandemic and it was the perfect storm for independent retailers and restaurateurs, taking down even the Cohen family's century-old Army & Navy Department Store chain.

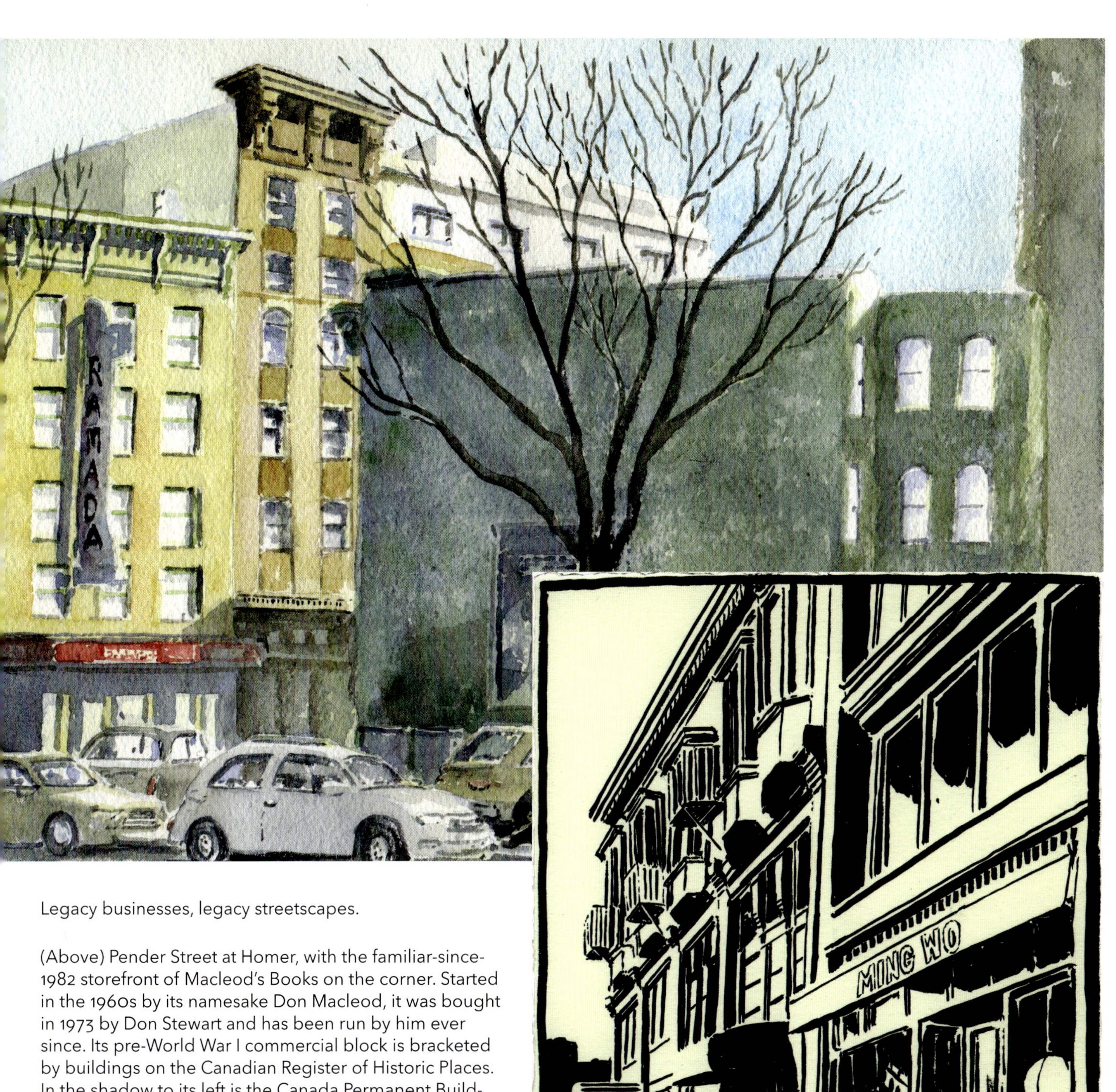

Legacy businesses, legacy streetscapes.

(Above) Pender Street at Homer, with the familiar-since-1982 storefront of Macleod's Books on the corner. Started in the 1960s by its namesake Don Macleod, it was bought in 1973 by Don Stewart and has been run by him ever since. Its pre-World War I commercial block is bracketed by buildings on the Canadian Register of Historic Places. In the shadow to its left is the Canada Permanent Building of 1911, when Hastings Street was the financial centre of the city – banks could not lend money for mortgages until changes to the Bank Act in 1953. On its right is the former Niagara Hotel, built in 1912, renowned until 20 years ago for its cascading Niagara neon sign and now rebranded as the Ramada.

(Right) The original Ming Wo cookware store, established in 1917 at 23 East Pender, closed in the winter of 2020, an event greeted with genuine mourning and considerable discussion over the fate of Chinatown and the impact on it of chaotic Hastings Street a block away – the epicentre of the Downtown Eastside. Ming Wo continues to operate elsewhere in the Lower Mainland.

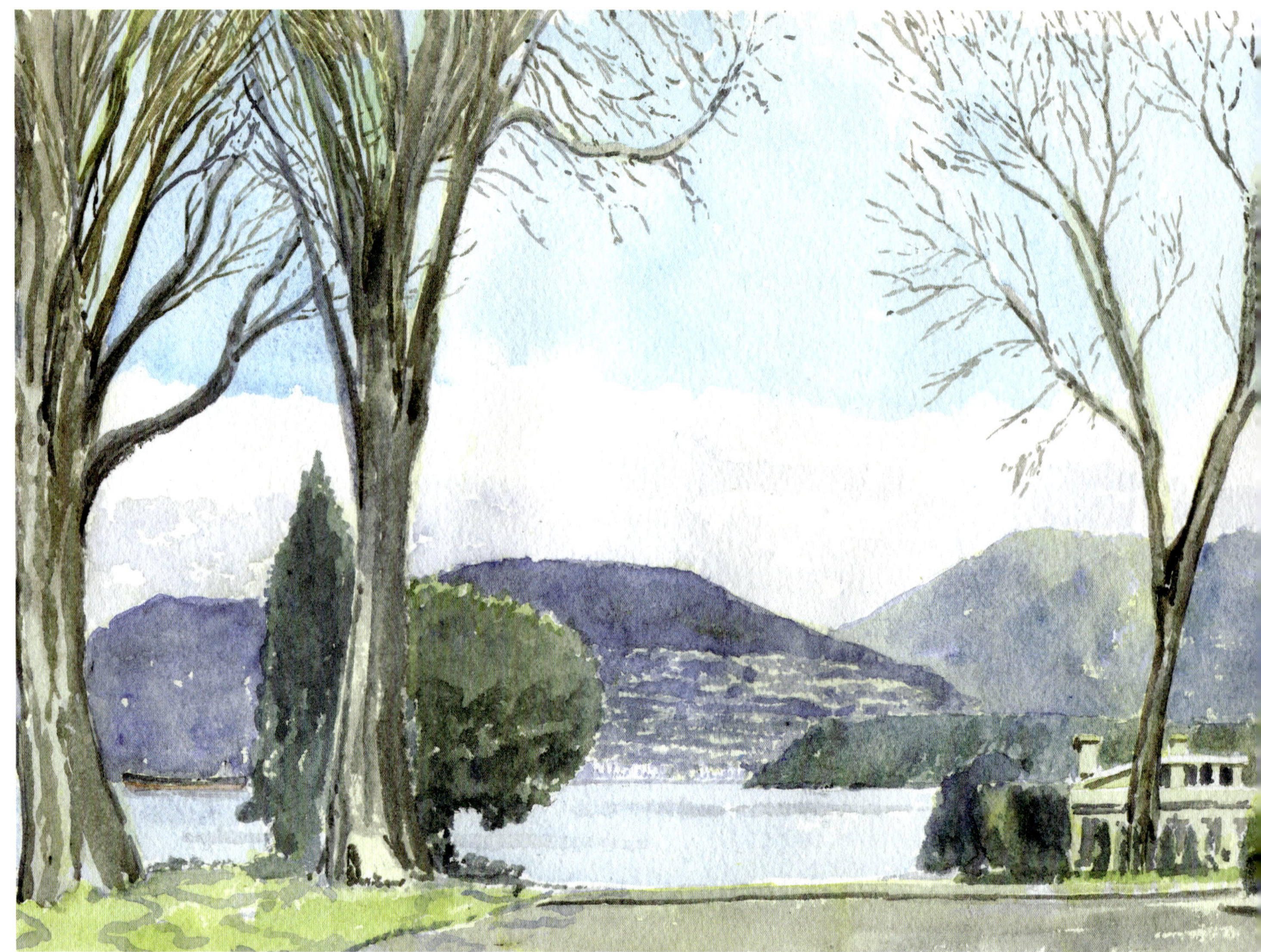

The two-block section of Point Grey Road west of Kitsilano Beach and north of Cornwall is a magical place, and not just for the lucky and wealthy who live there. At the foot of Trafalgar Street – the scene here – the view opens spectacularly across English Bay, a sweep of mountain-framed water extending from Stanley Park to Bowen Island.

The foot of Trafalgar was the "end of track" for the Canadian Pacific Railway's transcontinental line, and the western boundary of its 5,800-acre (2,350-hectare) land grant, which stretched east to Ontario Street. The CPR intended for a time to build wharves and tracks farther to the west and construct a terminus at Jericho, a plan re-promoted unsuccessfully for Spanish Banks in the 1910s by the Vancouver Terminal Company. A plan from the 1950s, touted by mayors Rathie and Campbell as a Centennial project, would have put a "glamour parkway" between the beachside homes and the water. Highrise apartments began to sprout on nearby blocks in the 1960s but citizen protests stopped them in the early '70s.

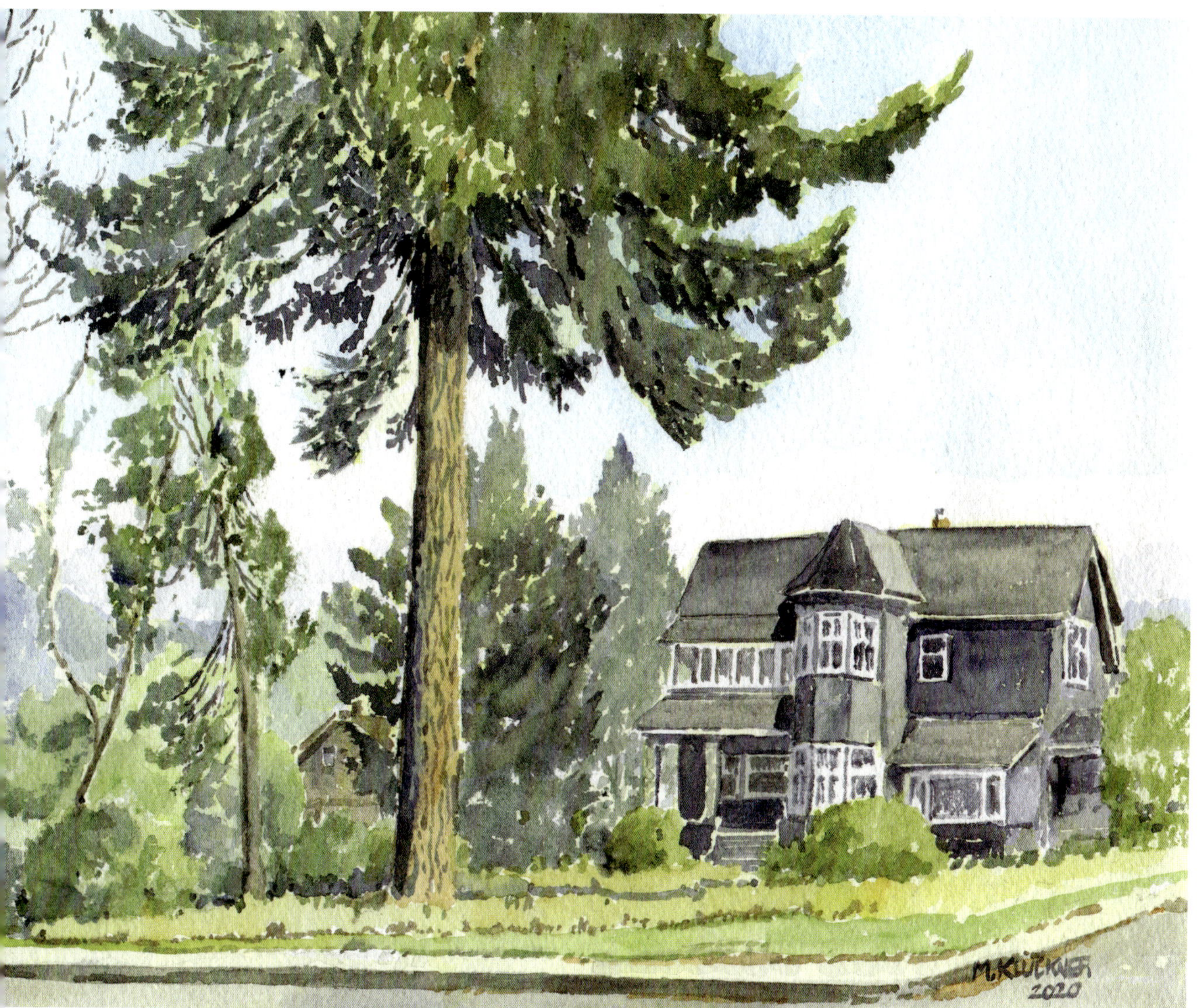

The foot of Vancouver's Trafalgar Street, with the fine old house at 2590 Point Grey Road, on a sunny day in January 2020.

The old house on the right sits at the back of its property on an extraordinary swath of land – more than 125 feet of frontage on three lots – and is angled picturesquely toward the summer sunset. Built in 1908, three years after streetcar service began to the Kitsilano Beach community, it is one of the oldest houses in the area. Its first owner, a property speculator and CPR agent named William Forrest, lived there until 1917, followed by Captain John Cates and his wife. Cates was a character of some renown, promoting Bowen Island as a summer resort and developing tugboat and shipping businesses that are still identified with the North Vancouver waterfront.

I painted this scene not because the house itself is in particular jeopardy but because its expansive garden is likely to be infilled with townhouses. I went there with the intention of painting just it and its splendid Douglas fir, but it became a panorama onto a second piece of paper because the light that winter afternoon was sublime.

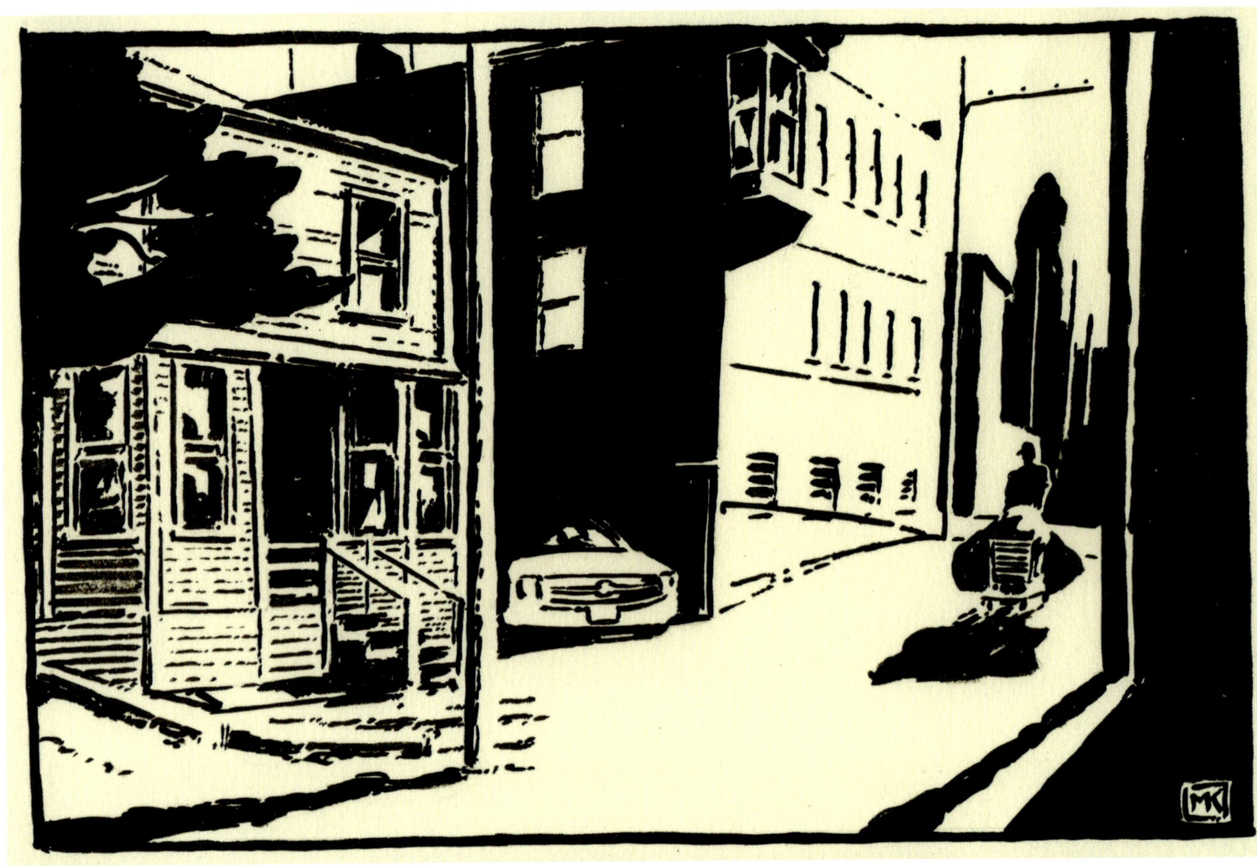

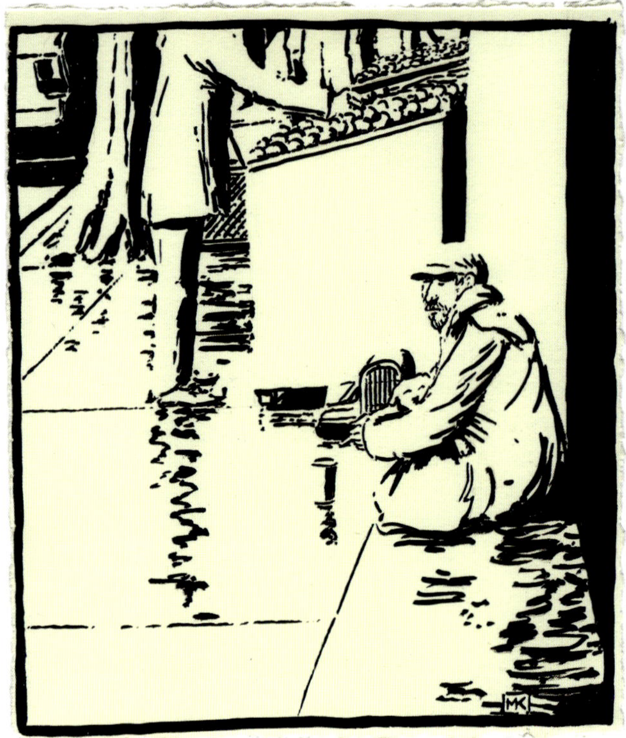

(Above) Kitsilano Beach village at the foot of Yew Street developed rapidly as it was near the terminus for the streetcar line to downtown along a right-of-way midway between Cornwall and Creelman on Kits Point. The City purchased the first piece of the beach from Yew to Balsam in 1909, and the neighbouring owners packed in small houses, lane cottages, and apartment buildings rather than selling big lots to wealthy people. A local developer named Theodore Calland, who had built himself a fine mansion above the beach just west of Trafalgar in 1903, built the Suffolk Apartments (in the middle of the drawing) in 1910, soon after the duplex (on the left) went up in the lane. More than a century later, in 2019, the tenant community in the duplex and apartment block survived an eviction threat when the owner of the property withdrew an application to construct a five-unit condominium project.

(Left) Until his death in 2020, panhandler Mike Lorimer and his little dog were a fixture on the sidewalk in front of Church's Chicken and Donald's Market on Hastings at Nanaimo. A former highrise window washer whose injuries apparently led him into substance abuse, he chatted with passersby, calling them (and me) by name. He lived at the Orwell Hotel on East Hastings and wryly described himself as "one of the lucky unlucky ones." When I drew him in 2013, he was mobile and rode a bike, carrying the dog in a small cage. A couple of years later he was partially paralyzed in a car crash, and thereafter held court in a wheelchair at his familiar spot. The *Georgia Straight* of May 30, 2020, noted the memorial service held for him in a nearby park.

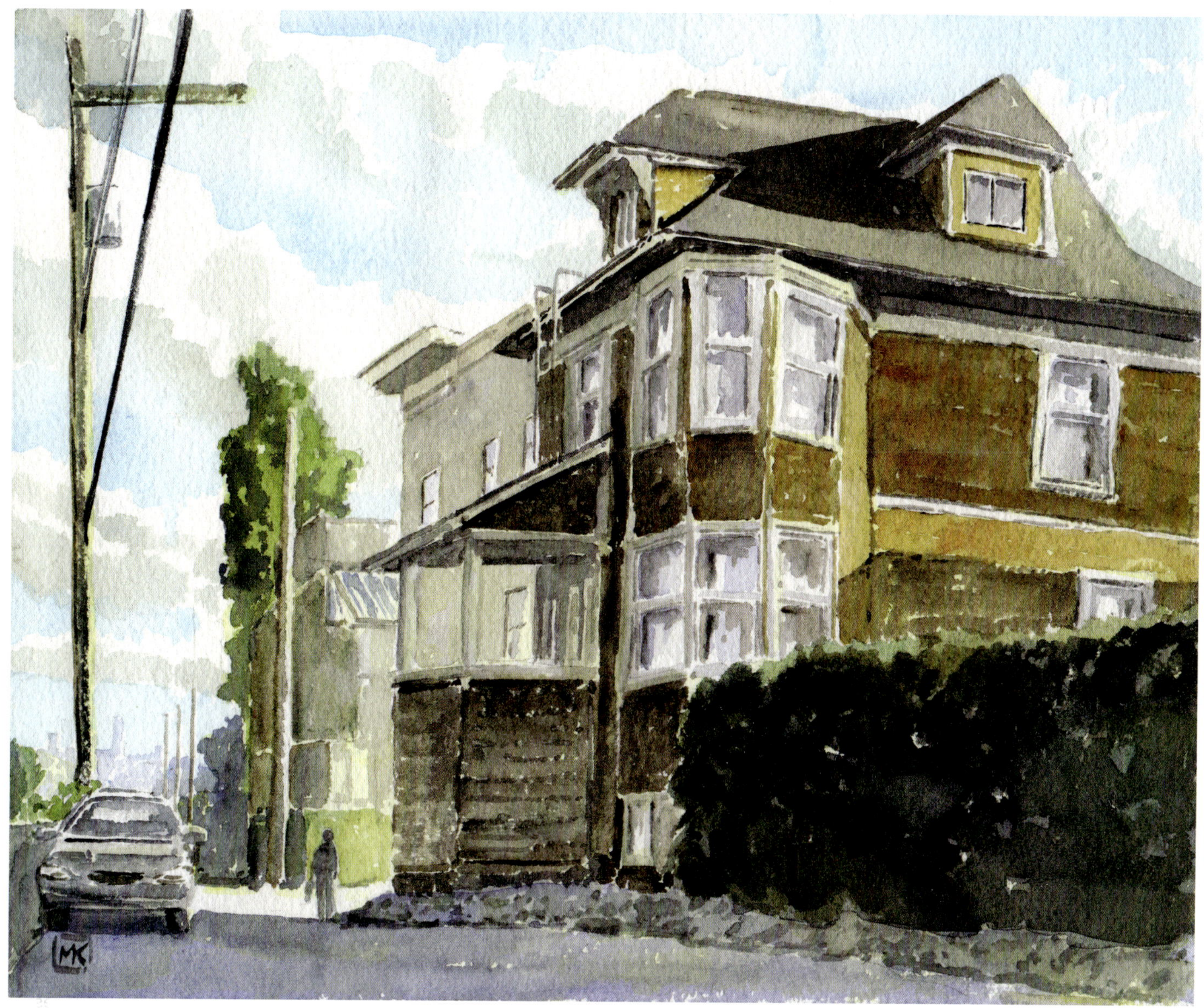

The Le Feuvre house in the lane off Yew Street in Kitsilano. Built in 1905, the year that the CPR named its suburb "Kitsilano" after the Squamish chief Khahtsahlano, it is a very early survivor of settlement in that part of the city. The 4th Avenue streetcar began service four years later, in 1909. Maxwell & Le Feuvre were real-estate brokers with offices on Granville near 6th.

Vancouver has a problem with bland, homogeneous, repetitive streetscapes, one that becomes worse with the passage of time as zoning rules and rigid building codes chew away at surviving examples of diversity. For better or worse, a century ago people built more or less what they wanted. But lest one think that such a libertarian attitude should be repeated, it was truly a different world then – individuals and small firms designed and built, not big corporations. Architects were, perhaps, not so sheeplike. There was little "financialization" of property, at least compared with now. Everything today is "built to the max"; generations ago, most people built only what they needed. It was hard to borrow money. Or so it seems from the surviving evidence.

Odd small places survive on streets and lanes in Strathcona and Mount Pleasant, and there are even a few left in Kitsilano. The house above, unusually set in the lane between 2nd and 3rd west of Yew, started life facing Yew but was skidded around the back in the 1920s when the owners decided to build the Manoa Apartments on the balance of its three lots.

On the facing page, the Suffolk Apartments and its lane duplex are another curiosity that survives as of this writing in 2020.

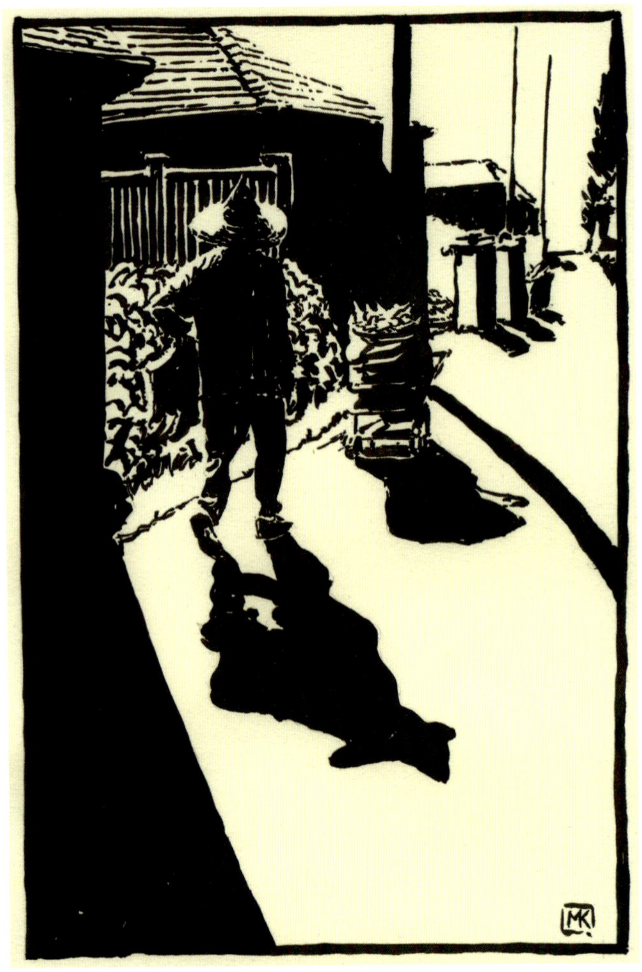

The Chinese bottle lady, with her conical woven hat and cart loaded with discarded bottles and cans, stands out from the throng of "binners" in our East Vancouver neighbourhood, most of whom make their rounds on bikes. "Bottle lady" seems like a polite Canadianism compared with "trash-picker," a term common in other parts of the world, but it is a term used even in New York City. Cheery and friendly but with little English, she works the lanes year-round, regardless of the weather, keeping busy and making a few dollars a day. One bottle lady on the Downtown Eastside, Gia Tran, was featured in a CBC piece in 2018, and a Marcus Gee article in the *Globe & Mail* in 2016 described them in Toronto.

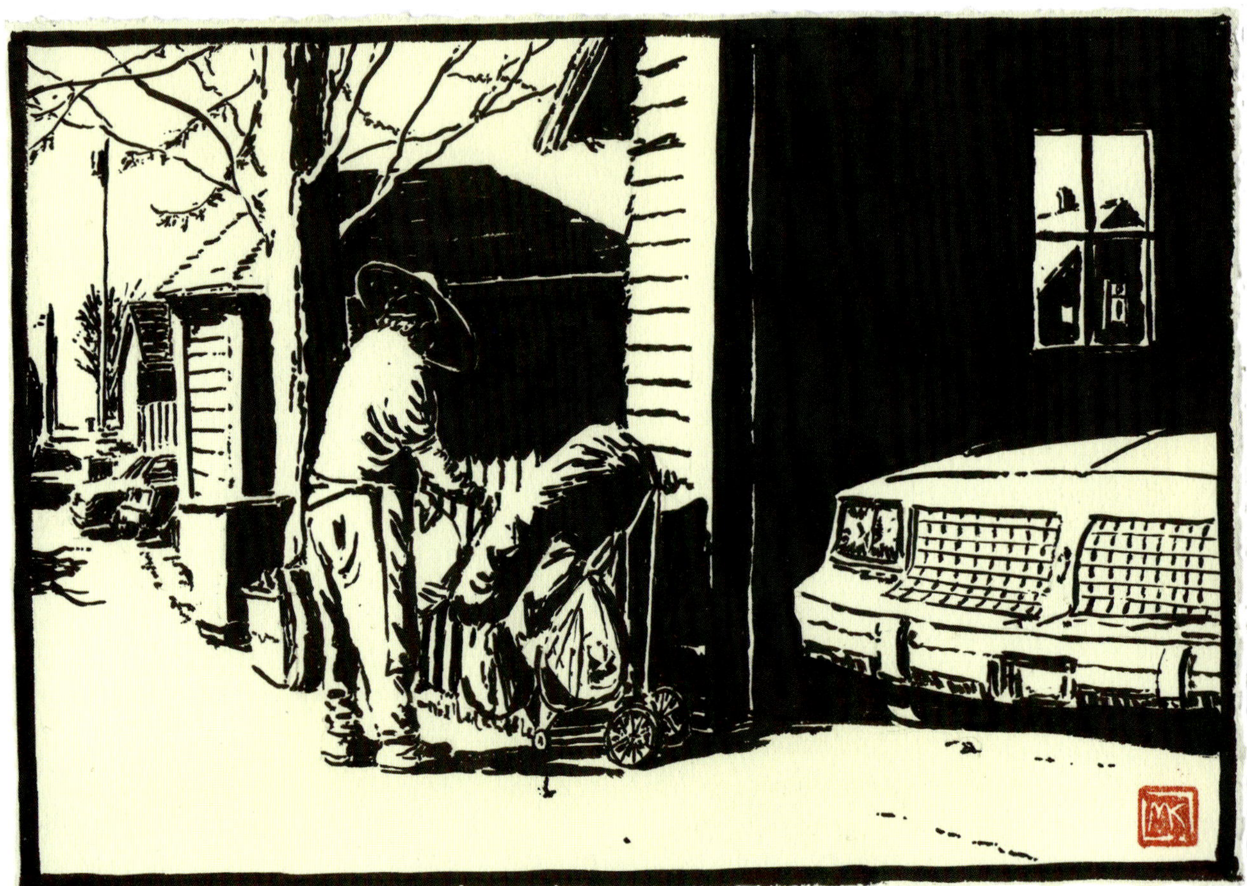

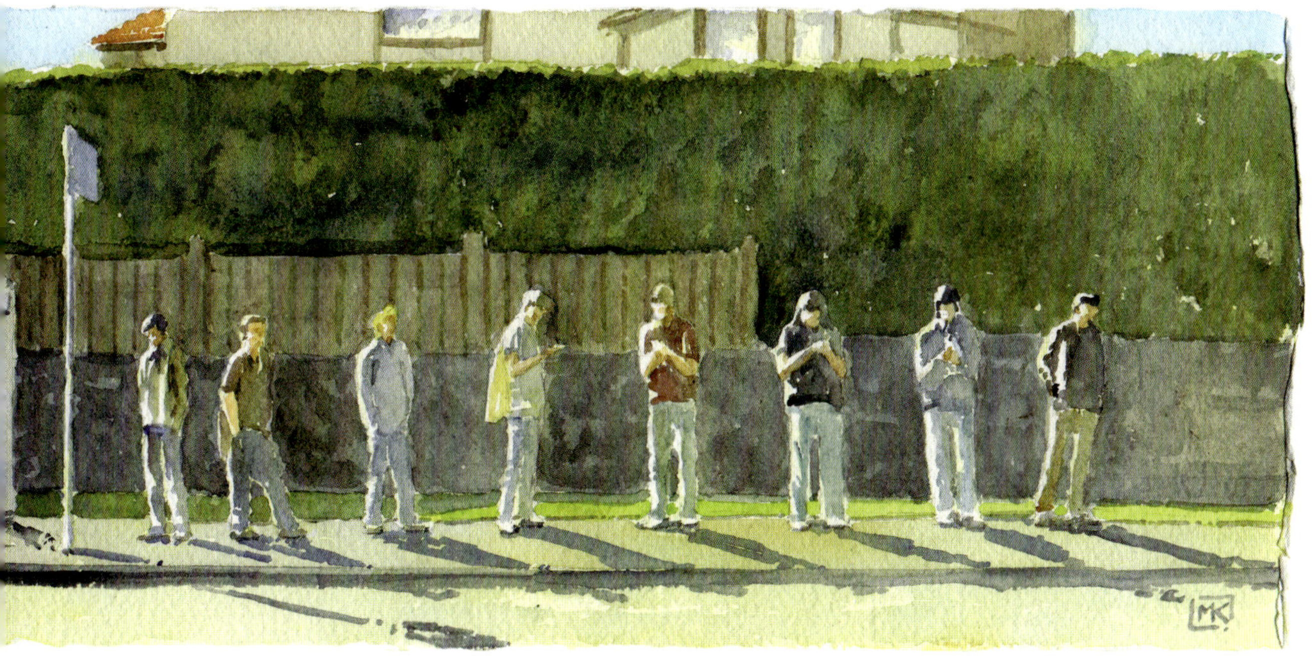

(Below) Rooming house as landmark: the house on 1st Avenue on the hill above Clark Drive stands dramatically above the vacant land on the corner. Built in 1910 by the Fairview Hardware Company, it had an unimpeded view to the west over the False Creek Flats, which at that time were a tidal inlet in the process of being drained and filled for trackage by the Great Northern Railway. Its location became less desirable after 1938, when the City completed the viaduct to connect Terminal Avenue and downtown with the arterial road system being built to the east. The house's site, the neighbouring grassy sward, and properties continuing up the hill are slated to host a controversial detox and social housing centre to be built by the City and provincial health department.

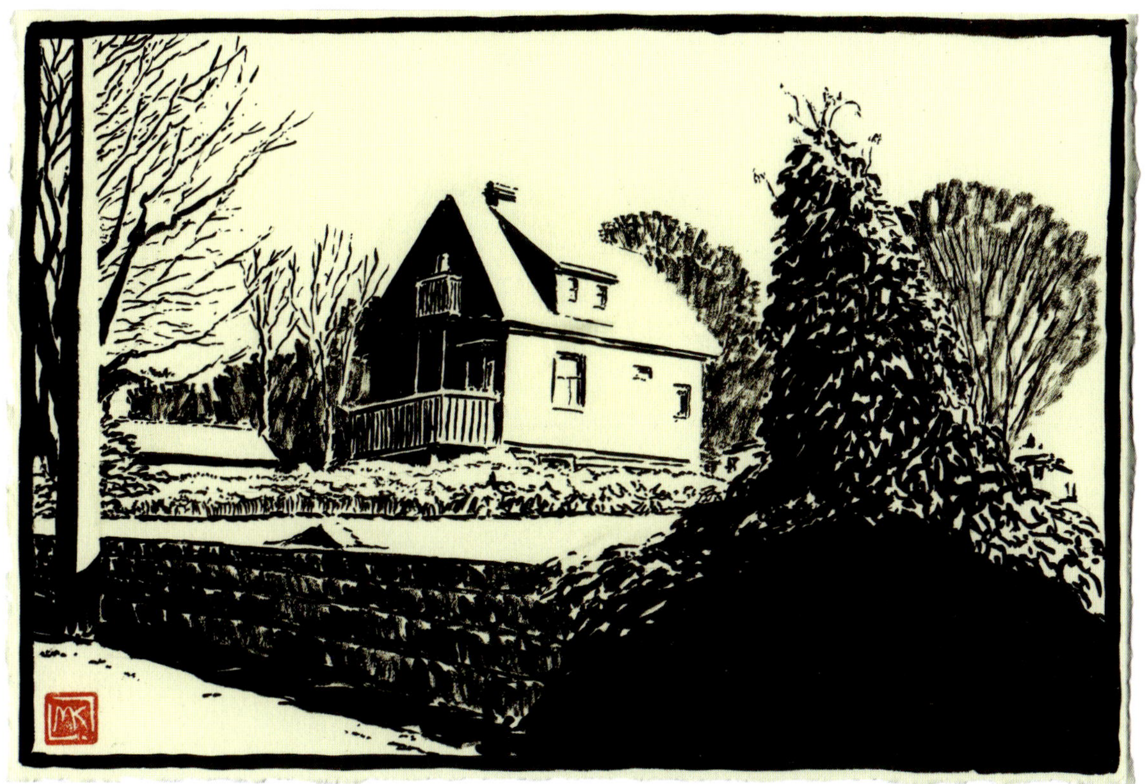

The rather grand house at 220 Salsbury is a rare concrete block structure, erected probably in 1908 by Alex J. Ross, a blacksmith; next to it on Pandora Street, he built a two-storey workshop in 1912. Today, the area is a mix of factories, many of which process food, and tech companies. In the distance on the waterfront are the orange cranes of VanTerm's container facility and the historic Dominion #1 grain elevator complex, built at the time the Panama Canal opened in 1915, which turned Vancouver into a grain port.

*From the frontispiece of his *Vancouverism* book published in 2019.

One of the biggest disappointments of Vancouver's evolution over the past 30 years has been the disconnection of its port from the daily awareness of its citizens. Other than its noise, which penetrates both day and night into homes a mile away, the port is invisible behind chain link and has been since the security lockdown in the wake of the 9-11 attacks.

A century ago, the Burrard Inlet waterfront was a mix of foundries, fish-packing plants and small mills, with a few landmarks including the B.C. Sugar Refinery and the Lapointe Pier complex of federal government grain elevators. Japantown established itself along Powell Street because it was close to the major employer of Japanese workers: the historic Hastings Mill at the foot of Dunlevy. Workers' cottages and tenements filled the streets of Strathcona and north Grandview, a short walk from waterfront jobs.

The Coal Harbour shoreline was industrial, too – occupied by tugboat companies, boat builders and chandlers. False Creek was even more heavily industrialized, with shipbuilding supplementing the usual tangle of sawmills and smoking sawdust burners.

This grit and bustle were a part of daily life in a Vancouver worlds away from the yachts and bike paths of today's Coal Harbour and False Creek – Vancouver's new self-image as an international resort. In former city planner Larry Beasley's words: "The experience of Vancouver is one of urban life on the water."* Not this stretch of water. Not in East Van.

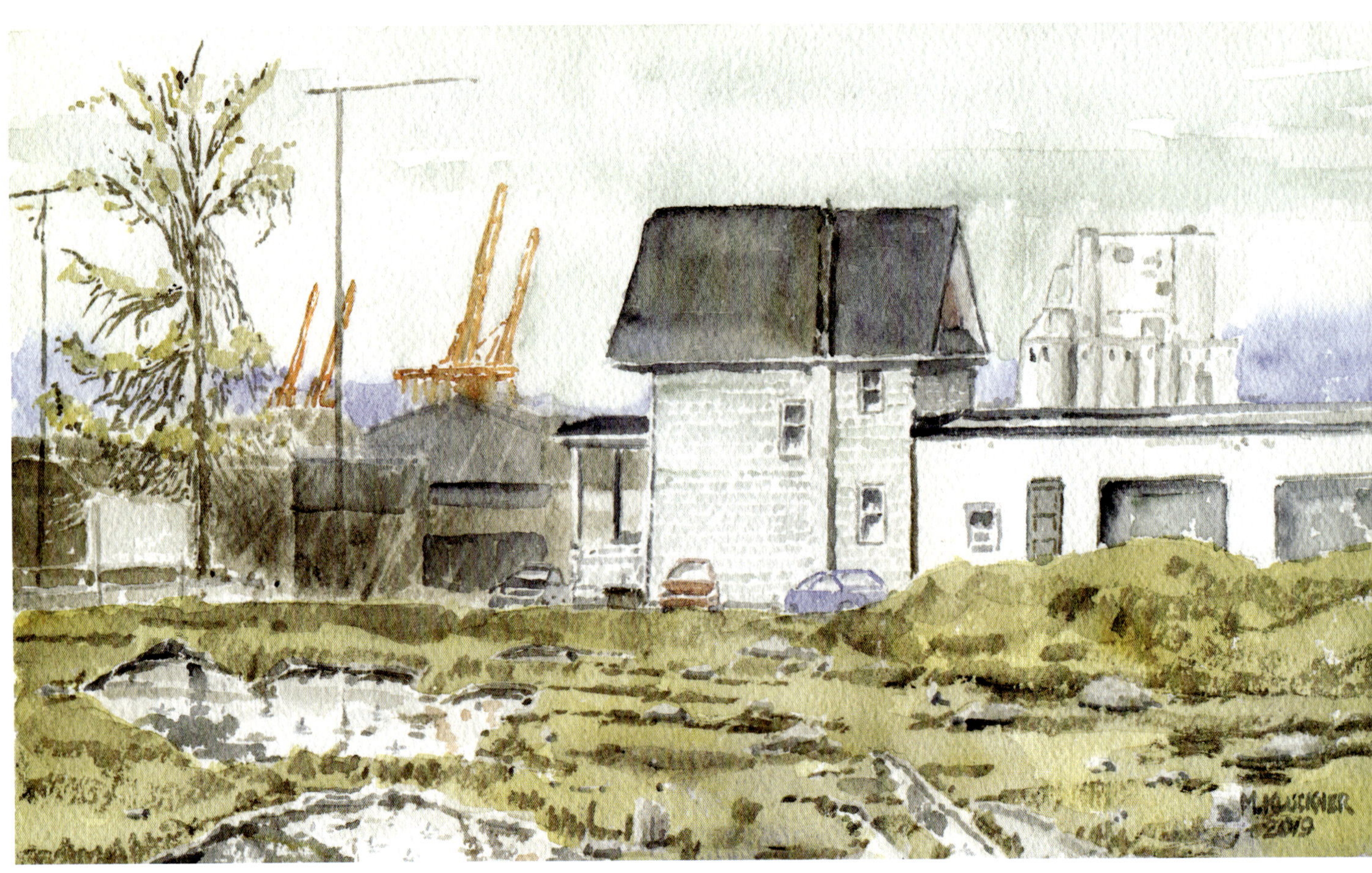

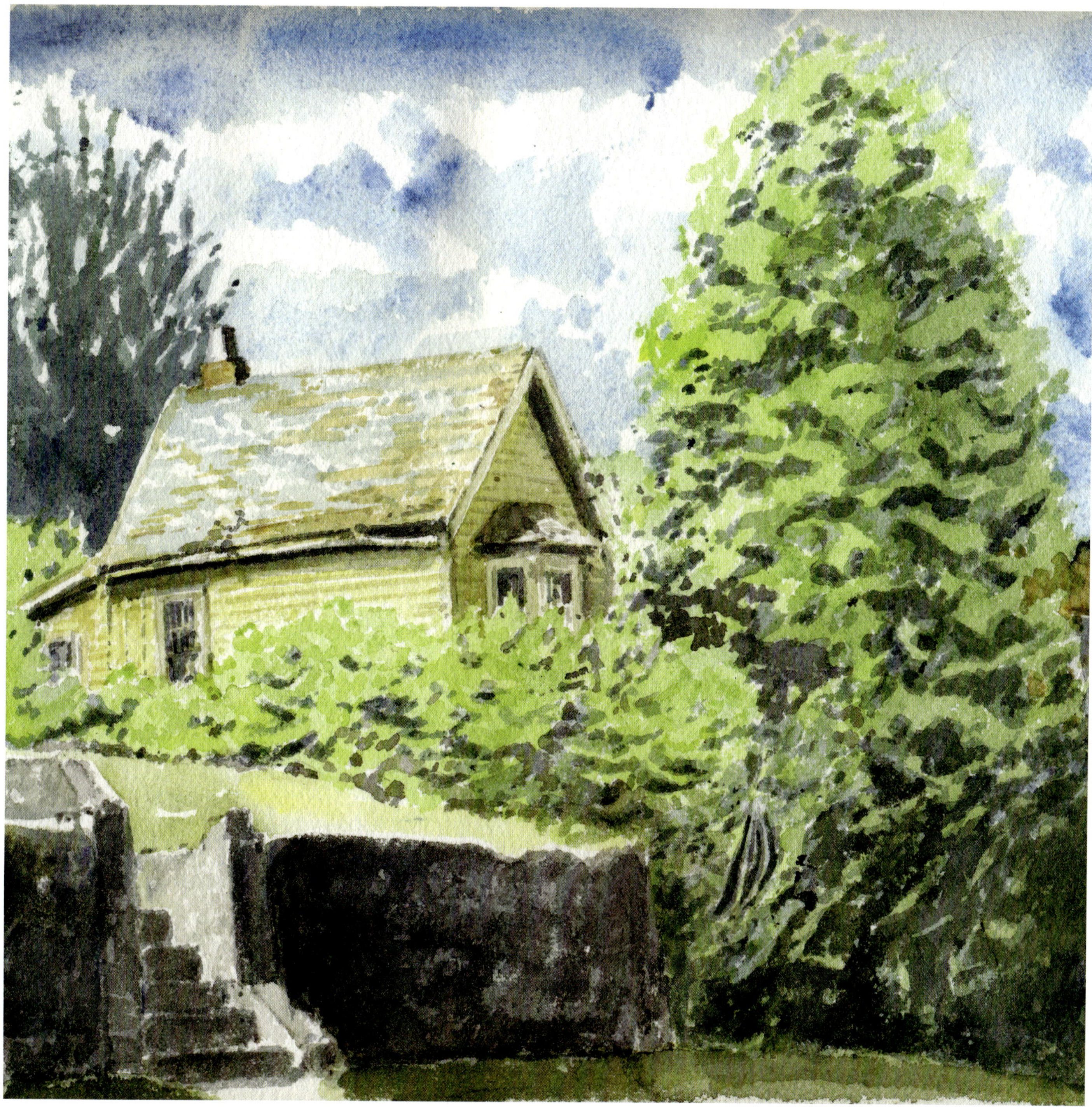

Vancouver's industrial land base in East Vancouver has been fairly well protected from the "highest and best use" onslaught of the condo builders who have taken over other "brownfield" (former industrial) areas such as False Creek and Coal Harbour. In these industrial areas, especially near 1000 Parker Street – a former furniture-manufacturing building – there survive most of the artists' studios and performance-rehearsal spaces in the gentrified city.

That slower pace of change has left a few relics to catch the eye of people like me, including the scenes on these pages.

1832 Franklin Street – a cottage probably built in 1905 for an iron moulder named Alfred May. I painted it in 2000. I wrote at the bottom of the sheet, "Burnt out but still standing in 2012." It was demolished the following year. In 2020 it and neighbouring lots were used for parking by the Hallmark Poultry plant in the next block.

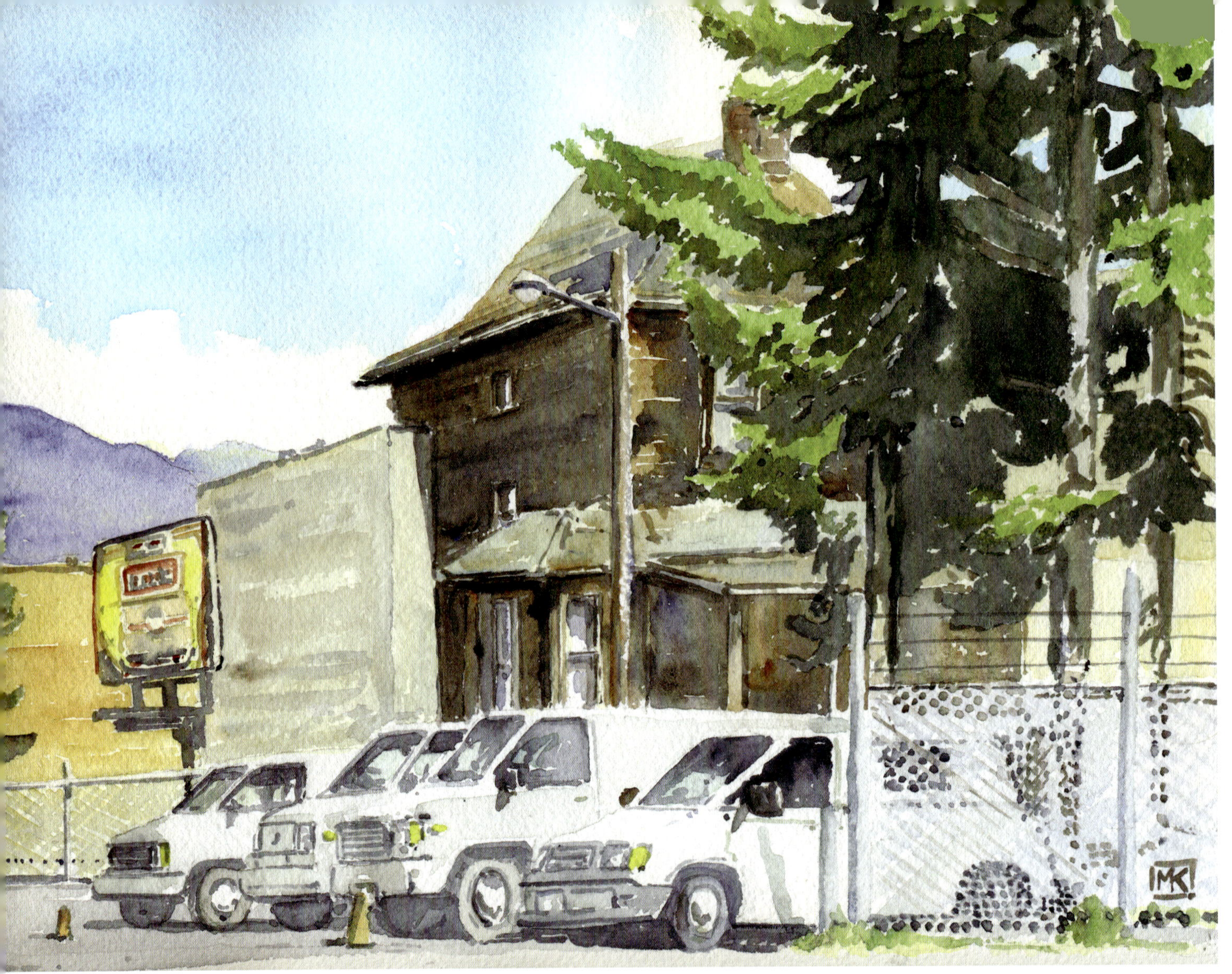

The house at 350 East 10th Avenue in the summer of 2013, one of a handful of buried houses – that is, houses that have had commercial buildings added to their front yards – left in the city. Telus trucks park in the vacant lot beside it. In the distance is the ochre-coloured wall of Kingsgate Mall.

The style – the "built form" in planner's jargon – of the blocks around the historic triangle of Main, Broadway and Kingsway has been hotly contested for the past decade. This Mount Pleasant village dates back to the 1880s and is the oldest suburb in the city, becoming settled so early because it was on the route to the Westminster Road (Kingway) to New Westminster, the colonial capital founded 25 years before the railway arrived in Vancouver.

So far, Main Street has remained intact, but the approval of a high-rise condo on Kingsway at 10th in 2014 was bitterly fought by many in the neighbourhood. Since then, the pending arrival of a subway line with a station at the southwest corner of Broadway and Main is certain to push Mount Pleasant in the direction of a downtown-style cluster of highrises.

A big question mark is the Kingsgate Mall property east of Kingsway on Broadway. It is the site of the Mount Pleasant School, torn down in the early 1970s, and is still owned by the School Board but leased to the mall.

Amidst all this change, a handful of curious old places has lived on in the shadows. One of them is the buried house illustrated above at 350 East 10th, on the bike route that runs on the south side of Kingsgate Mall. There was a café in the 1950 concrete block addition on the front of the 1909 house until a few years ago. Properties on either side of it are used by Telus; since 1912, the B.C. Telephone Company's Fairmont Exchange building has stood on the Prince Edward corner just to the east.

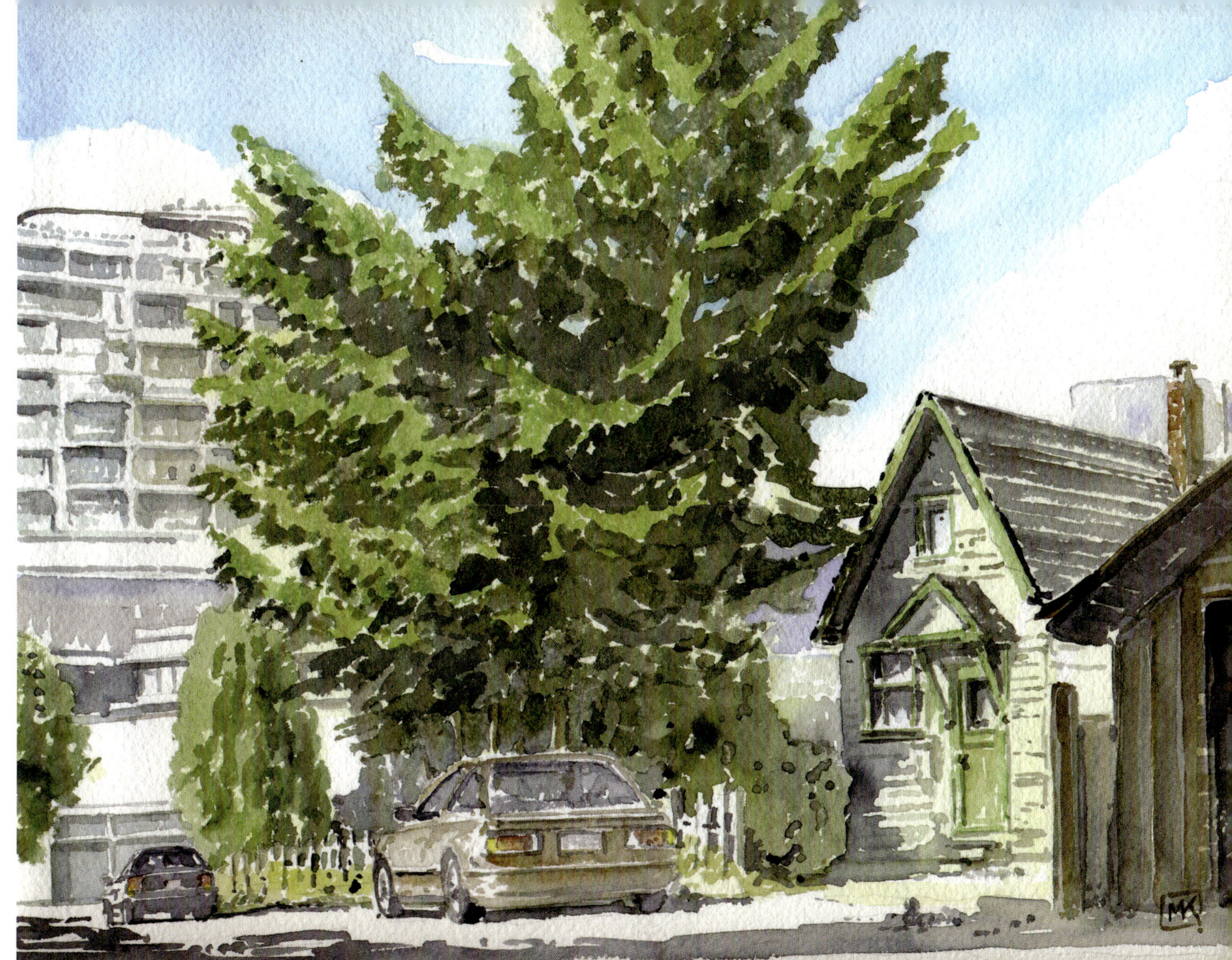

Just a couple of blocks south on the curve of 12th Avenue was another relic – a cottage dating back to 1909. It sat behind a larger house that faced 13th Avenue on a triangular lot formed by two lanes, one on the north-south grid and the other parallel to Kingsway's diagonal. Kingsway is just out of sight on the right of the watercolour: the condo building on the left side of the image has its main frontage on Kingsway but its side, visible here, faces 12th Avenue.

It gained its weird position when 12th Avenue was "smoothed" in accordance with road improvements recommended by the Harland-Bartholomew Plan of 1927–30. Before that time, 12th Avenue dead-ended at Sophy Street, as it was then called; on the east side, 12th Avenue stopped at Kingsway where it created a 5-way corner with Kingsway and Prince Edward. The new arterial path of 12th just clipped the corner at the bottom of the cottage's garden.

Records are unclear but appear to show that a man named J.C. McMillan built it in 1909 for $150; he built a larger house later that year for $2,000 facing onto 13th Avenue.

The lane cottage just south of 12th Avenue between Sophia Street and Kingsway in the summer of 2013. The big new city crept closer each year. The cottage was in ruins in 2020 but still standing.

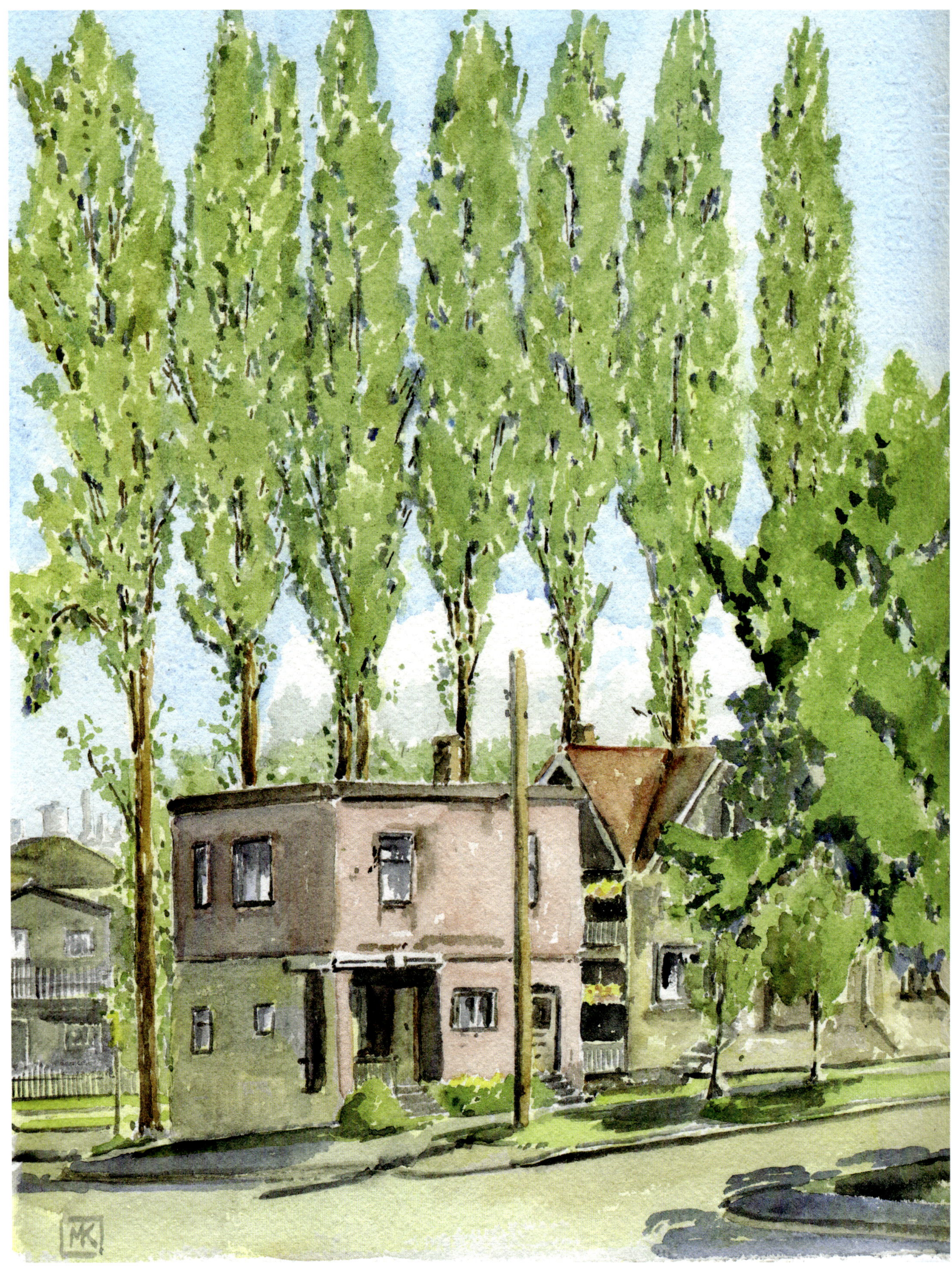

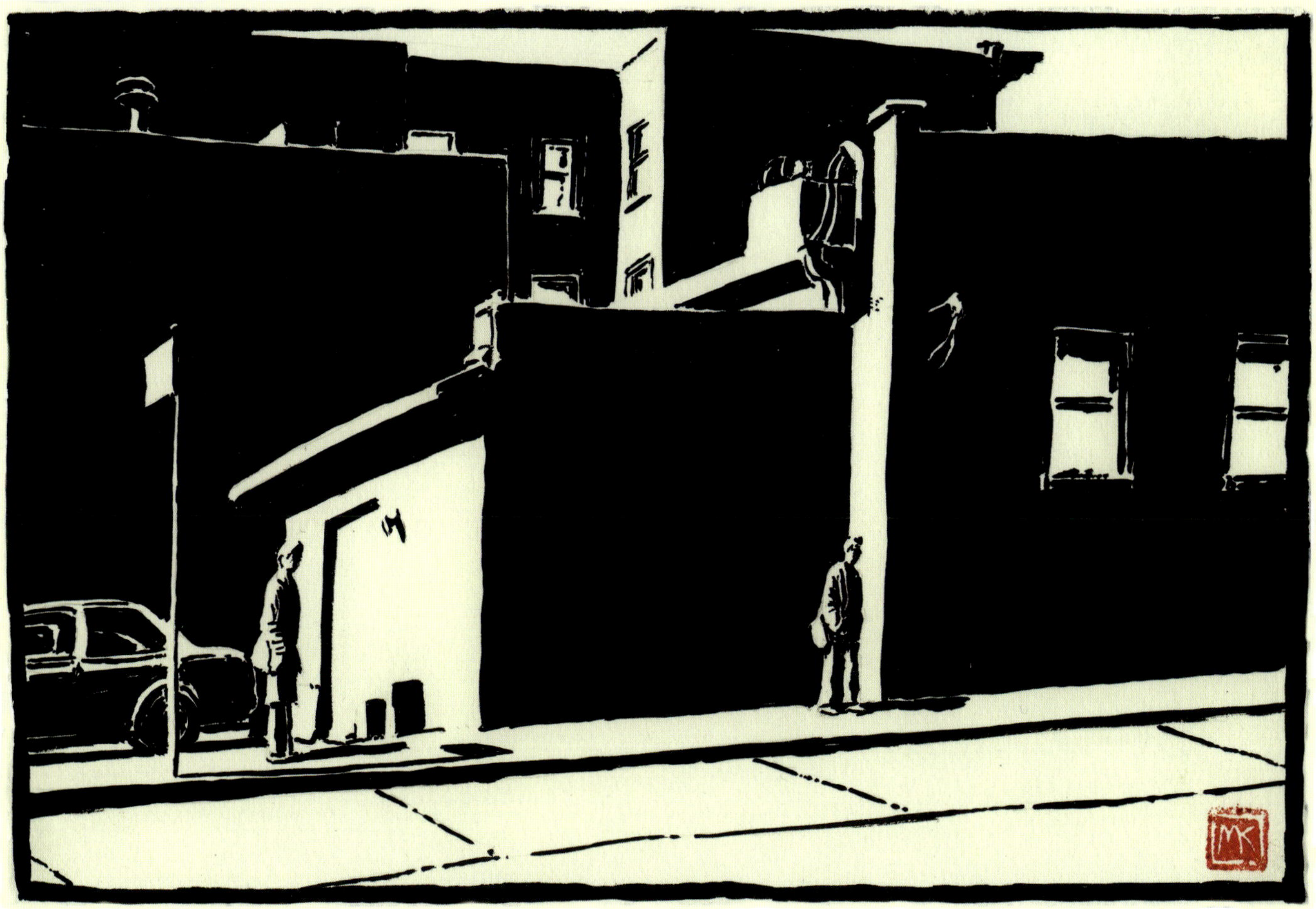

(Above) Bus stop – King Edward and Main.

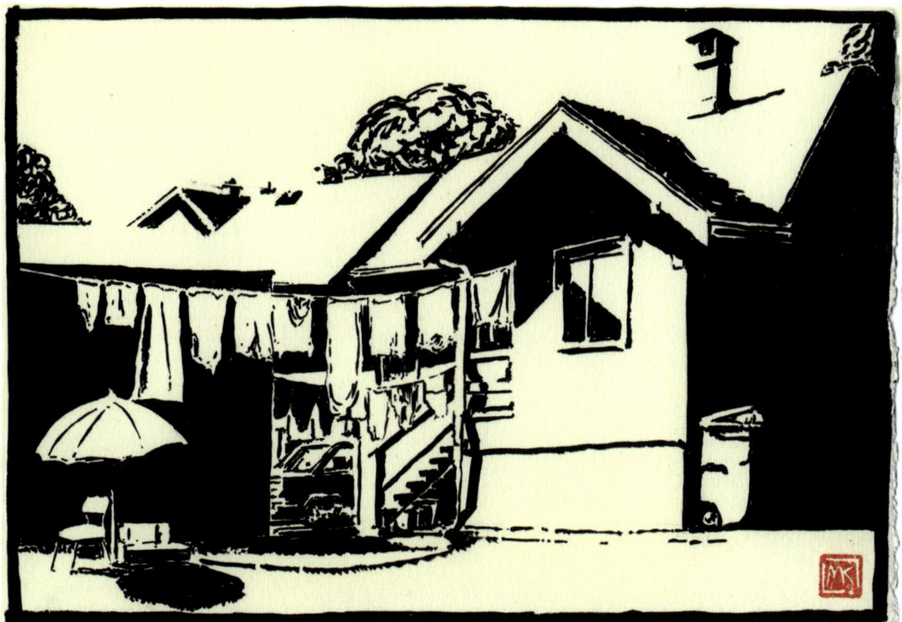

(Left) A Vancouver paradise: a lawn to mow, laundry to hang, and a chair in the sun. A brush-ink drawing from 2018.

(Previous page) You would travel far before finding a homelier building than the little stucco-covered box wedged onto the 32-foot strip of land on King Edward between John and Prince Edward streets, two blocks east of Main, an anomaly left from the chaotic subdivision patterns of the old Municipality of South Vancouver. It first appears in the 1913 directory as the home of Arthur Choquette, a builder, and Joseph Choquette, an employee of the Perfect Concealed Bed Company. Around that time, someone planted a row of poplar trees on the remainder of the lot, visible today from miles away.

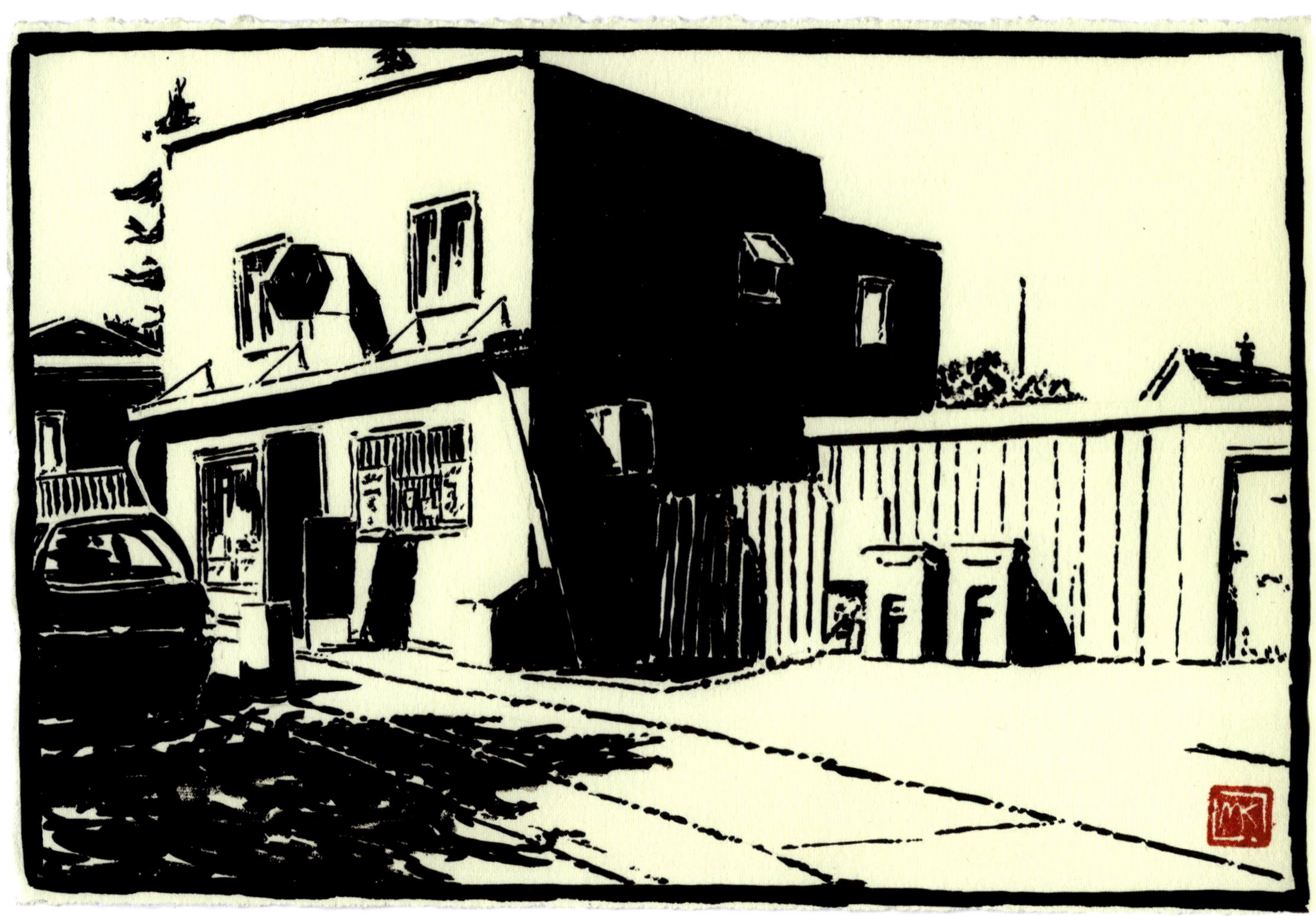

A rare survivor: a store built in 1930 on East 35th at Windsor Street in an area once called Kensington Heights, drawn in 2018. East 35th was originally called Kensington Avenue. Recently relaxed City policies will allow it to be renovated and reopened as some kind of café and store – a gathering spot amidst the quiet residential streets east of Mountainview Cemetery.

*I wrote in detail on corner stores in the 2012 *Vanishing Vancouver*, pp. 71–4; and on the Fukuhara family's store on Main Street, which they lost in the WWII internment, in *Vanishing British Columbia*, pp. 38–9.

The saga of Vancouver's corner grocery stores is instructive for anyone wanting to understand the evolution of the city over the past 125 years. Before 1930, with no zoning regulations in place, little stores sprang up throughout the city's residential areas on corners, occasionally mid-block, sometimes in the main floors of modified houses, other times as front-yard additions on standard houses. There were, of course, many more stores on the streetcar strips of main streets such as Hastings and Commercial Drive.

They were live-work spaces that suited widows, of whom there were many in the first two decades of the 20th century with few options other than running boarding houses. By the 1920s, however, stores had become a kind of port of entry for many Chinese and Japanese immigrant families, providing housing and an income, kept open for long hours by everyone in the family pitching in.* In retrospect, they were hugely significant culturally. For example, an acquaintance of mine whose family immigrated from Hong Kong in the 1950s grew up behind the Cardero Grocery in the West End and is now a successful corporate lawyer – an arc of achievement in a single generation that ought to be a badge of pride for Canadian society to complement our earlier history of racism.

The other saga of the corner grocery is the City's long resistance to them. Beginning in 1930 when Vancouver adopted its first formal zoning plan, "intrusions" of small stores, as they were described in the Harland-Bartholomew City Plan for Vancouver, were actively resisted. Existing ones were "grandfathered," but the orthodoxy of planning at the time insisted that residential areas should be strictly residential and commercial uses should be only on main streets.

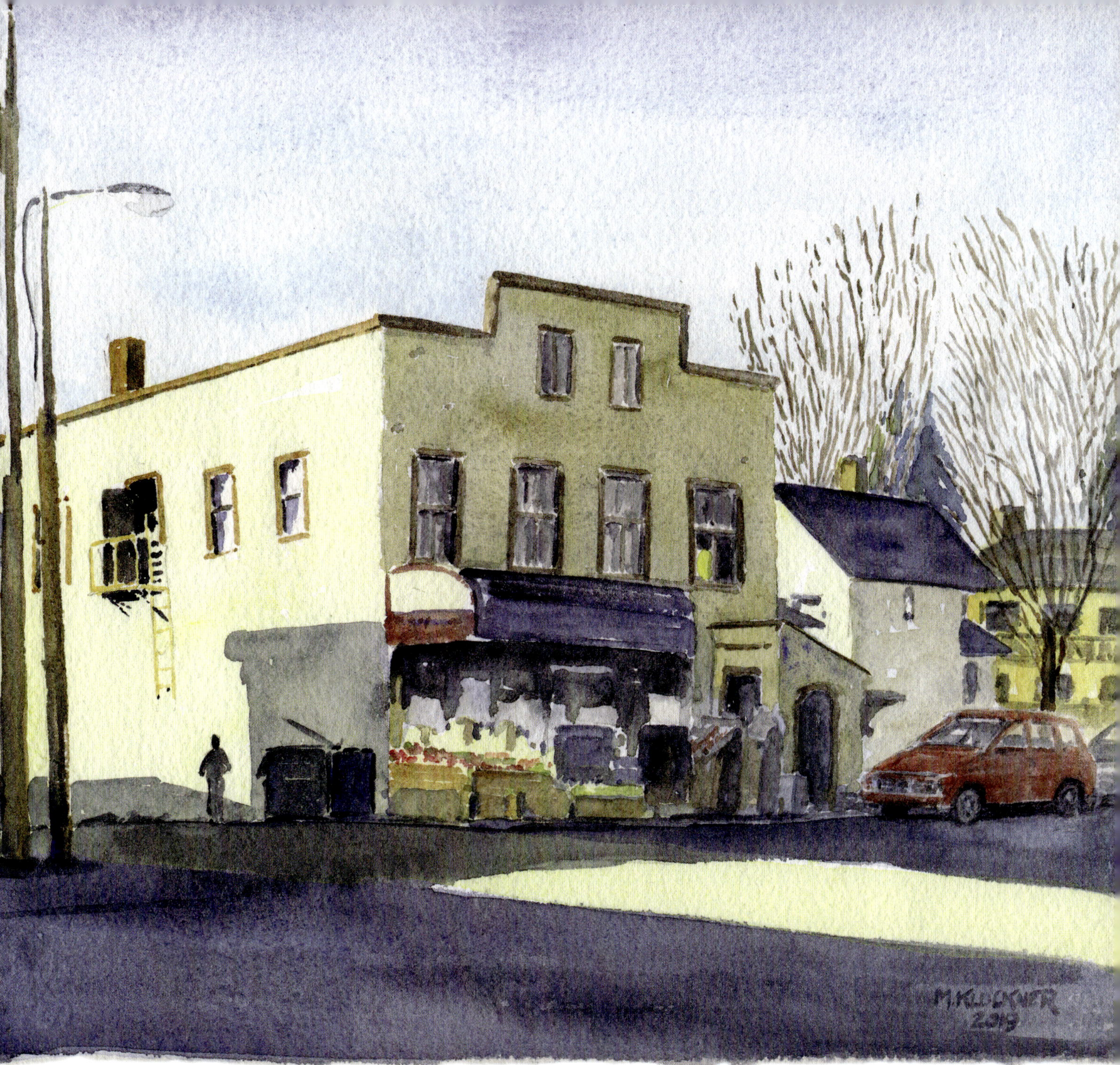

Then came the shift that began a lifetime ago to chain-owned supermarkets, and more recently to the 7-11 type of convenience store, creating a milieu where most of the little independents disappeared.

A recent *cause célèbre* was Le Marché St. Georges, an old grocery store on East 28th that was threatened in 2015 when a conflict erupted over what permits were required for it to be a café; a social media storm helped turn the tide in its favour. One old store that has operated since 2002 without any controversy is the former Arbutus Grocery at 6th and Arbutus, a popular coffee shop and neighbourhood hangout.

Still going strong: the North Templeton market near Cambridge Street in the blue December shadows. Built in 1914 for $3,500 by R.D. McKenzie, who lived nearby at 2231 Oxford Street but was listed as a logger in the city directory, it originally did business as the Oxford Meat Market and Bayly Bros. Grocery.

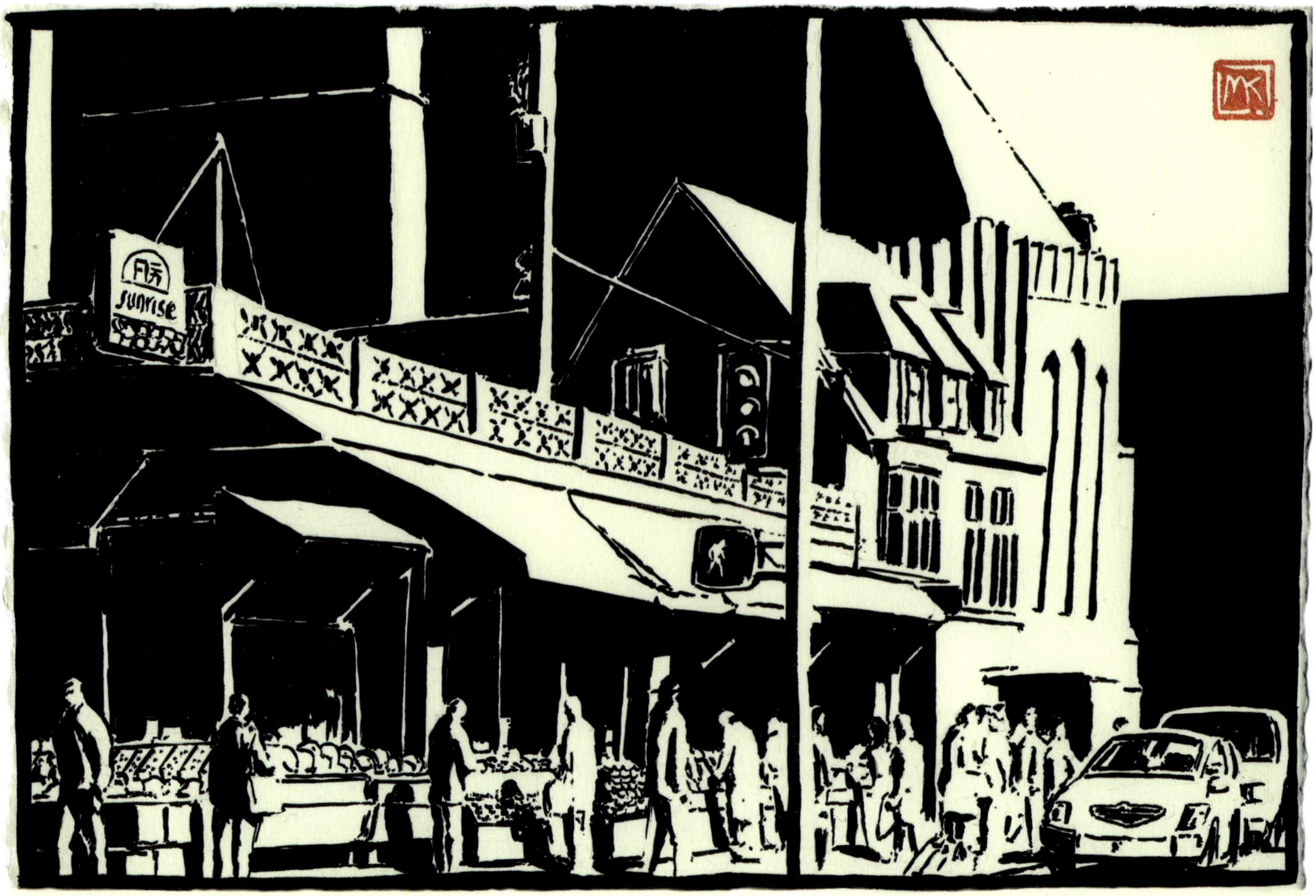

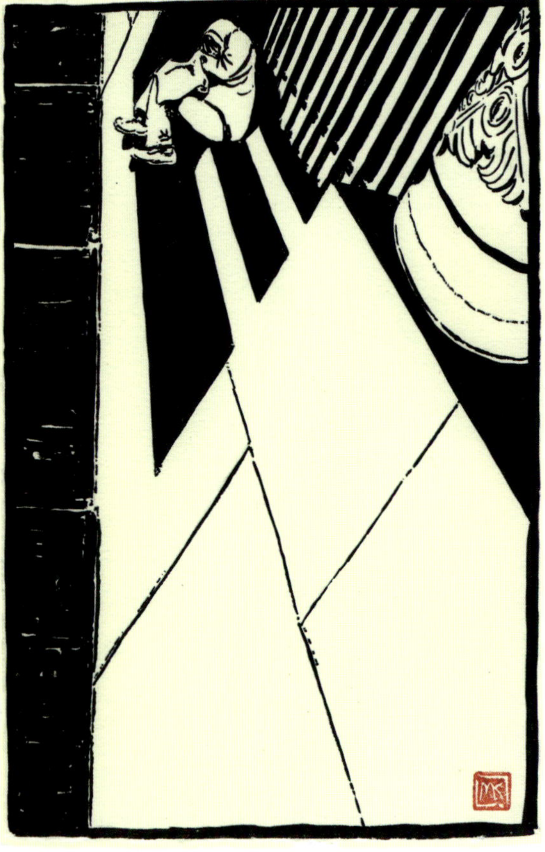

(Above) The venerable Sunrise Market on Gore at Powell, framed by St. James Anglican Church and its dormered parish hall: a semblance of traditional Vancouver existing a block west of the Oppenheimer Park tent city which lasted for two years before being cleared out in May 2020 during the pandemic. Leslie and Susan Joe started the grocery store after immigrating to Canada in 1956; their Sunrise Soya Foods is Canada's largest manufacturer of tofu.

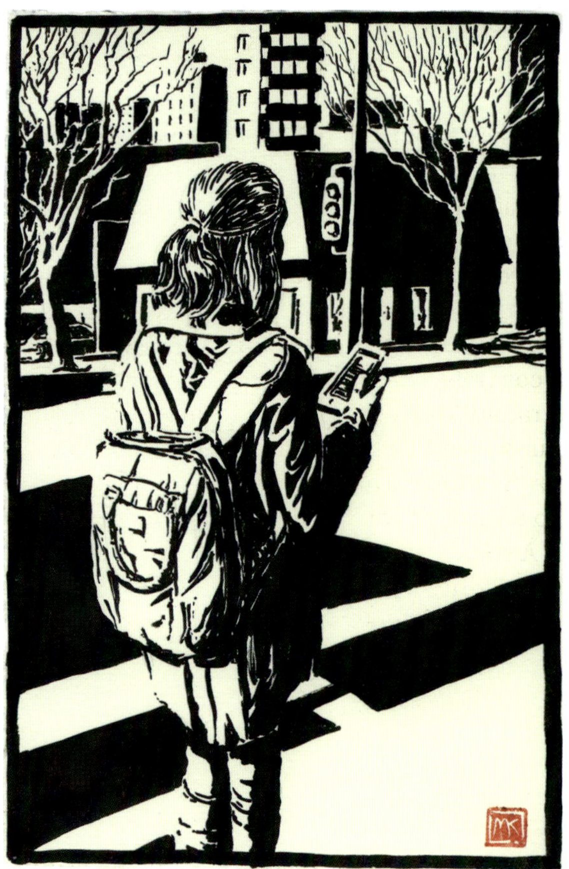

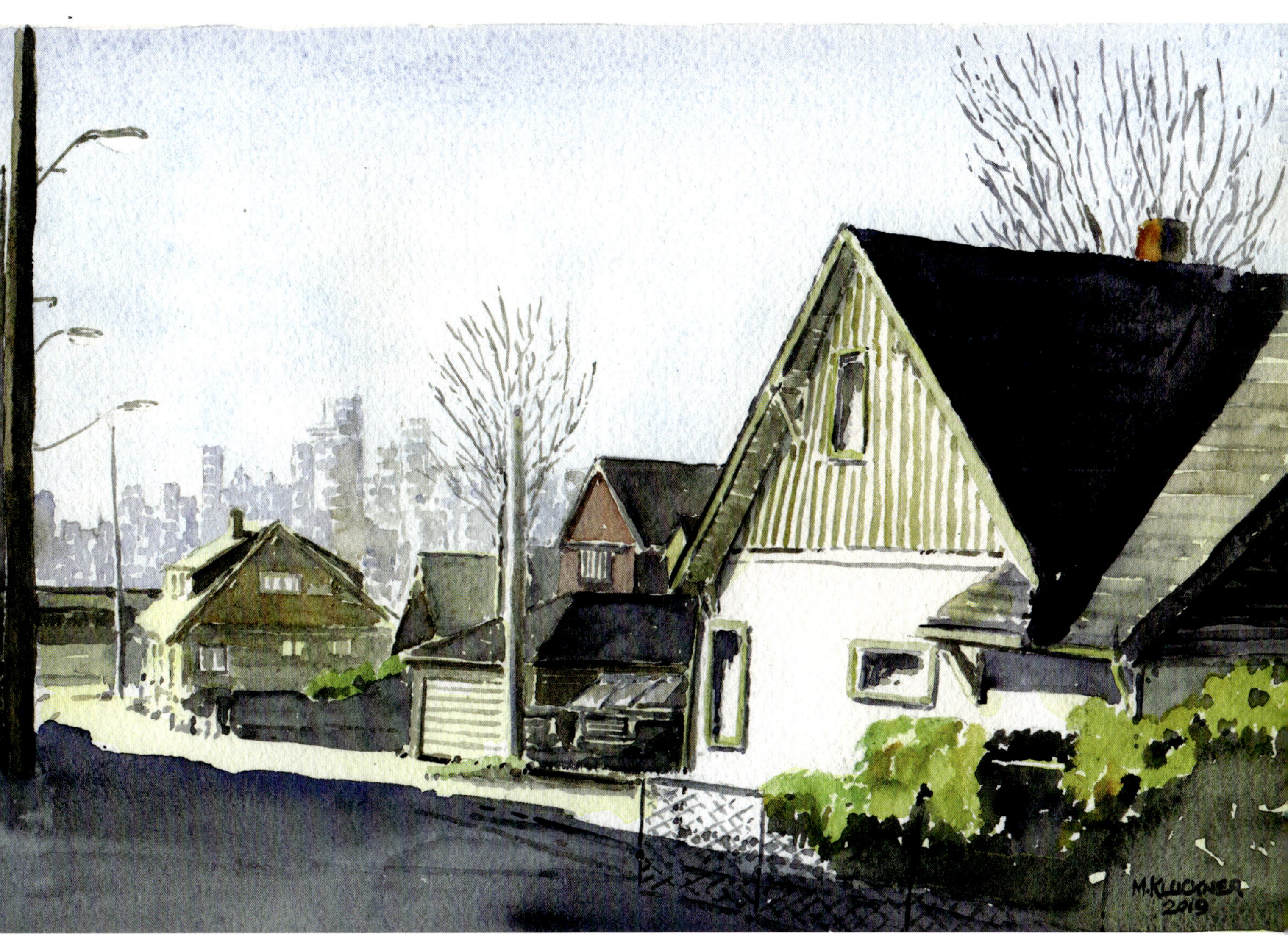

The blue shadows of a clear December day in 2019: a view down the lane north of busy Hastings Street from Templeton Drive toward the glass forest.

Long views from old to new are a trademark Vancouver scene, aided by a topography of slopes and hills such as the Hastings Street area near Nanaimo (above), or from nearby Grandview (page 28), or from the south slope of False Creek in the Mount Pleasant and Fairview neighbourhoods.

I could not have imagined Vancouver becoming such a city of contrasts even 30 or so years ago when I was writing the original *Vanishing Vancouver* book. Certainly, it was in its buildings – the West End had already become a concrete forest when I was a teenager, a forest that became glassy and strata-titled as it expanded through the downtown peninsula in the 1990s. But the city still seemed to be a middle-class kind of place, a yin and yang town of towers and apartments for some and wooden houses for others. To a large extent, it reflected the choices available all across urban Canada.

A society of haves and have-nots? That was the USA, Canadians said smugly, not here. But no safety net is able to catch all the people who fall through the cracks in the 21st-century city.

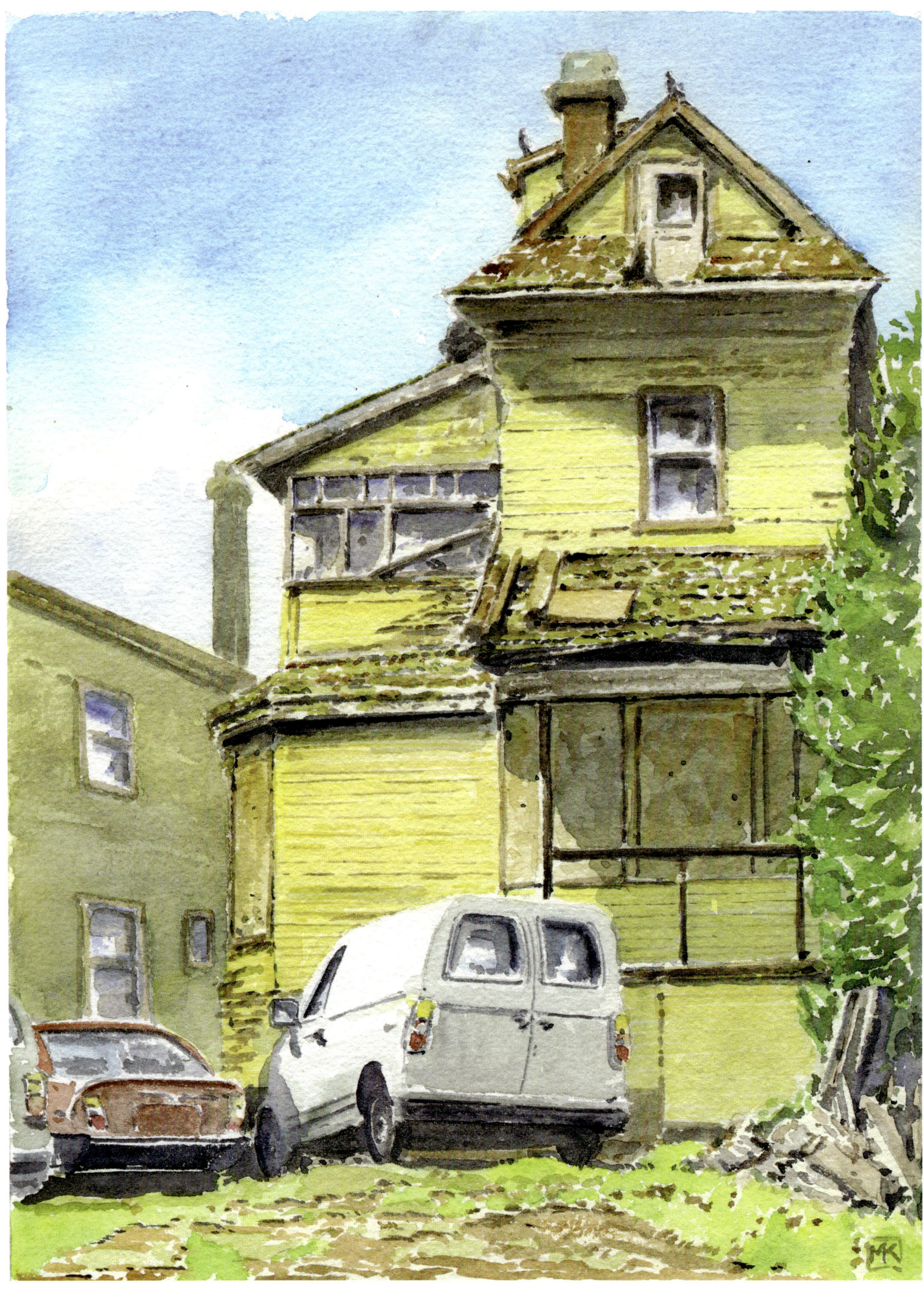

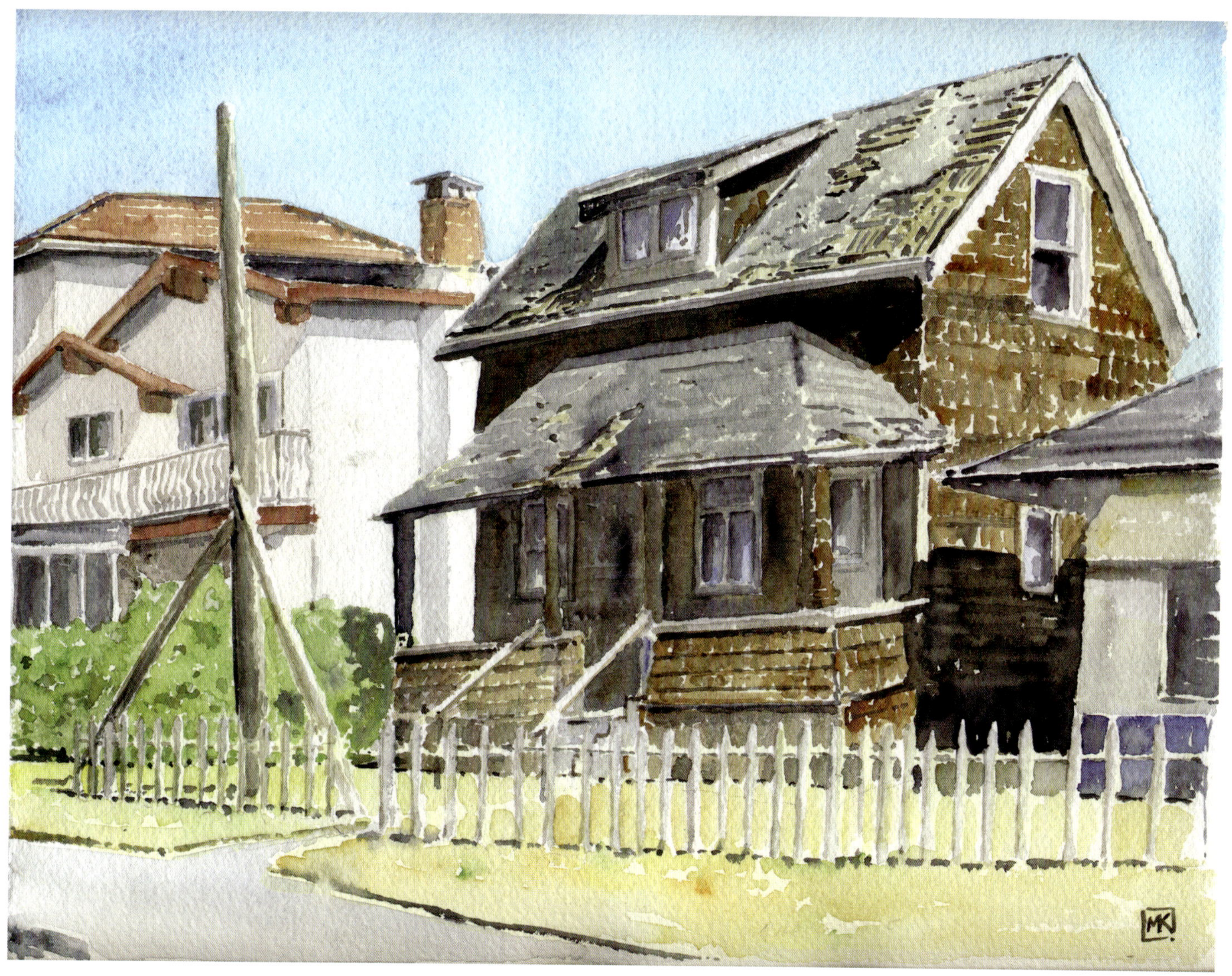

(Above) 4966 Rupert Street in the summer of 2013, shortly before its demolition.

(Previous page) A 1903 house at 1431 Haro Street painted at its 110th birthday. Built by J.P. Matheson, the father of a partner in the celebrated Townley and Matheson architectural firm, it was foundry owner Charles Lightfoot's home, later becoming a rooming house. It has been restored and stood until recently across the lane from the Landmark Hotel – an astonishing recent demolition of what was, in the 1970s, the tallest building in the West End.

Romantic-era artists in 18th- and 19th-century Europe lingered over picturesque ruins that would evoke melancholic thoughts on the passage of time and the frailty of human endeavour. Their Vancouver successors have to be quicker on their feet, as nothing sticks around here for long.

When I ask myself why I would paint such things, which few people want to own and hang on their wall, I usually get an answer that is partly to do with their pending erasure and is partly their textures and weathered colours – such a contrast with the bland glass and stucco of much of the city.

I fancifully imagine them having a kind of kinship with the Japanese concepts of *wabi* and *sabi* – the former meaning a rustic simplicity such as the house above that was built way out in the sticks north of Kingsway (the Westminster Road) in 1910. It was one of a number of small cottages along the street because the Collingwood West interurban station was a half block to the north; there is no station today, but the right-of-way is now the Expo line. One old cottage survives on the block.

Sabi means the beauty or serenity that comes with age, when the life of the object and its impermanence can be seen in its patina and wear. But there is little of that kind of serenity in Vancouver.

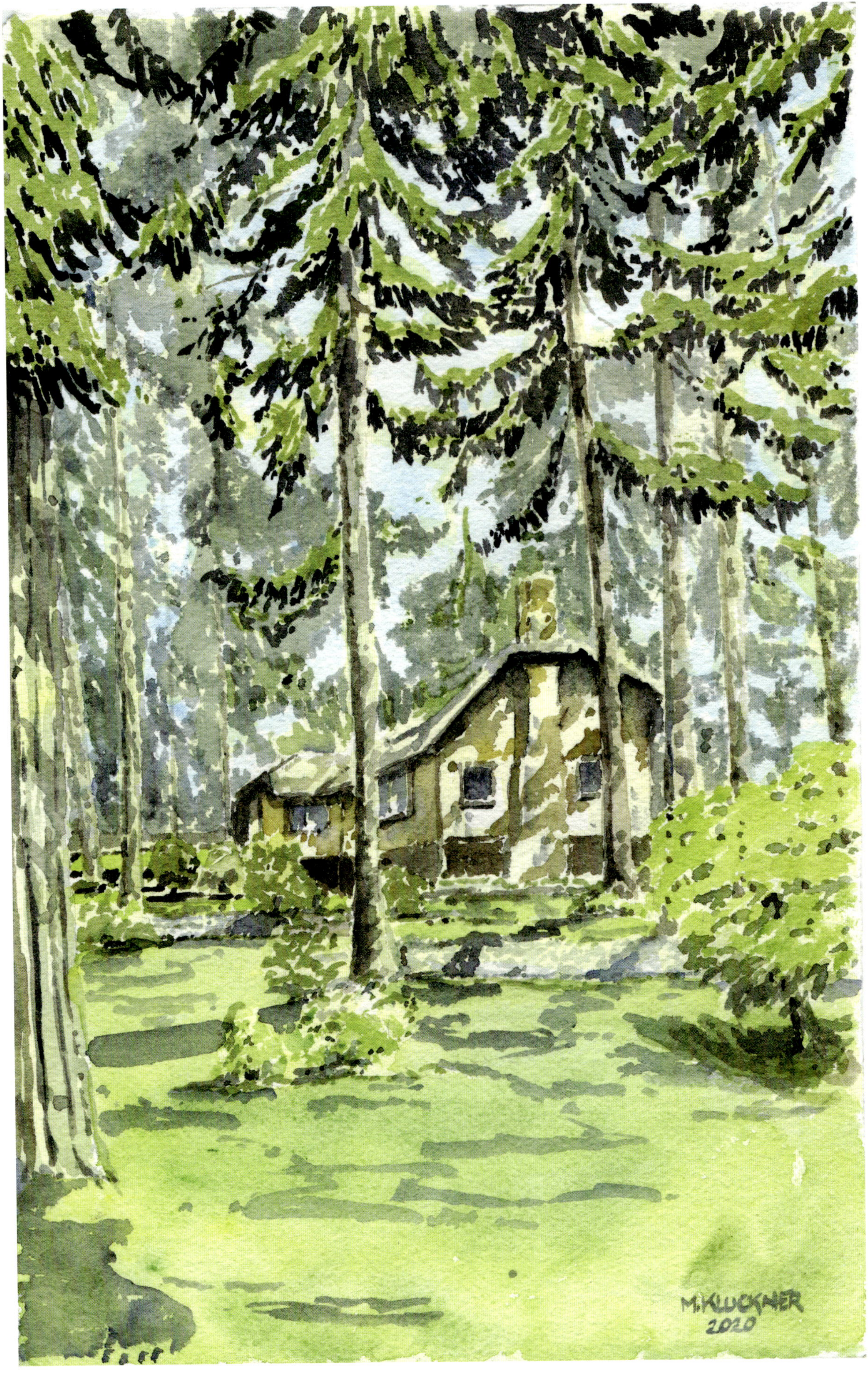
M.KLUCKNER
2020

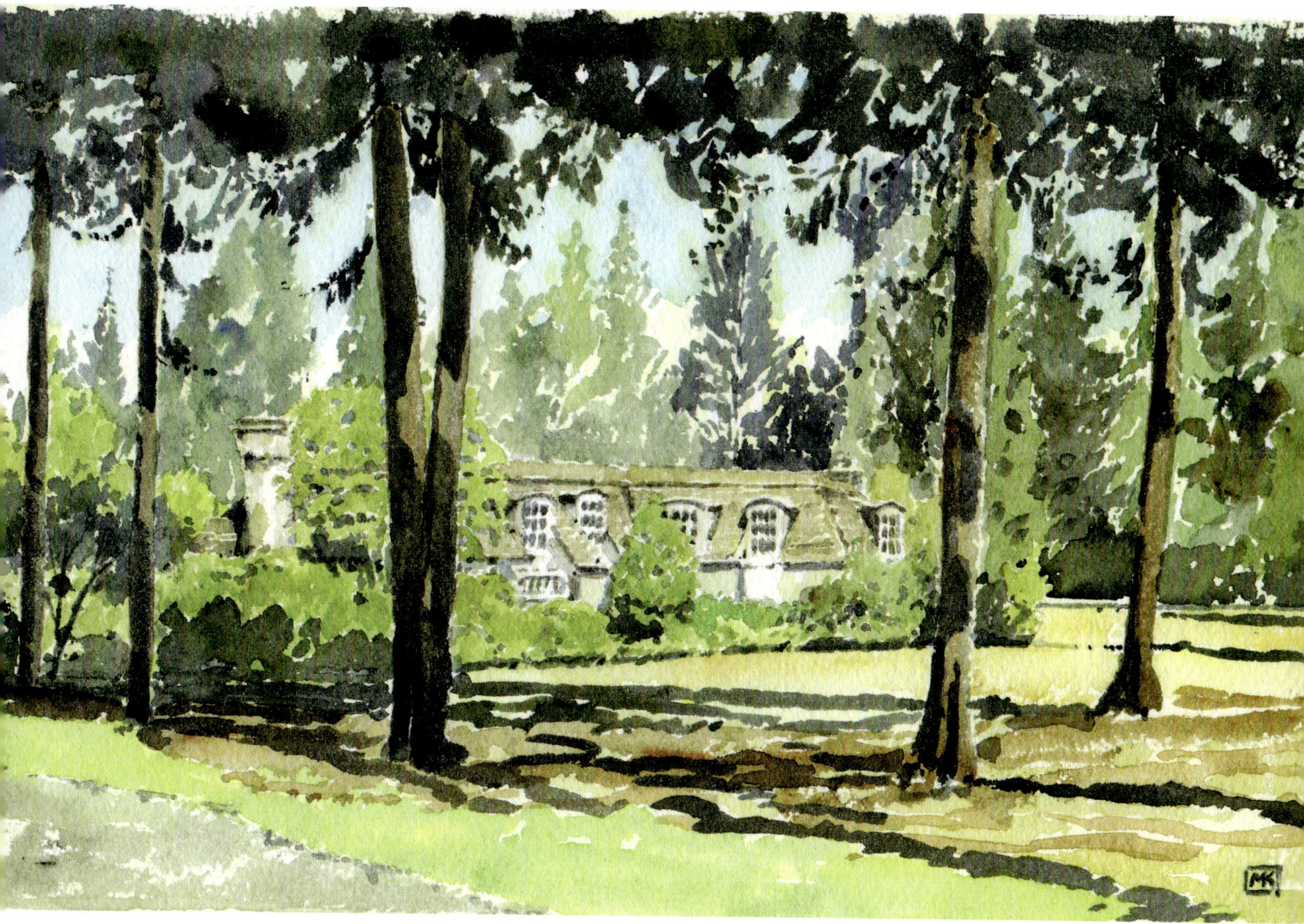

In July 2010 I was painting a commission in the area and came upon this abandoned estate at 1784 Drummond Drive. It was an unusual French Provincial-style home, built in 1949 for Dr. S.T.R. Serjeant. It sold in 2015 for $17,550,000 and, still vacant, was torched in an arson fire in November of the following year – the second empty-home fire in a month in the area. In 2020, the next time I returned, there was evidence of construction on a new home.

Curiously perhaps, even the bastion of uber-wealth in the northwest corner of Vancouver above Spanish Banks presents a disrupted and shabby face. Houses that are obviously empty with abandoned grand gardens dot posh Drummond Drive. Evidently even the rich can't maintain a stable neighbourhood. One owner on nearby Belmont Avenue, Yi Ju He, the wife of an international businessman, filed suit in June 2019 against a $249,000 vacancy tax bill on her $25 million property, arguing that the renovations she wished to do on the 1937 house (assessed at only $10,000) had been delayed by the City.

Shaughnessy Heights – now called First Shaughnessy, which was named a Heritage Conservation District in 2015 to preserve its historic homes and apply some maintenance standards to the many properties that are sitting empty – looks positively settled by comparison.

(Previous page) A house on Drummond Drive built in 1926 for K.G. Nairn, president of a real estate and investment company. Vacant and going to seed in 2020, the house and its 1.34-acre grounds were on the market for $21.5 million with annual taxes of just over $106,000. Almost a bargain.

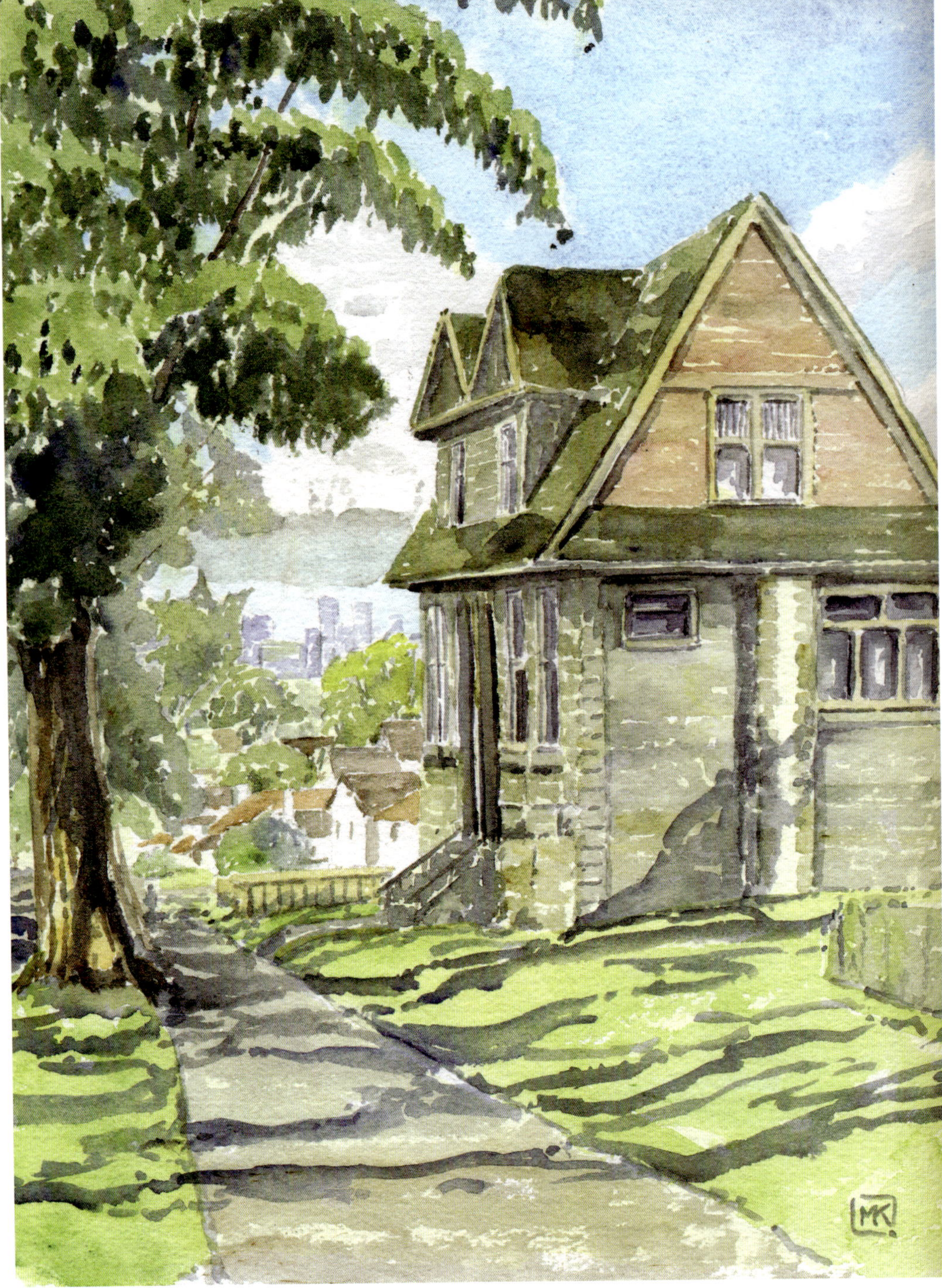

Most buildings in Vancouver conform to fairly standard setbacks, shapes and sizes. The occasional anomaly tells a story, such as this house at 2033–35 East 2nd Avenue on the steep hill east of Victoria Drive. It is unusual both because it is a side-by-side duplex built in 1912 from concrete blocks – a rarely used handyman-type of construction technique (see page 14) – and because it sits almost on the sidewalk. Its neighbouring houses have much deeper setbacks, and almost all of them on the two blocks between Victoria Drive and Lakewood are postwar ranchers. Why? Because the Burnaby Lake interurban railway line, which ceased operation in 1952, ran on a diagonal right of way from 2nd and Victoria Drive through what was then an empty block in the distance and actually passed through the backyard of this house. It joined First Avenue near Nanaimo and proceeded eastward into Burnaby along the grassy median, which still exists today.

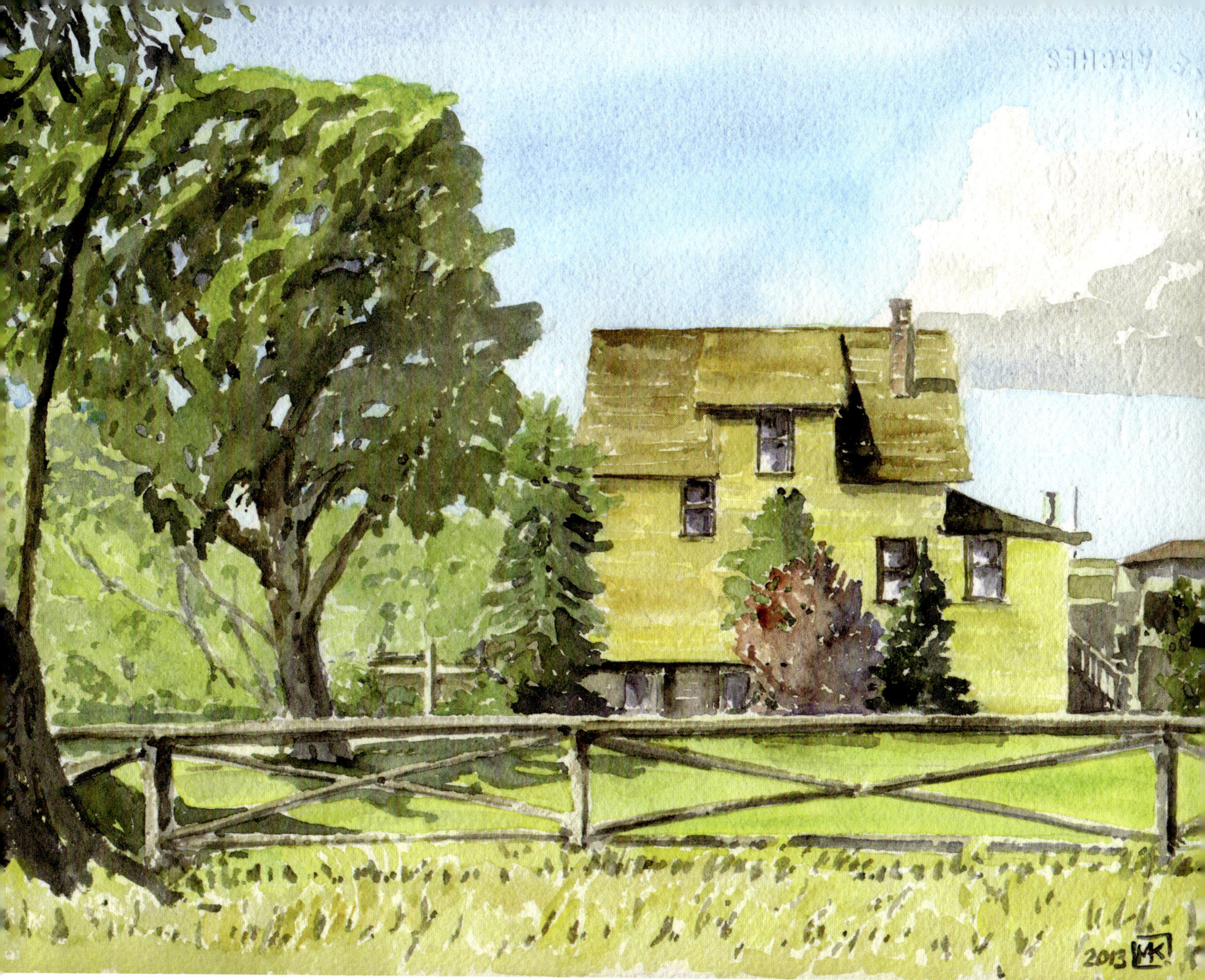

The 1908 Avalon Dairy farmhouse at 5805 Wales Street, just south of 41st Avenue, in 2013.

A unique piece of Vancouver's semi-rural past was "saved" several years ago, in the sense that the operation was a success but the patient died. The lawns and trees that surrounded the old Avalon Dairy have been completely replaced by townhouses, leaving the farmhouse standing in a central plaza with a handful of raised garden beds in front of it. The view of the farmhouse that I painted here in 2013 from Wales Street is now obliterated except for a peephole corridor through the red-painted townhouses of "Avalon Mews." Its agricultural past is commemorated by three metal cutouts of grazing cows – the public art component of the redevelopment.

Jeremiah Crowley moved west from Newfoundland's Avalon Peninsula in 1906 and rented a house on Wales Street near Kingsway that came with six cows. Life as a dairy farmer appealed to him, and two years later he moved with his family to this property. He soon had 30 cows. By 1916, bottled milk delivered by his horse-drawn wagons replaced a system where neighbours would bring their own containers and buy milk and cream by the dipperful.

Jeremiah's sons expanded the business. Everett Crowley was the most prominent of them and is commemorated for his community service and political work by a park in southeast Vancouver. The company continues in operation in Burnaby, specializing in organic dairy products.

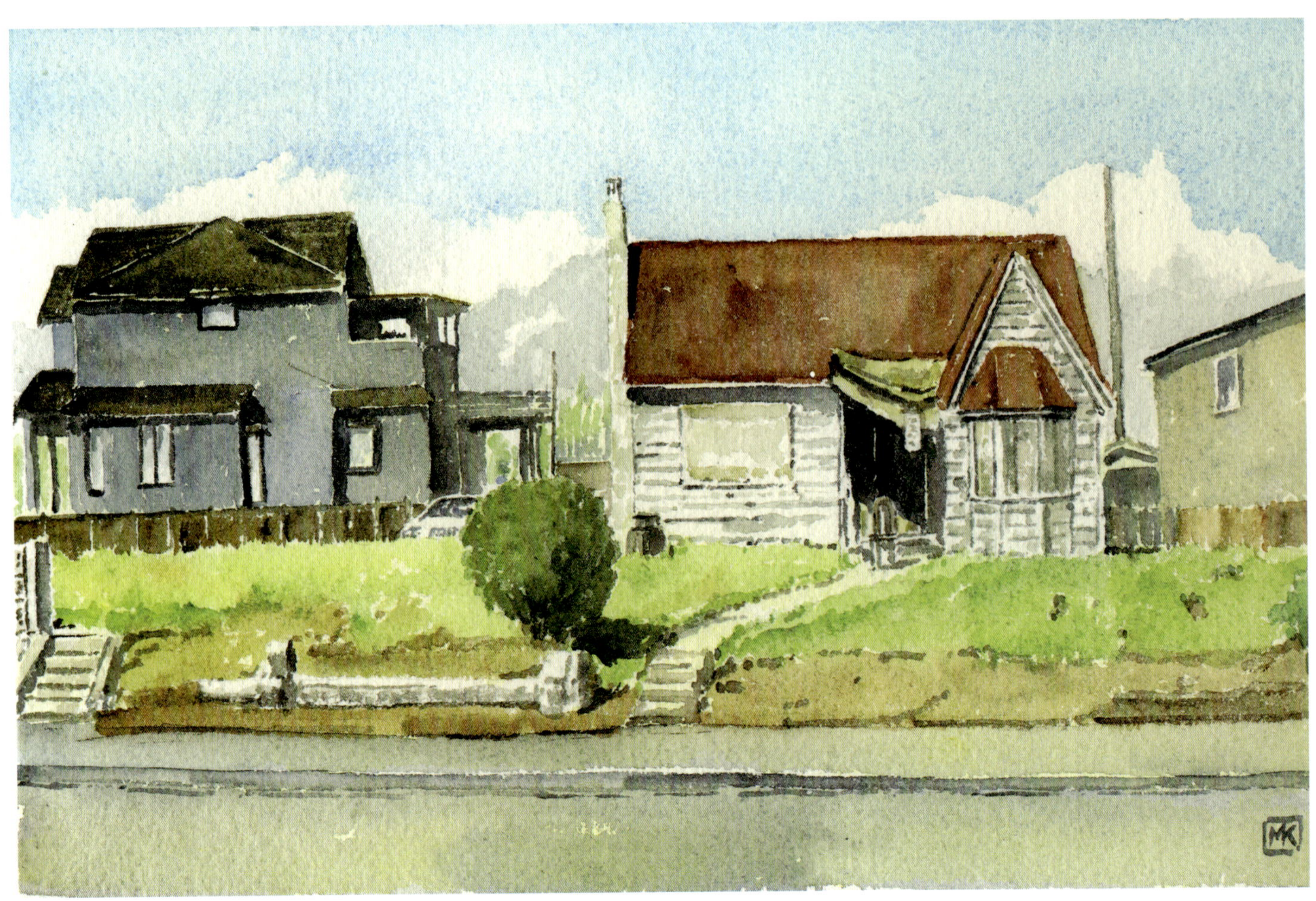

The 1941 house at 4459 Rupert Street and the vacant lot beside it – site of a 1945 house – in the spring of 2020.

The occasional tableau of abandoned vs. new can still be seen on the streets of East Vancouver and tells of the changes in prosperity the city has witnessed over a lifetime.

The boarded-up little house at 4459 Rupert was built in 1941, probably by its first occupants, carpenter Paul McNamara and his wife Lillian. It was one of the relatively few houses completed as wartime restrictions on labour and materials clamped down on the domestic market. Postwar in 1948, several blocks to the north, the federal government's Central Mortgage & Housing Corporation built 600 homes for returned veterans and their families in a new Renfrew Heights subdivision, dubbed Diaperville by the locals, a nickname it shared with Fraserview, the 1950 CMHC development south and east of Victoria Drive and 54th.

These were the birth houses of the baby boomers – small, with shared bedrooms, one bathroom, one phone, big yards to play in, new schools a short walk away. Throughout East Vancouver, most of these modest houses from the '40s and '50s have been swept away by a second generation of much bigger homes, such as the one in the background that faces onto 29th Avenue.

Part of the change is demographic – waves of "non-British" immigration, of multi-generational extended families wishing to live under one roof – and is the story of the Vancouver Special house style beloved of Italian families in the '60s and '70s and many other ethnicities since. And part of it is prosperity – the ability to have the Great Indoors that was out of reach of most wage earners a lifetime ago.

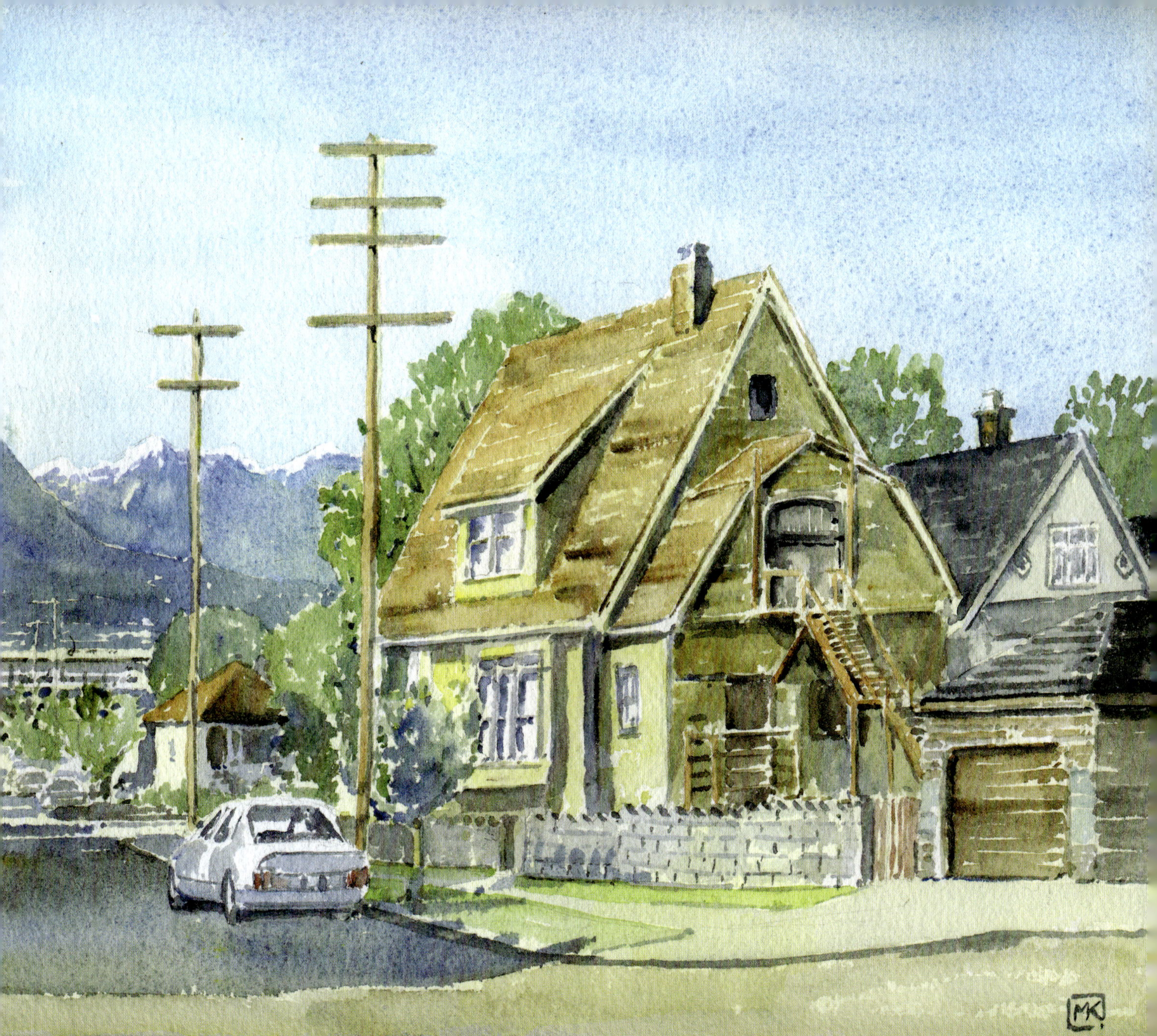

The debate about housing affordability has run like a river through Vancouver for the past half-century. Even in 1967, realtor Henry Block told a reporter that "only 40 percent of our society can afford to buy a home today."* In this century, with scads of money flowing into the city from overseas investors, prices have skyrocketed and caused immense pressure especially on young people unable to buy homes and compete for scarce apartments.

The city's surviving stock of affordable rentals includes old rooming house conversions such as this one at 2104 Venables. Built as a single-family home by R.R. Hintz in 1910, it adapted to changing times along with much of its Grandview neighbourhood. Rents stay affordable in part because of deferred maintenance; the houses are deteriorating slowly – appealingly to my painter's eye. Some tenants are the kind of people I once was, the "wilfully poor" as I described myself on page 3 of this book, the "creative class" in writer Richard Florida's expression, who he says are the harbinger of a neighbourhood's gentrification.

Looking north on Lakewood Drive to Venables and the North Shore mountains on a spring evening with snow still on the mountains and the "golden hour" sunlight casting long shadows across the road. The old stone wall indicates the house was once a grand residence; the fire escape attests to its conversion into a rooming house.

*Quoted in *Vanishing Vancouver: The Last 25 Years*, p. 31.

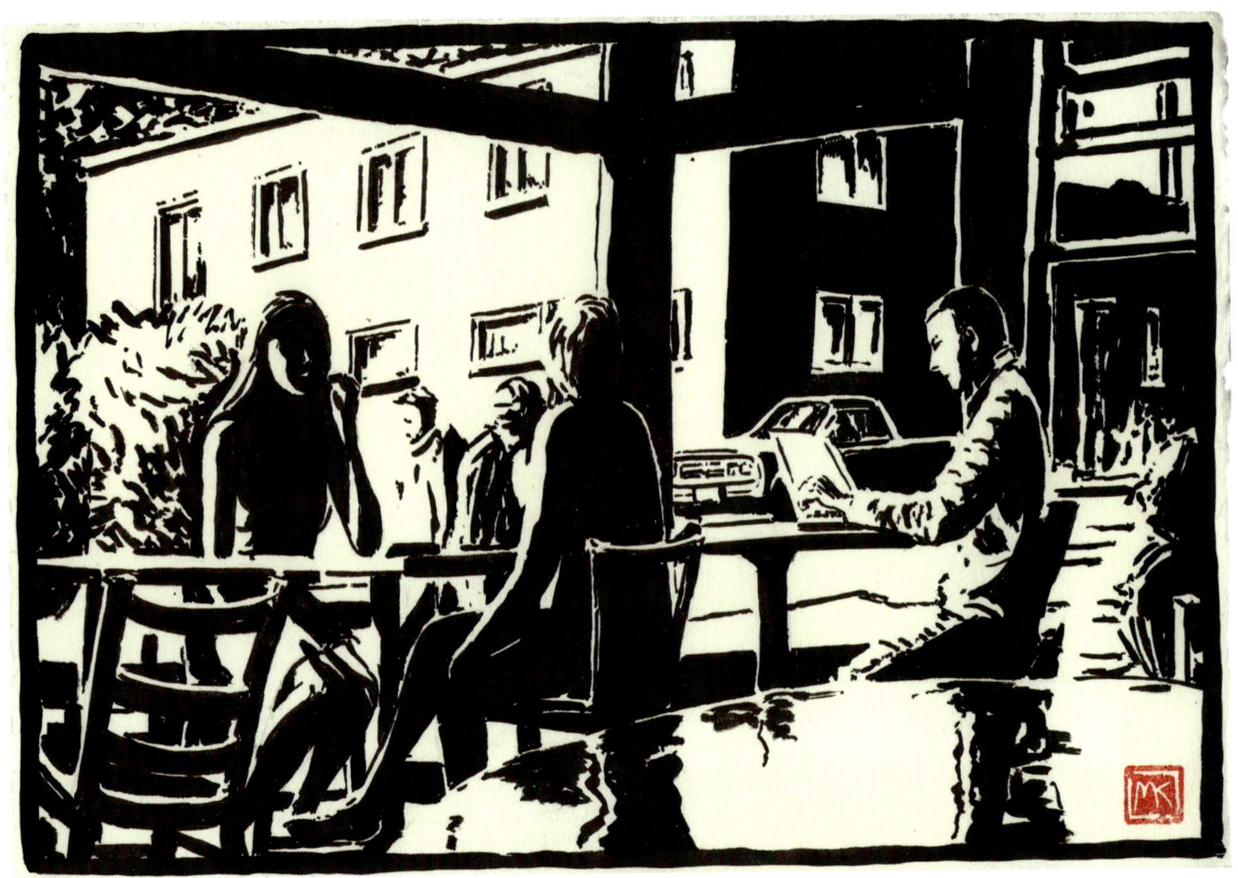

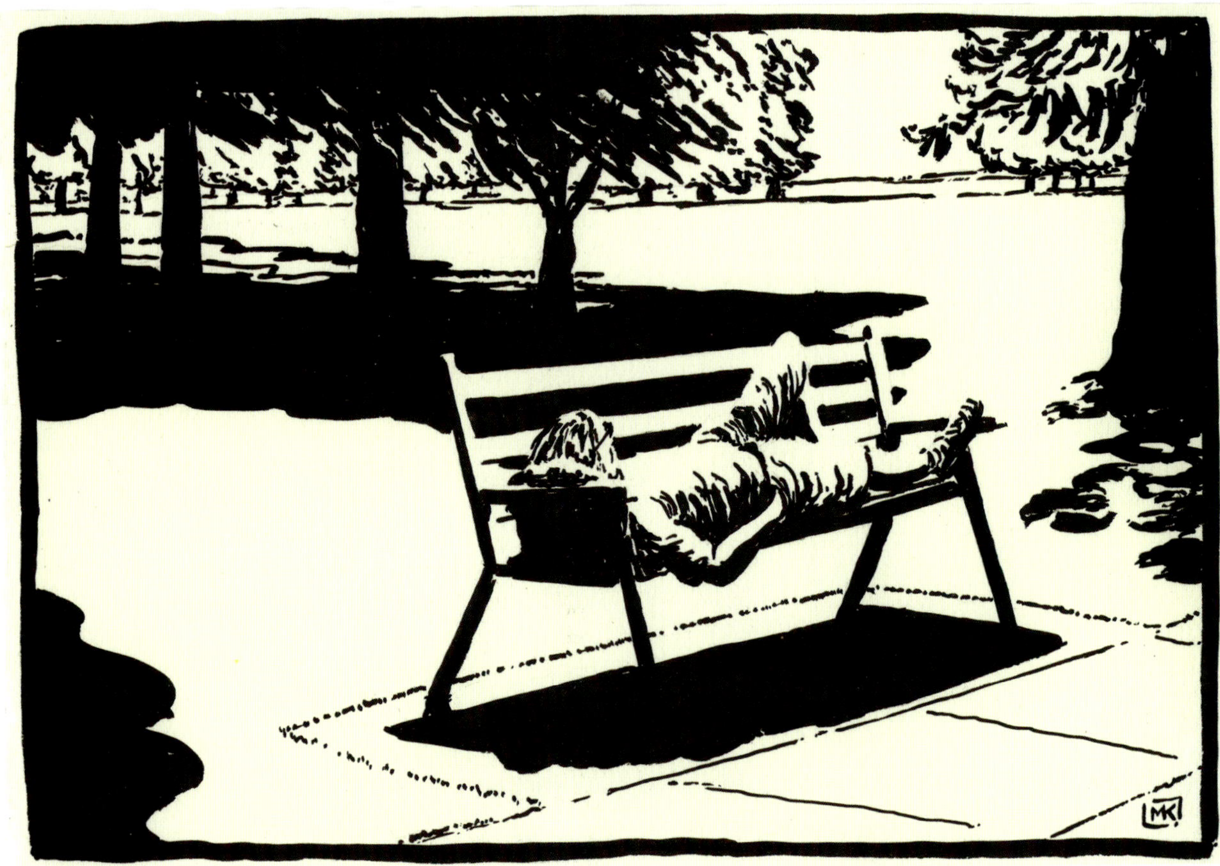

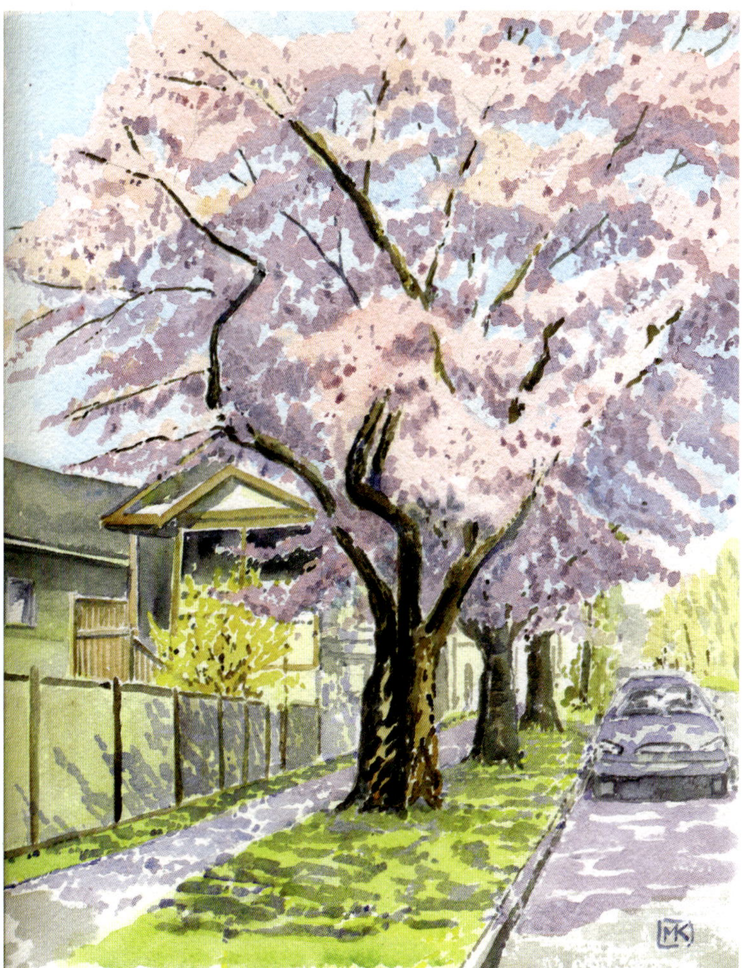

Vancouver's best places are available to everyone for free or, say, the cost of a coffee. At a workshop held in 2019 to discuss the forthcoming City Plan, participants were asked to describe their favourite event or experience. People spoke of the Folk Festival, the Jazz Festival, the Film Festival, and the recent mural painting extravaganzas in Mount Pleasant. The legendary retired city planner Ray Spaxman, however, described the sunsets.

These natural rituals define the place for some of us: in November, the white line on the North Shore mountains from the first snowfall of winter; the quiet summertime gatherings at Kits Beach to watch the sun go down (above); and the spectacular cherry blossoms of March and April, such as these Kanzan cherry trees on Victoria Drive near the Trout Lake Community Centre (left).

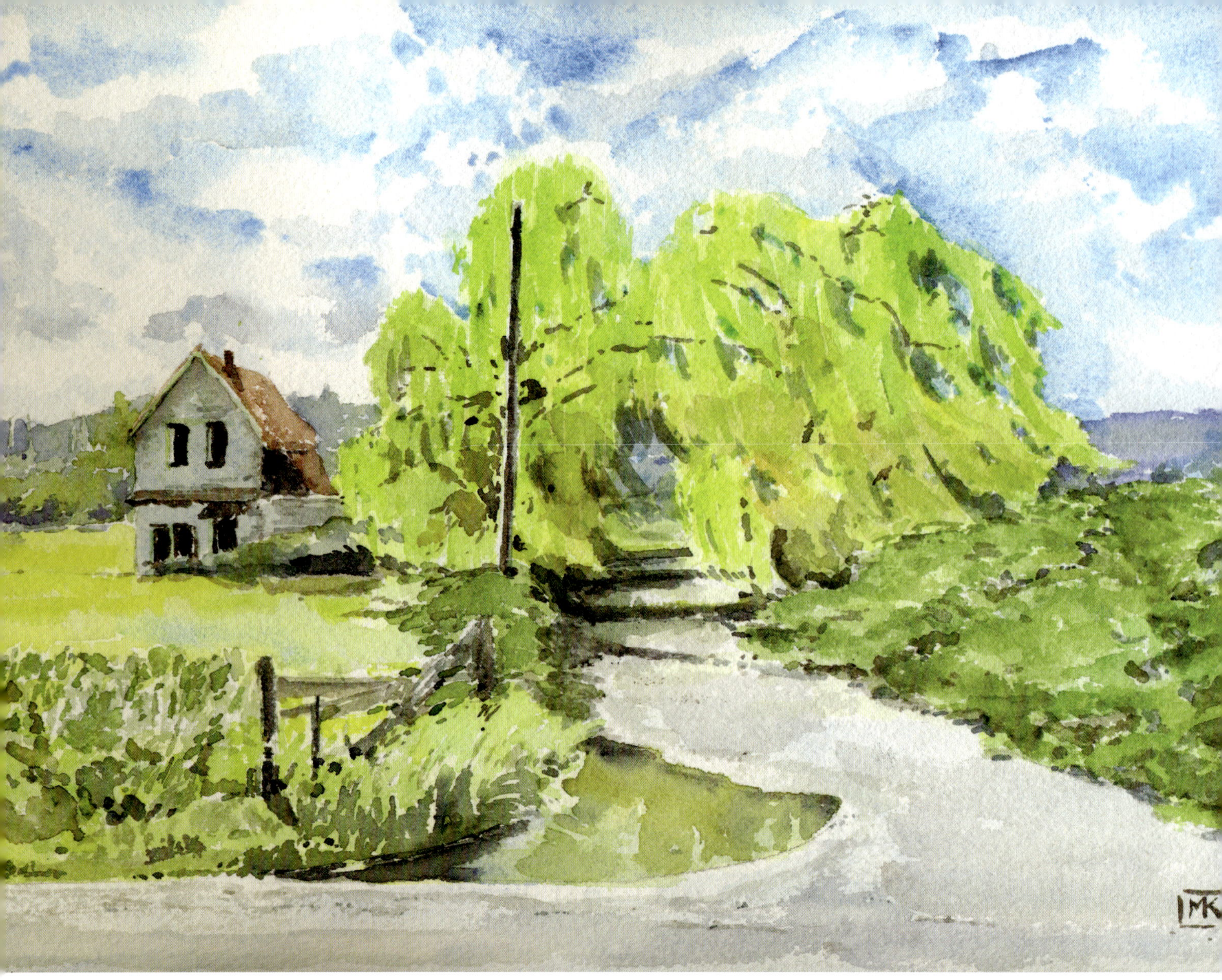

Farm on 8th Avenue in the Hazelmere Valley, Surrey, about 2000.

"I had a farm in Africa, at the foot of the Ngong Hills." So begins Karen Blixen's *Out of Africa*. Less exotically, we had a farm in South Langley where we lived from 1993–2006. Sheep, chickens, and old-rose cultivation occupied us, inspiring me to write *The Pullet Surprise* (1997) and *Wise Acres* (2000) and Christine to write *A Year at Killara Farm* (2013). Our neighbour was a boutique winery set picturesquely on the hillside behind us.

Our surroundings changed comparatively little during those years as we were deep in the Agricultural Land Reserve. The speculators and subdivision builders were forced farther north in the Fraser Valley or west near White Rock's edge, closer to the freeways. But farmland was nevertheless amalgamated and old places abandoned. This property in the Hazelmere Valley, a few miles west of our place, had a large barn which blew over in a winter storm; subsequently, the abandoned house slowly fell apart.

As in the image on page 41, you recognize the trees first. Weeping willows – not native trees. Somebody lived here. And the thicket of blackberries isn't native either.

Gone

The idea of travel had never seemed so sweet as during the COVID-19 pandemic that flourished in 2020 while I was writing this book. Freedom to move, to experience new places and see new people, had always been something I had taken for granted. We could go away whenever we wanted, couldn't we?

We weren't incessant travellers but did cover a lot of ground in the 35 years since I first took art materials with me on a trip. Included in these adventures were some epic sojourns – three months in the Mediterranean in the winter of 1992–3 was one – as well as more than three years living in Australia in the 2000s. And there were multiple forays through Canada in the '90s, collected in the book *Canada: A Journey of Discovery*.

My never-ending travels with my sketchbooks have been through British Columbia, a series of which became *Vanishing British Columbia*. The watercolours that begin this "Gone" section were painted since its publication in 2005.

Over the years, the media I carry with me have changed: early on, being more robust, I carried quite large, heavy sketchbooks and full sets of watercolours and brushes; later, especially in challenging Asian countries, I took a small (8 × 5 inch) Moleskine journal for pencil drawings and words and carried only a few watercolour sheets. I have always used Arches cold-pressed paper: the "Aquarelle Arches" watermark is visible on the image on this page.

Some places demanded additional materials, such as *sumi* and *washi* (ink and paper) in Japan. We travel very light and it's getting lighter the older we get.

I have not laid out chronologically this selection of pages from all the sketchbooks from all the trips. If there is a theme, it starts with places that experience a lot of change, moving through to countries that, for whatever reason, have a timeless quality to their landscapes or cultures.

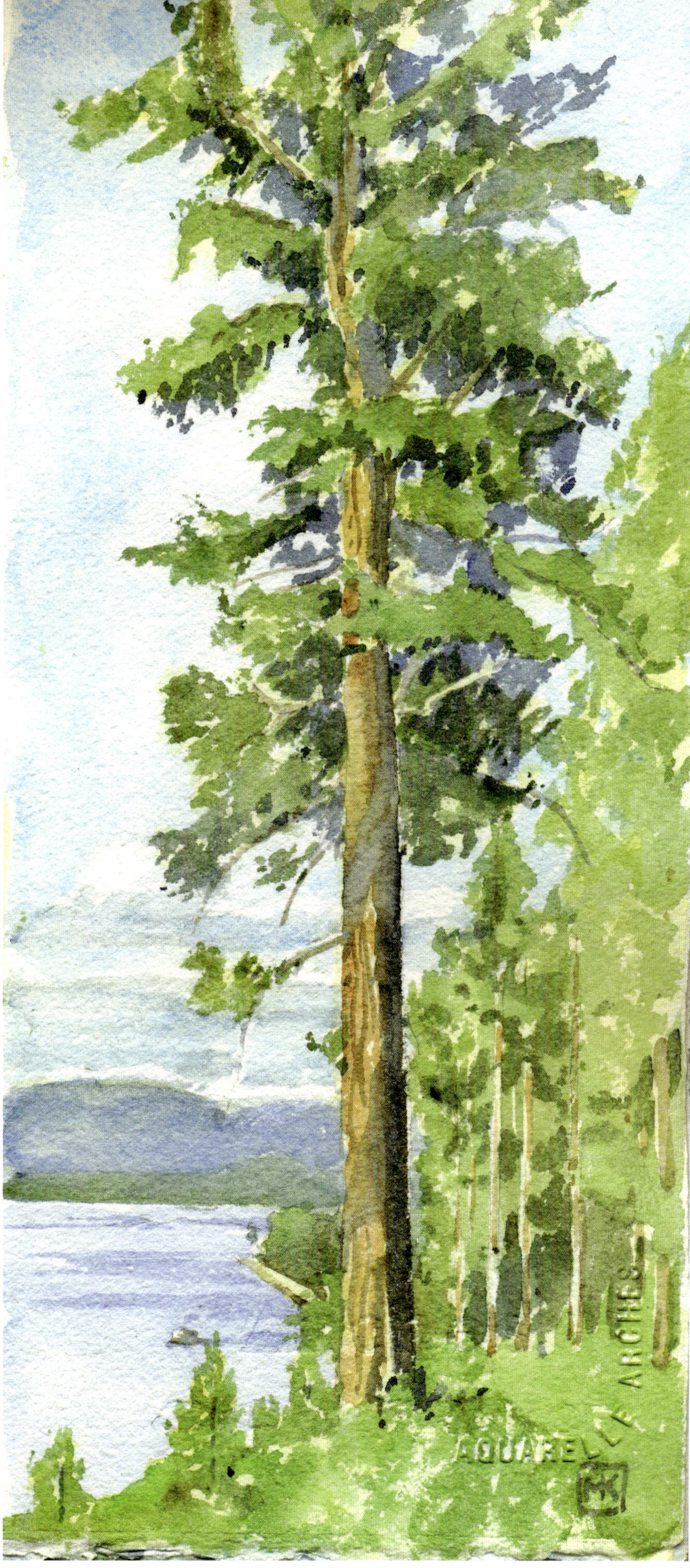

Douglas fir on Savary Island, 2004.

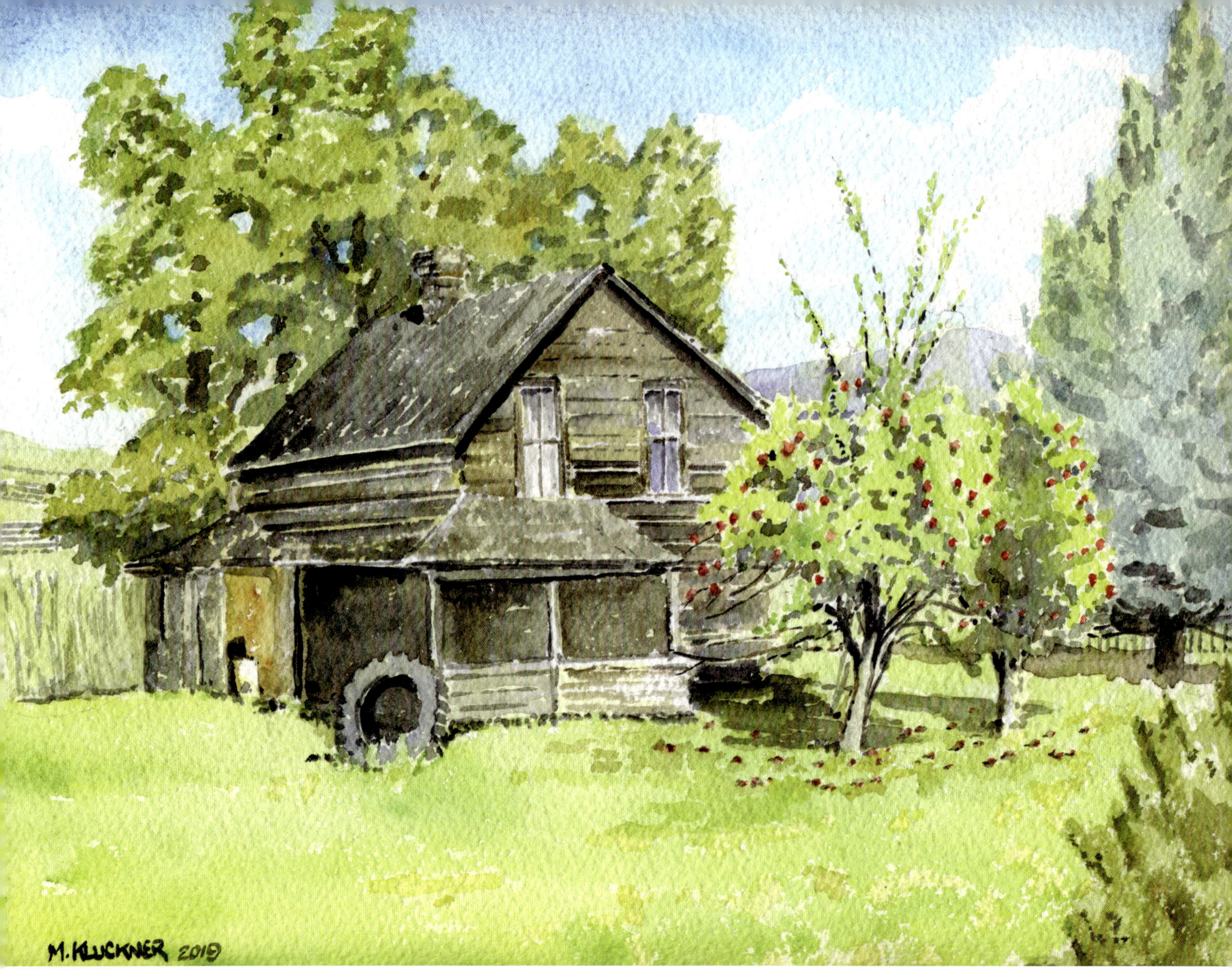

Homestead east of Cherryville, September 2019. All of the nearby pastures were still in use but this settler's house, built of squared logs, was empty. What struck me were the unpicked apples, and the memory of drying apples on a rack above a woodstove. I stopped, filled a bag with them, then started the watercolour.

*See *Vanishing British Columbia*, pp. 70–1.

A road less travelled crosses the Monashee Mountains. Highway 6 begins at Vernon, running east through miles of fine agricultural land and the communities of Coldstream and Lavington. The former was something of a Shangri-La for English expatriates, drawn there for the gentlemanly pursuit of orcharding by the example of Lord and Lady Aberdeen, he being Canada's Governor General from 1893 to 1898.

The Coldstream Estate Company, founded in 1906, built on work the couple had begun in Kelowna 15 years earlier and placed a genteel stamp on the land east of Kalamalka Lake that is still discernible amidst the ranchers and malls that have taken over the area.*

Farther east, the road passes through the busy town of Lumby and arrives in rougher, less cultivated terrain as it nears Cherryville. It is still good land, but more suited to grazing than farming.

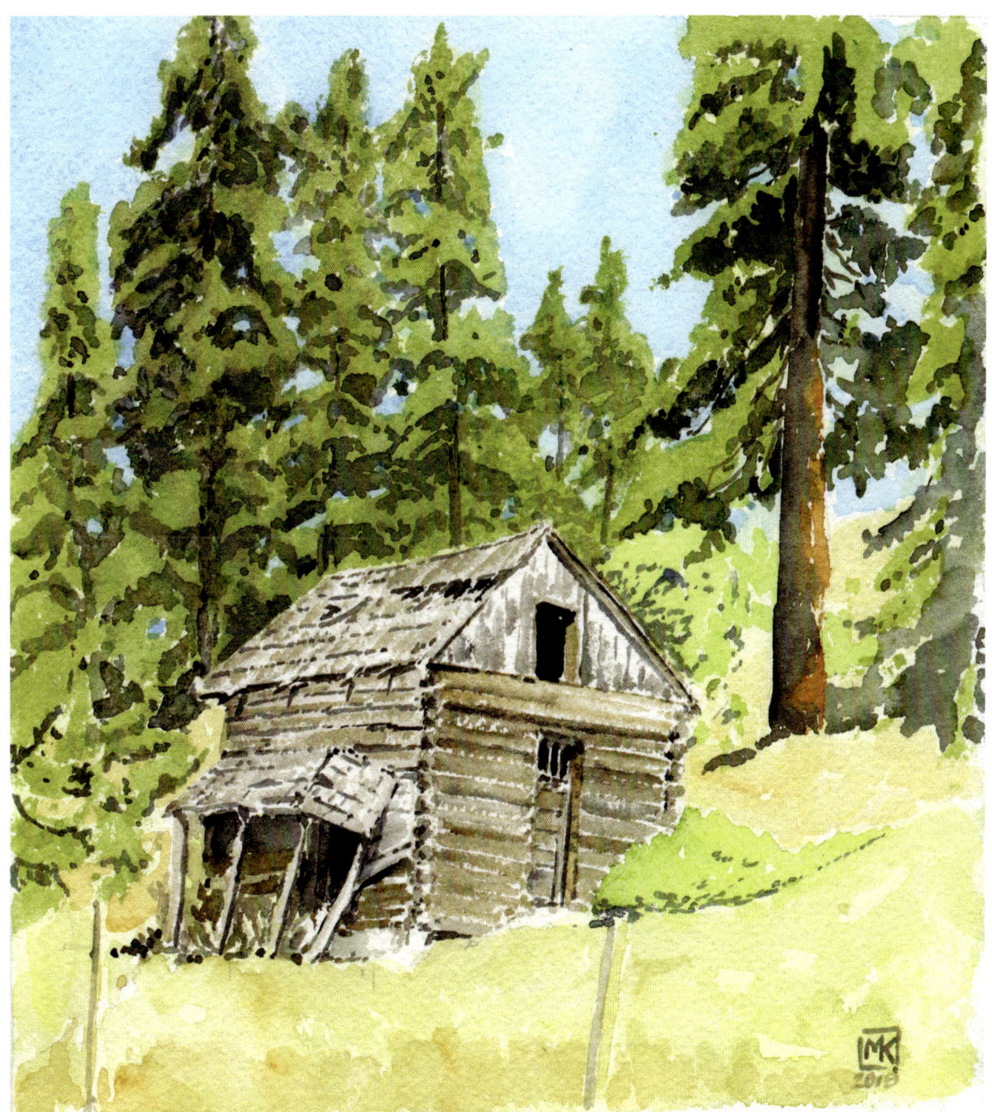

First shelter of a settler, maybe a solitary trapper or hunter? September 2019 in the Monashee.

If you pull off the road, walk along the narrow shoulder and then sit, as I did to paint the little shack above, dogs a half-kilometre away notice you and bark until you leave. Evidently, there are not many strangers passing through.

Relics of the homesteading era still dot the roadside until the highway passes the abandoned house with the apple trees and begins to climb toward Monashee Pass. Across that ridge it descends steeply in switchbacks before arriving at Arrow Lake, now a hydroelectric reservoir behind the High Arrow Dam miles to the south near Castlegar.

On that Kootenays side of the divide, it is harder to spot any evidence of early settlement because the old lakeside communities were drowned by the reservoir. Anne de Grace's 2005 novel *Treading Water* follows the lives of the people of Bear Creek from its founding to its extinction three quarters of a century later.

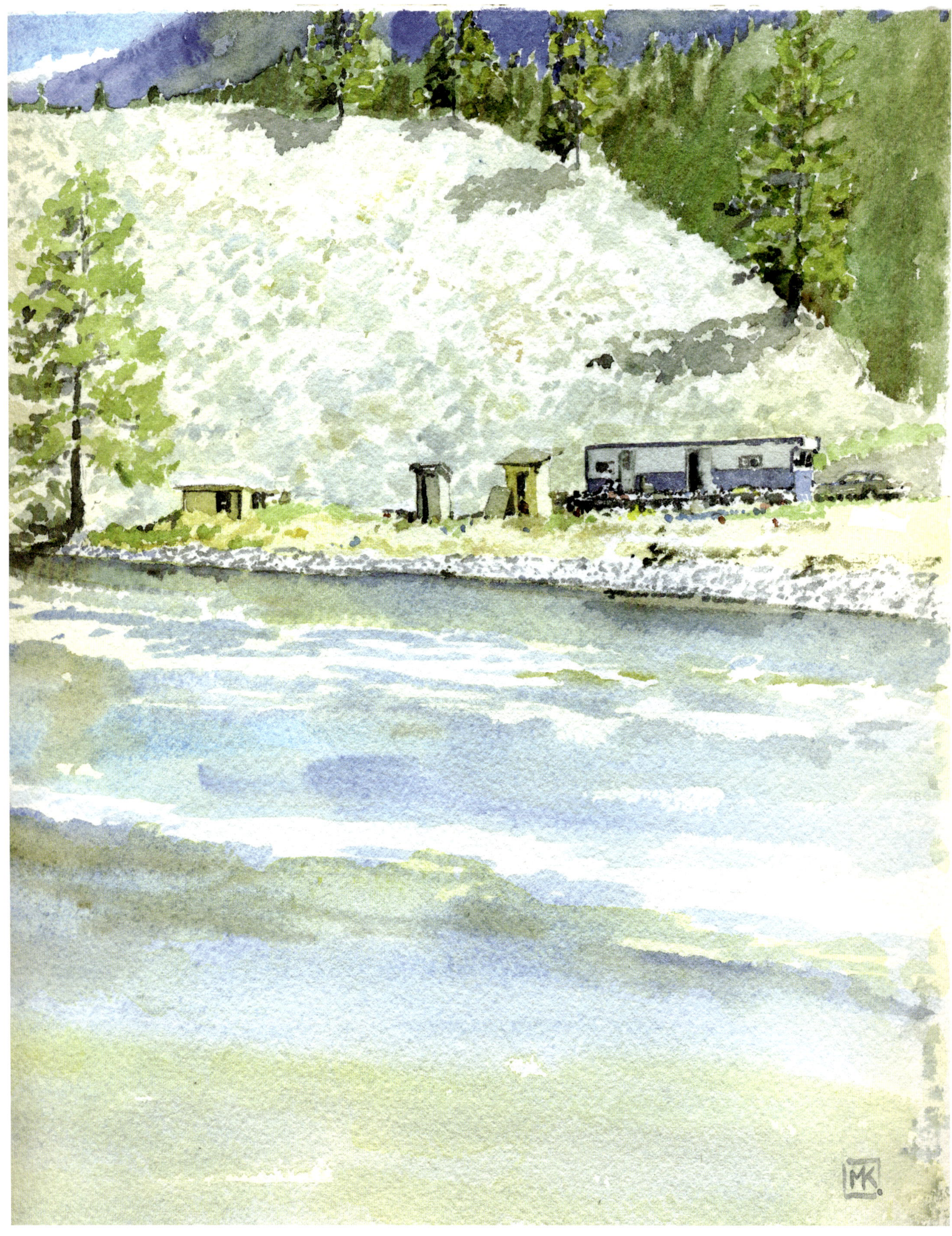

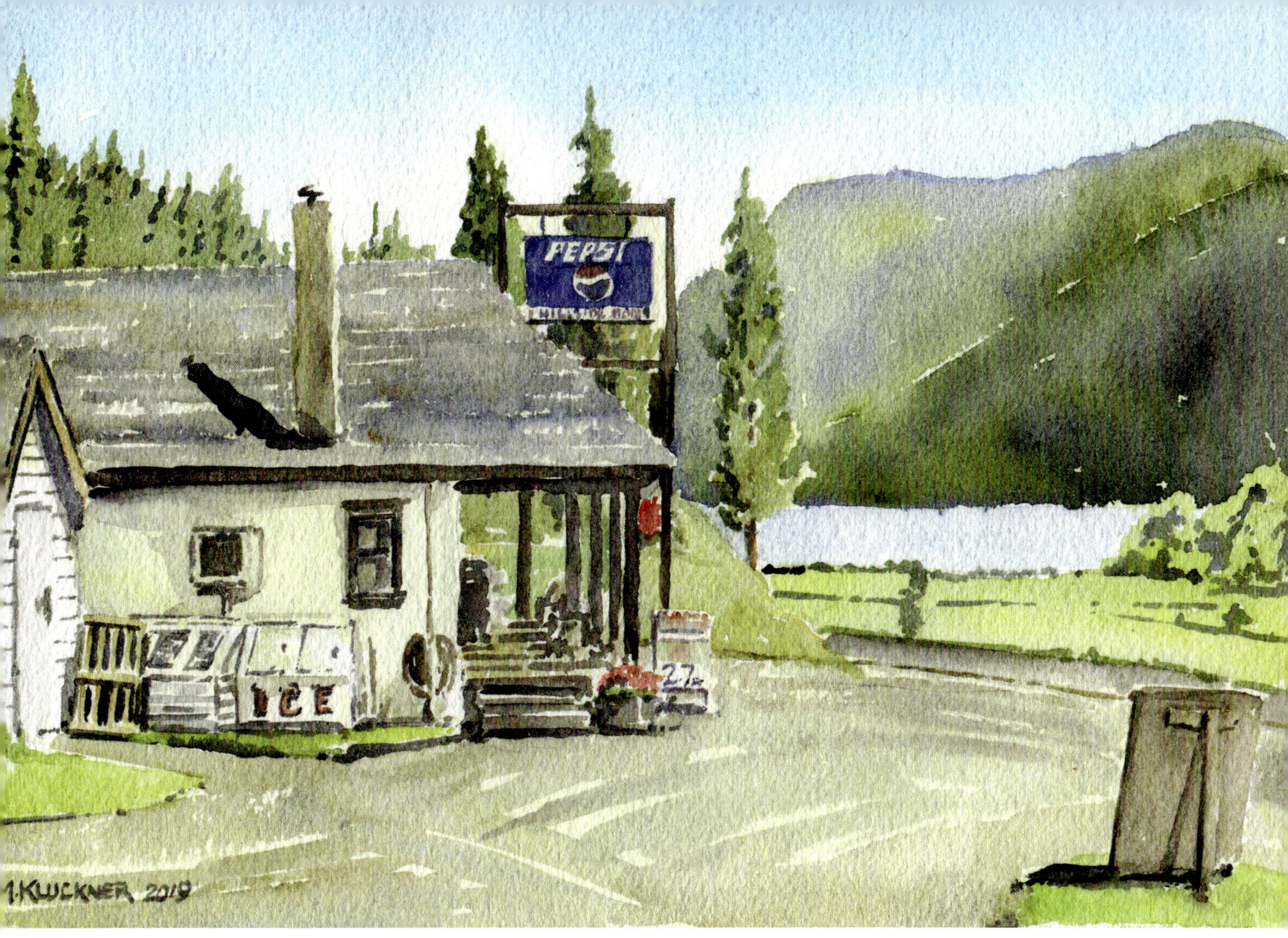

Monte Lake store, 2019. Dream job: own a country store? Monte Lake is on the section of Highway 97 between Vernon and Kamloops.

The ramshackle quality of rural and small town British Columbia disconcerts many Europeans and uninitiated urban Canadians who head out on a road trip to see the province's natural beauty. Much of it is a landscape of abandonment, of folks who tried to settle on bad land in a harsh climate and eventually moved on. Chasing the baubles and tasting the fruits of modern life usually requires an urban home and job, and Canada is amongst the most urbanized countries in the world. In the cities, change is caused by the relentless pressure of growth and development, not abandonment.

In the local lingo, if you live near fresh water you probably have a cabin; near salt water, such as the Gulf Islands, you probably call it a cottage. The cabin communities in the Interior, such as at Monte Lake (above), have a certain stability and tidiness. Elsewhere, like the encampment with the single-wide and the biffy, it's easy to move on when fortunes change or, perhaps in this case, when the Thompson River floods.

(Preceding page) Thompson River near Spences Bridge, high water, 2008.

A homestead on the riverbank
A biffy and a plywood shed
A generator, propane tank
An airtight in the trailer.
Mess and rusty metal spread
Who cares? they might have said.
You only see it if you wish.

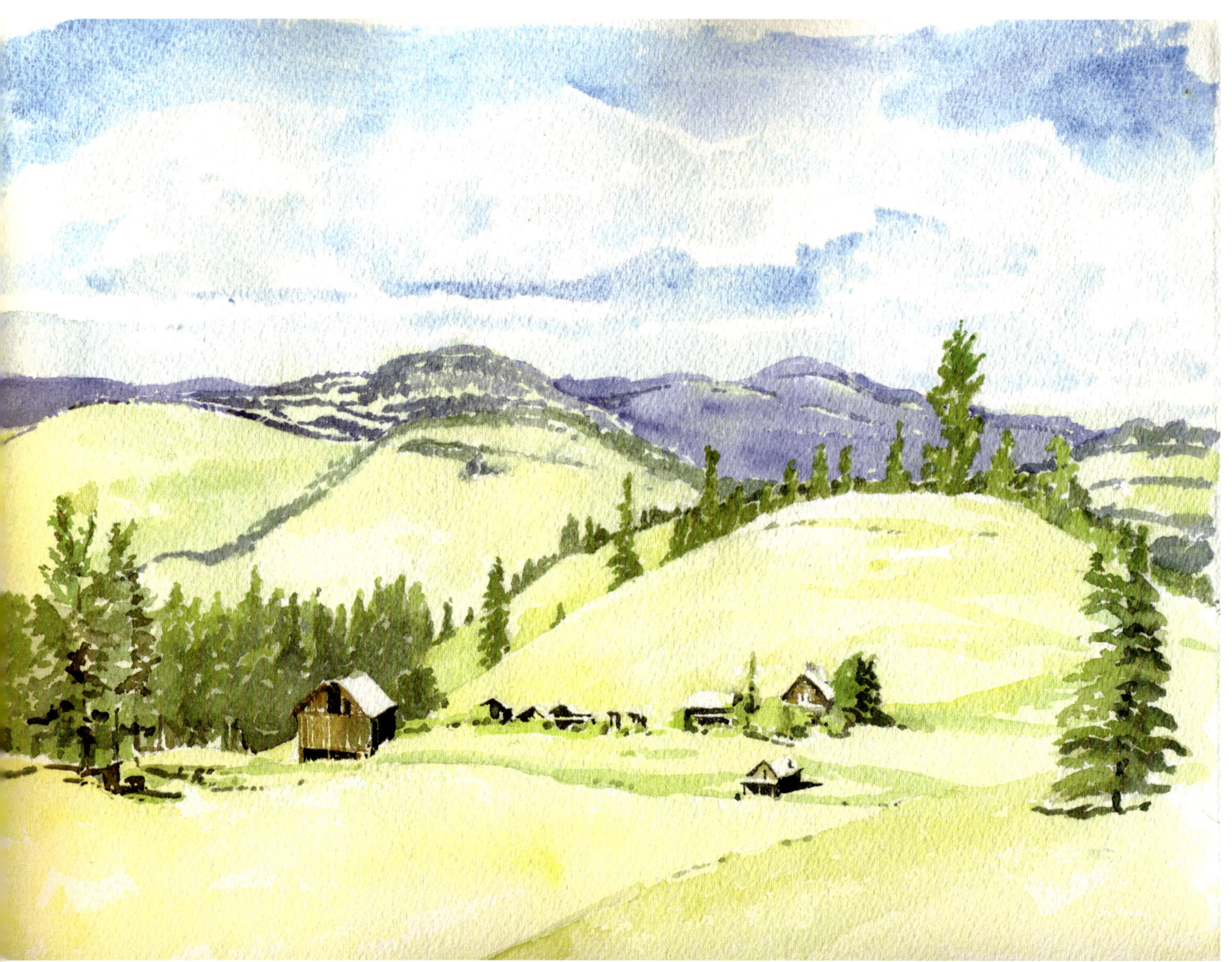

The Eek ranch near Rock Creek in 2005.

A favourite place to travel and paint is the Boundary Country east of Osoyoos Lake, a dry landscape with long views and a particular cobalt blue colour in the distant mountains caused by the sharp clear air. Settlers drove cattle from the USA in the late 19th century and established ranches. Bridesville, with a Great Northern Railway connection that lasted from 1905–35, became the spot of commerce and connection with the outside world. Relics remain visible on the grasslands as it is too dry for them to be colonized by trees, unlike many other areas of the Interior. The trees, mainly ponderosa pines, run in ribbons on slopes and settle in gullies where rainwater collects.

The ranch of Charles and Kathleen Eek was a landmark of sorts on the old Bridesville – Rock Creek Road that runs close to the US border south of Highway 3. I posted the picture on my website and in 2007 a reader noted Charlie's passing years before and stated that "it seems old Johnny Eek has died as well," which got a response from another reader that Johnny wasn't dead yet and had published a book of his cowboy poetry!*

Johnny Eek died in 2015 at the age of 91. As well as being ranchers, he and his wife Margaret were enthusiastic square dancers, and he played fiddle, banjo, guitar and harmonica.

**Cowboy Poetry and Wisdom from Boundary Country*, Kettle River Writers Cauldron, 2004.

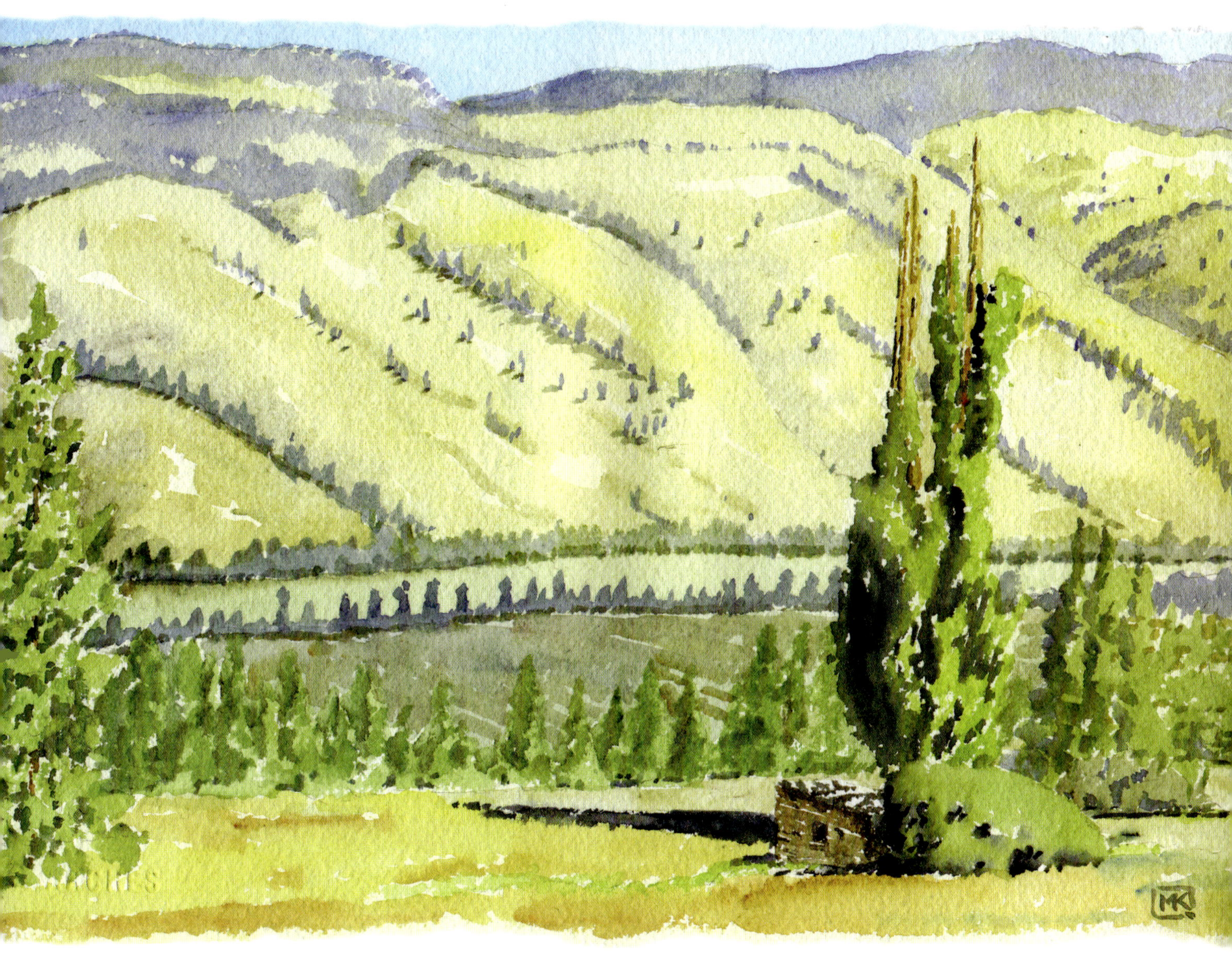

View down to the Kettle River, September 2013.

Not far east of the Eek ranch, the Kettle River emerges from the mountains and makes a left turn to run just north of the International border before flowing into the US at Midway. There is high ground south of the river – the viewpoint in this watercolour – and some good farmland for a way along the riverbanks near Rock Creek. Mainly, though, it's cattle country, with superb pastures on the treeless slopes on the north (far) side of the river.

It was the old poplar trees that caught my eye on Myers Creek Road long before I saw the ruins of a log cabin. In places all over southern BC, it's just the trees that survive from the attempts at settlement. Poplars were planted as windbreaks in this part of the province; weeping willows were a typical addition to roadhouses and motels in the Fraser Canyon. Neither type of tree is particularly long-lived. The landscape will return to a completely natural state once the logs rot into the soil.

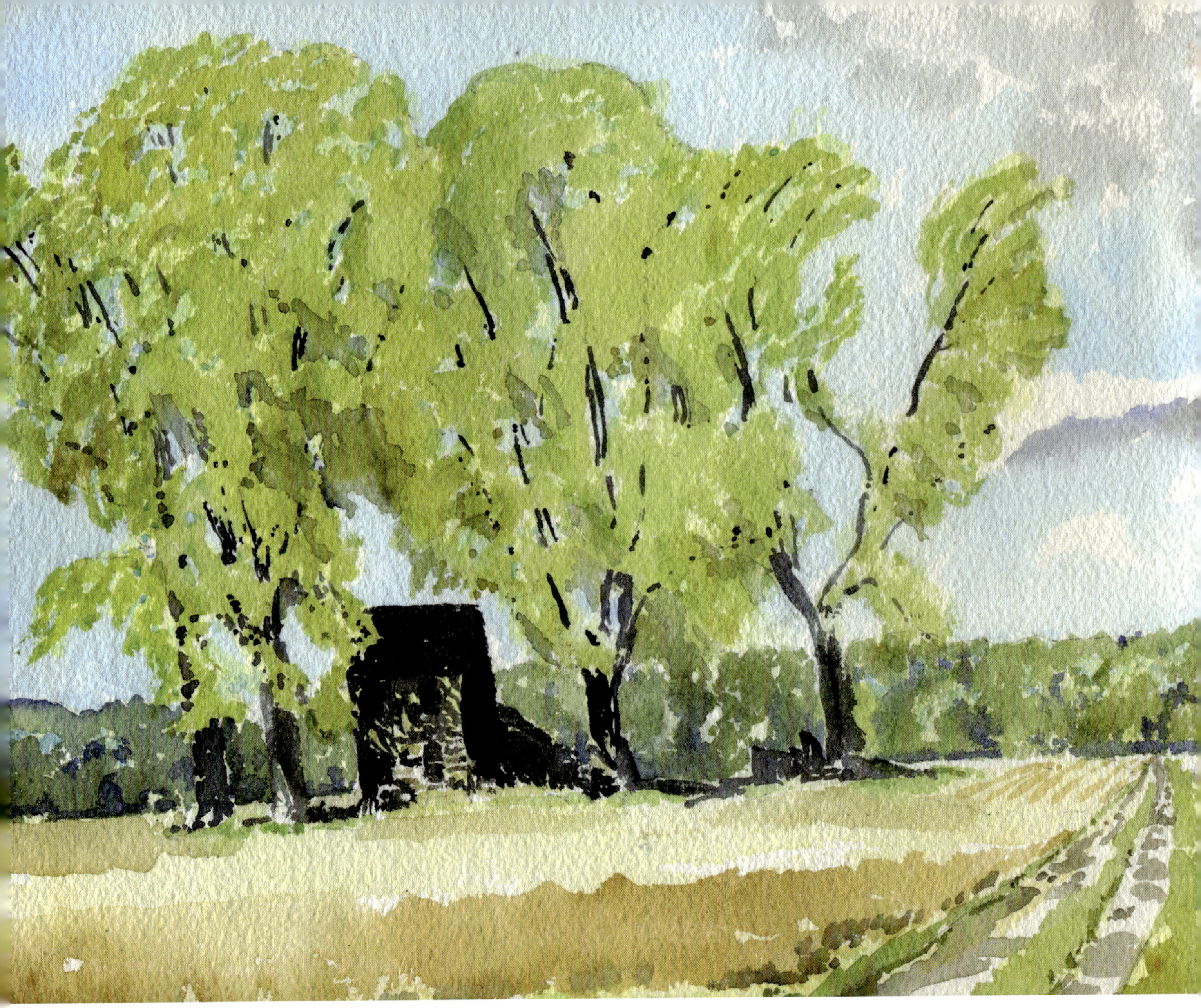

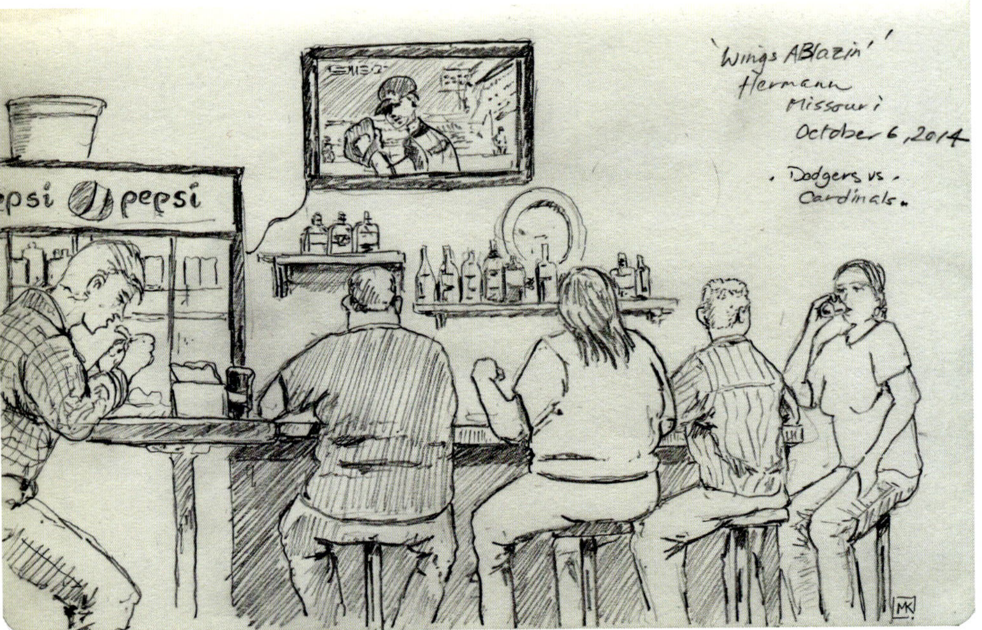

An island in the soybean sea behind the Missouri River levee (the line of trees in the distance) about 20 miles west of the charming German-flavoured town of Hermann. Places left behind, people moving on, farms consolidated – a kind of definition of the Midwest and West.

(Left) In 2014, both Missouri teams – St. Louis and Kansas City – were in the running for the World Series, adding some excitement to evenings spent in local taverns like Wings A-Blazin' in Hermann.

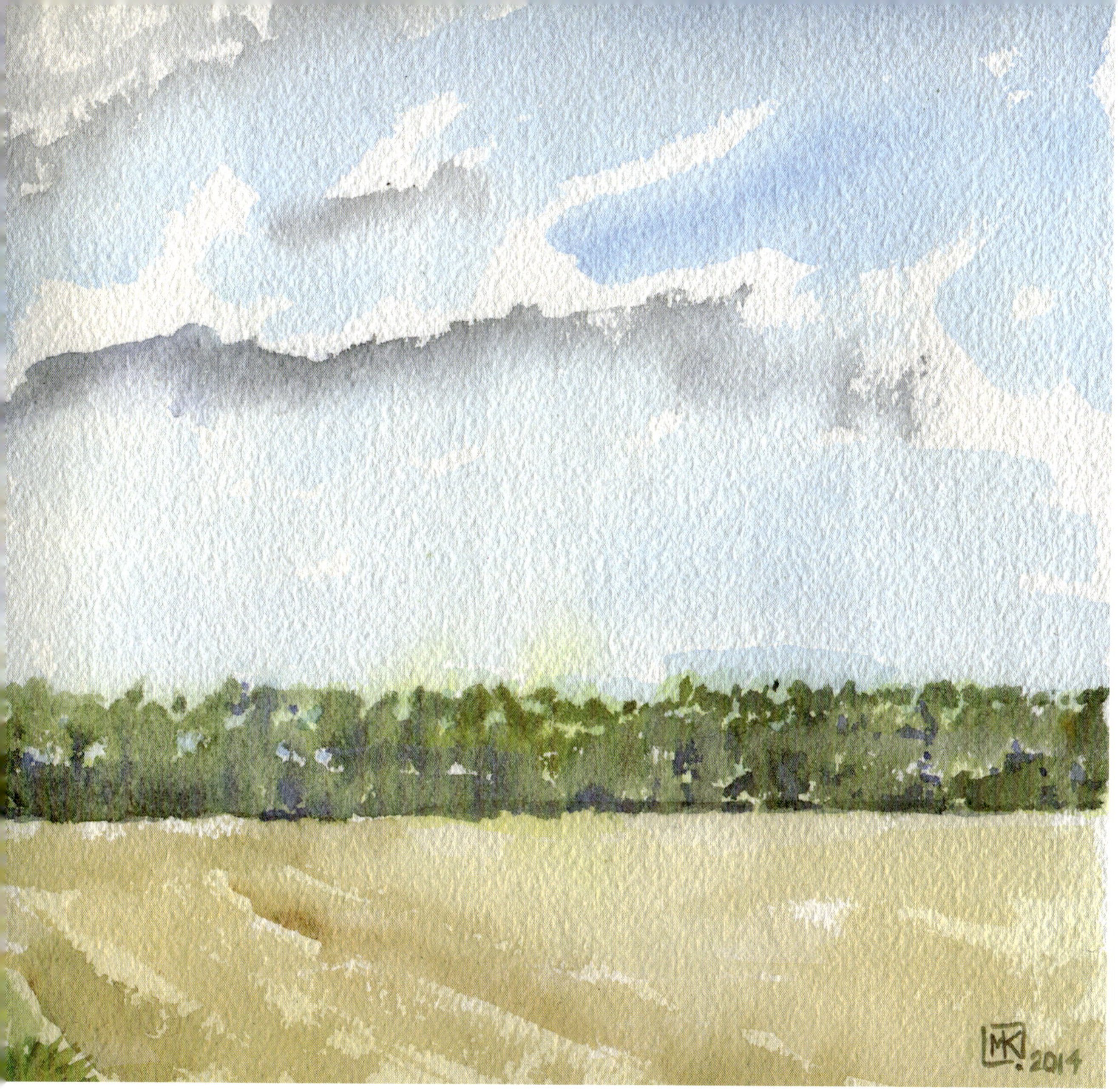

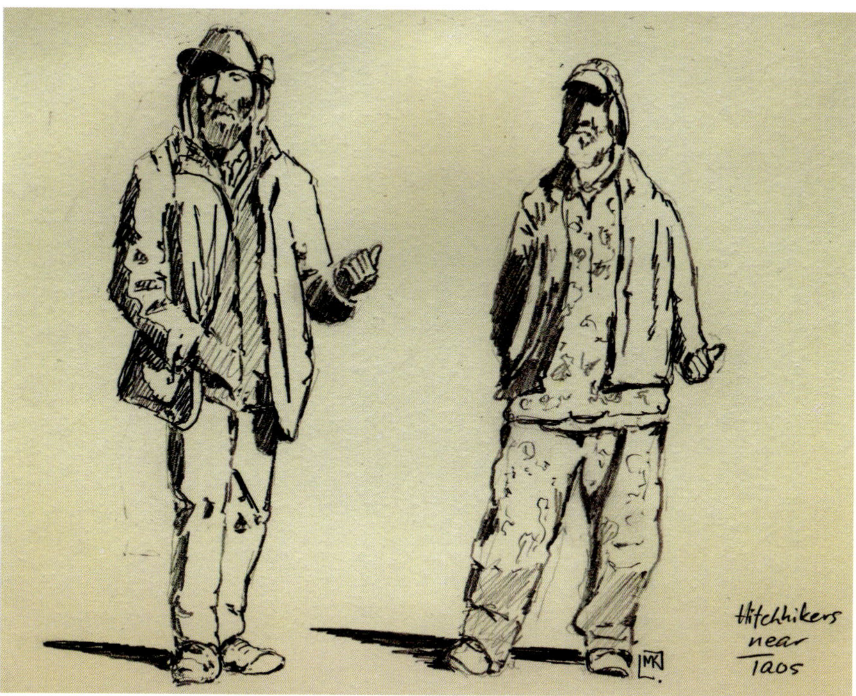

The sense of being in the USA is never far from one's consciousness when on the road, whether it's odd people wearing camo or Praise God billboards or signs lauding the right to bear arms. Not surprisingly, these hitchers – who could have been out of a Cormac McCarthy novel – posed for a long time waiting for a kindred spirit to give them a ride outside a café in New Mexico in 2013.

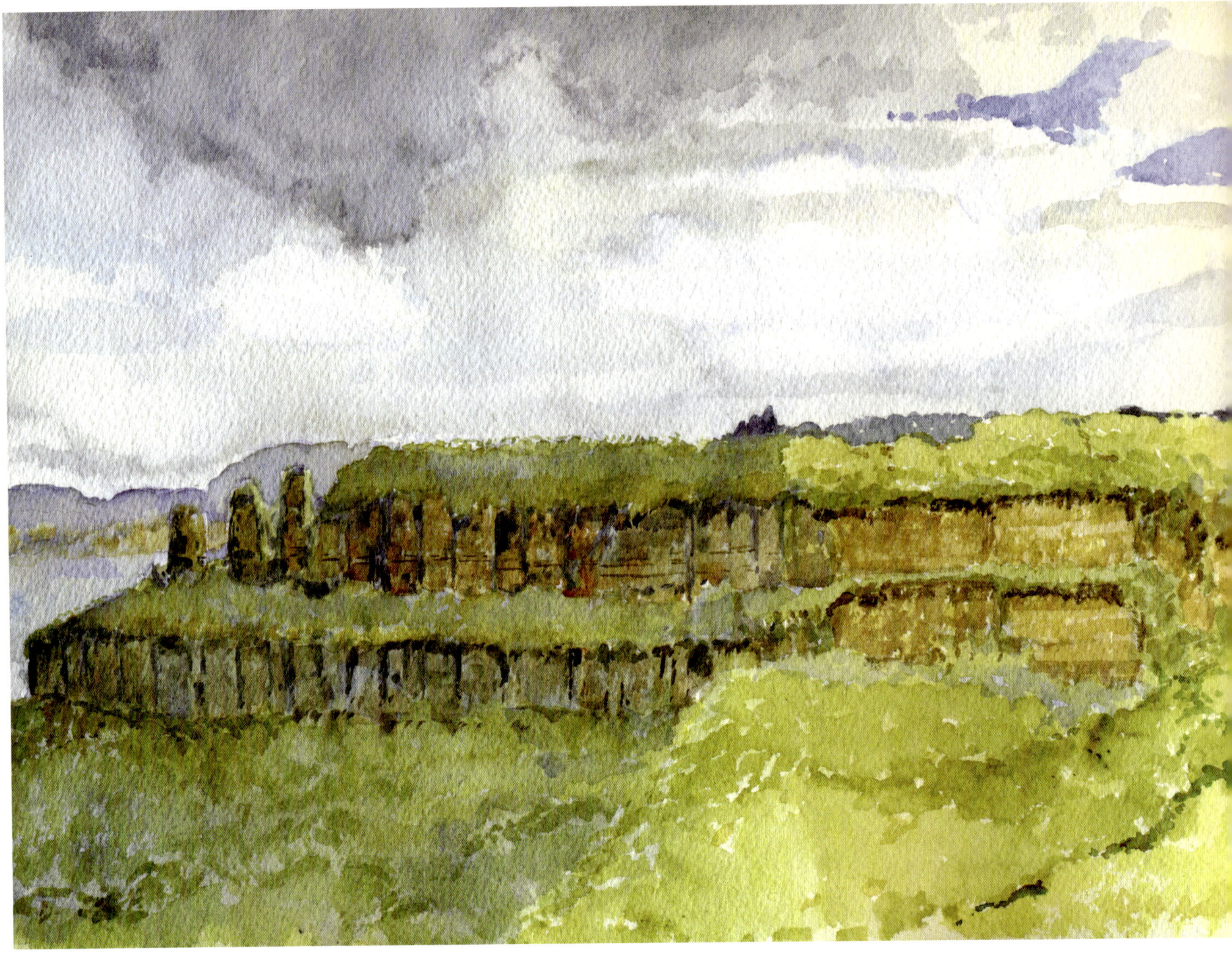

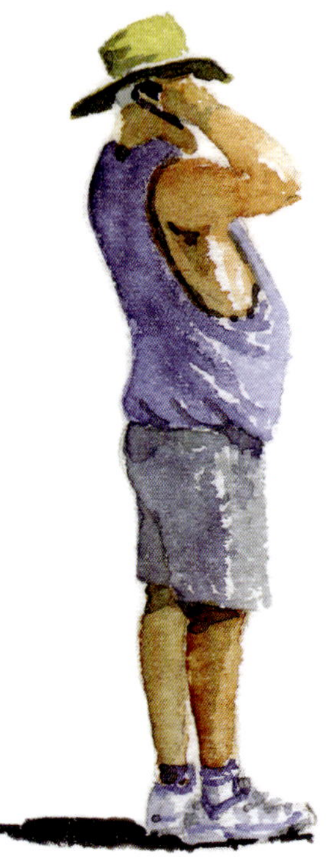

Australia is my second home as Canada is Christine's. We travelled there regularly beginning in 1979 and decided to move there, lock, stock and barrel, in 2006. Most of her family lived in Sydney, which was appealing but far too expensive for two itinerants with no jobs and episodic incomes from writing and art. So we looked to the west, about two hours by train or an hour and a half by car, to the Blue Mountains, and settled in its biggest town, Katoomba, population about 7,000, altitude about 1,000 metres or 3,000 feet. The climate is temperate for Australia.

The Blue Mountains are upside down in every sense: the rail line and roads and towns are on a plateau, not in the valleys; the valleys are almost impenetrable, cut deeply into the sandstone floor of an ancient sea and blanketed in eucalyptus forest. When you begin a hike you go down, and struggle to climb back out at the end when you're thoroughly exhausted.

All the towns strung along the rail line have their charms, with Victorian architecture mixed with art deco buildings and timber cottages. Katoomba is an arts hub; nearby Blackheath and Leura have a more exclusive, affluent feeling.

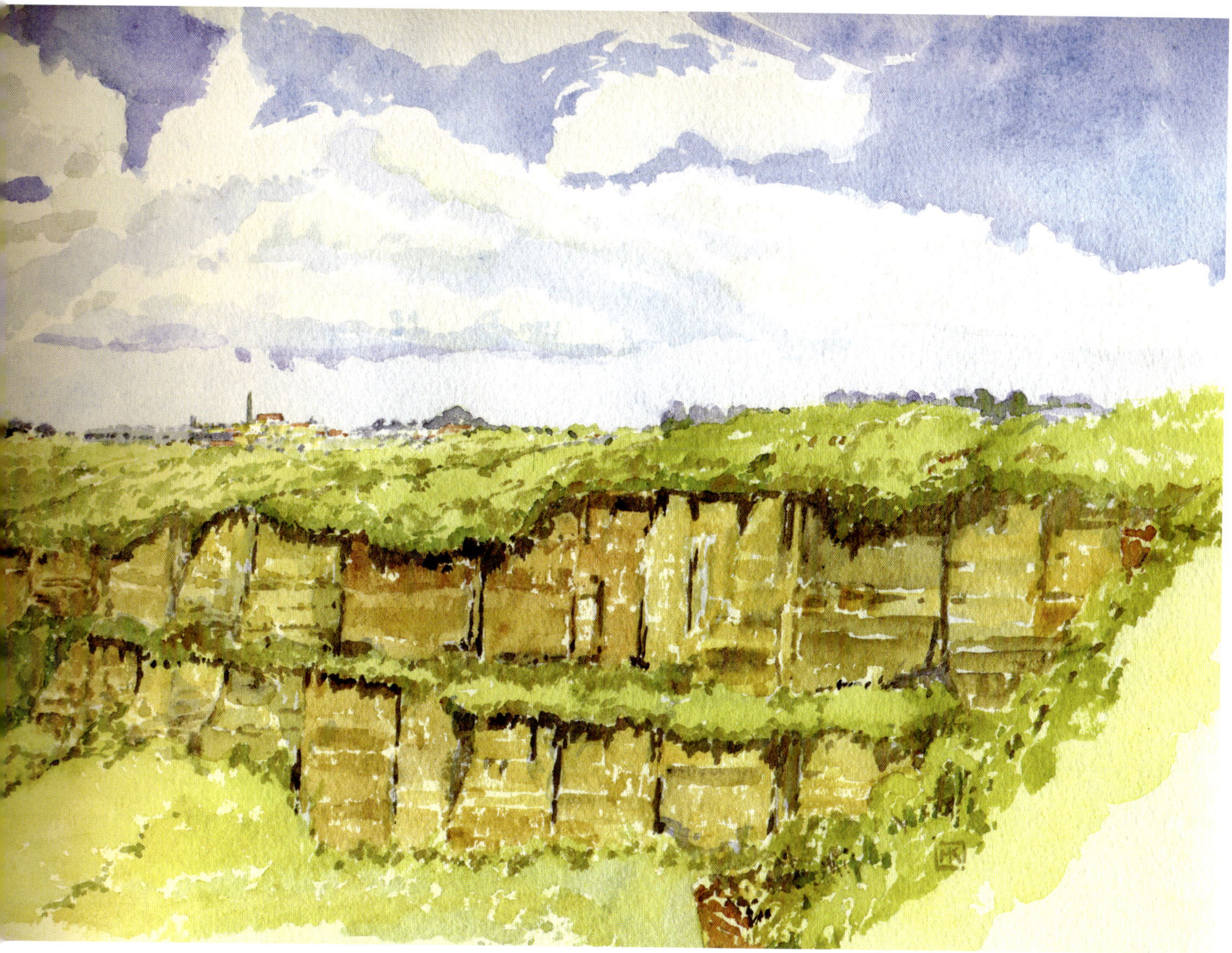

In the era before jet travel, they were all destinations for Sydneysiders eager to escape the steamy summer heat or to experience winter's tiny fangs. When we lived there, Katoomba celebrated "Christmas in July."

The scene above is from Sublime Point in Leura, looking across the gully to the escarpment of Katoomba. On the left in the shadow of a passing cloud are the famous Three Sisters, massive stone columns viewable from Echo Point at the end of the escarpment. The panorama there takes in the Jameson Valley, a World Heritage Site.

The landmark in the town is the Carrington Hotel with its exclamation-point chimney on the high ground near the railway station.

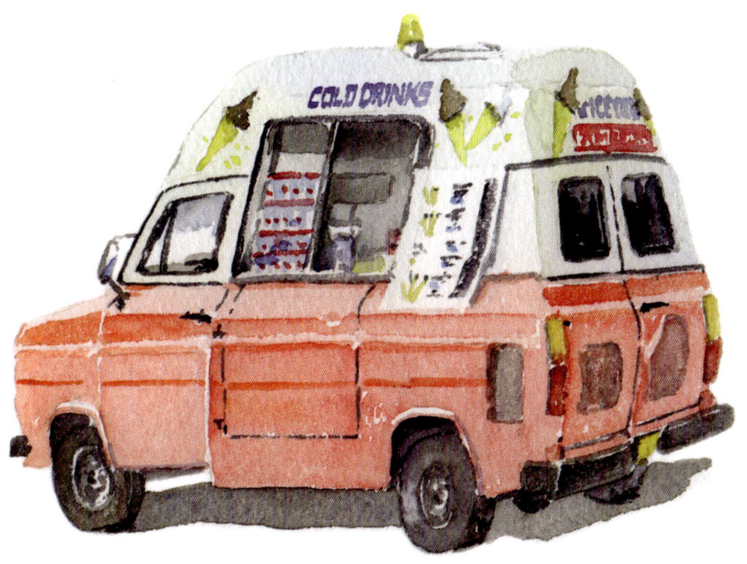

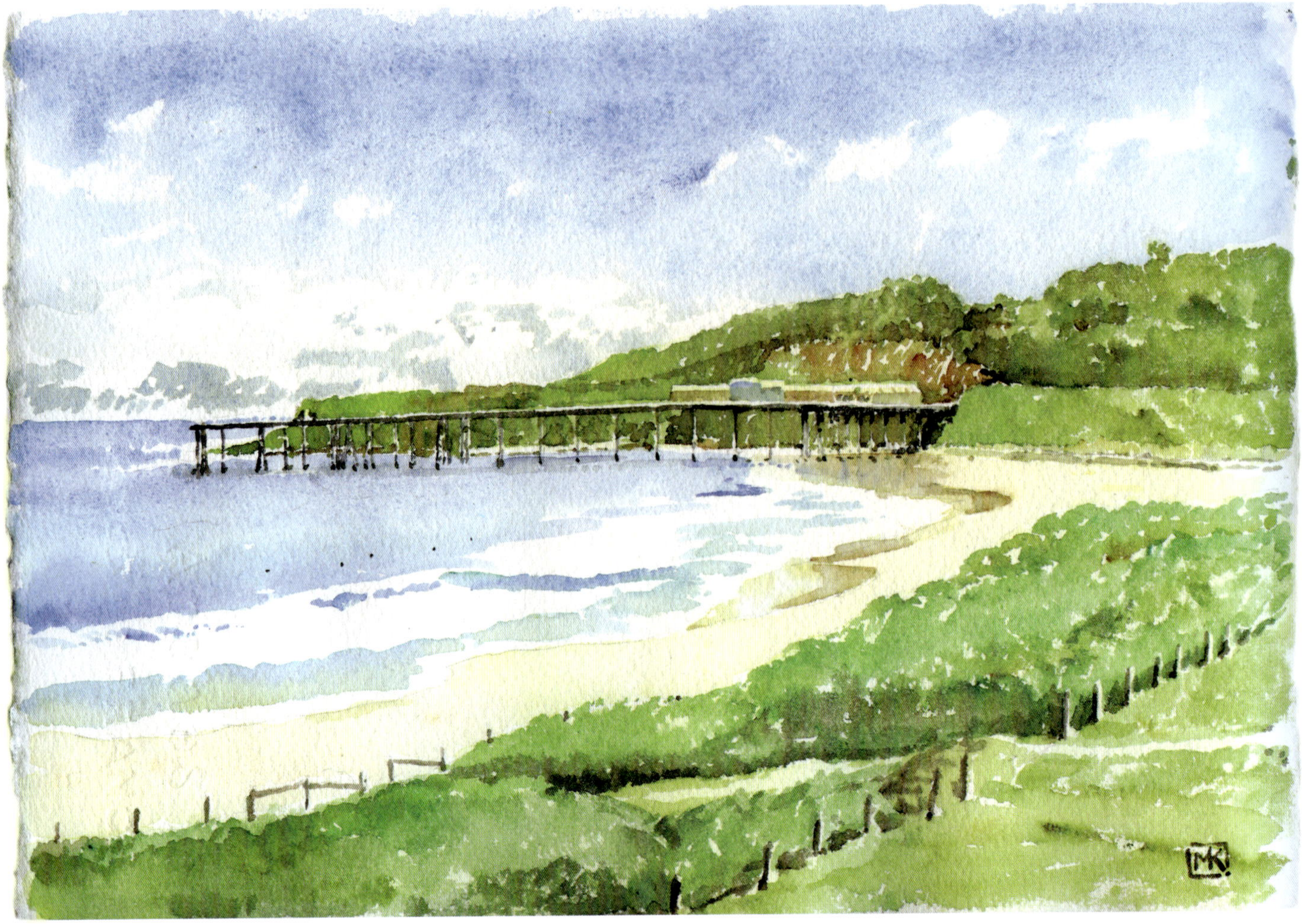

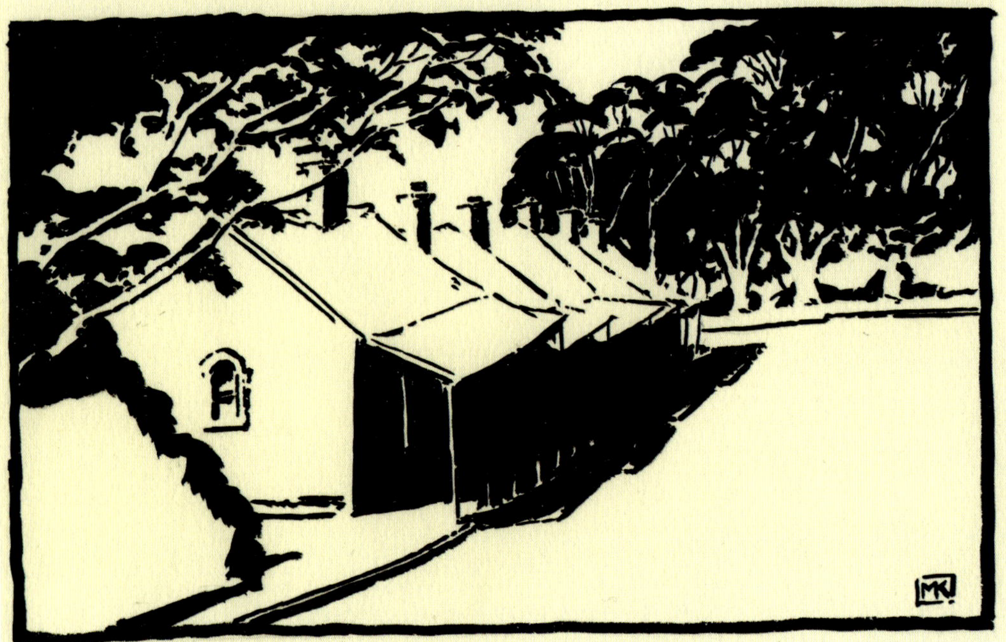

The industrial face of Australia.

(Above) Catherine Hill Bay is a 19th-century coal-mining town with a historic coal-loading jetty north of Sydney in New South Wales (NSW). Most places like it are now tourist spots (the dark spots I painted in the water were surfers), with a row of miners' cottages on the main street protected by state heritage laws.

(Left) One side of a quadrangle of miners' cottages called Paxton Square in Burra, a sleepy pastoral town in South Australia, settled by workers from the UK and Germany when a copper mine opened in 1848.

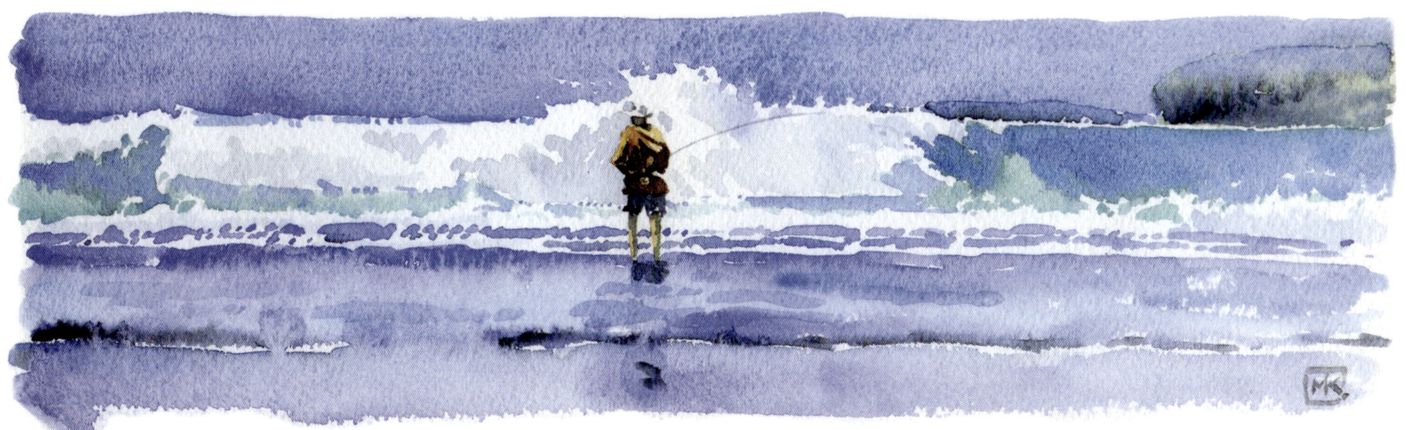

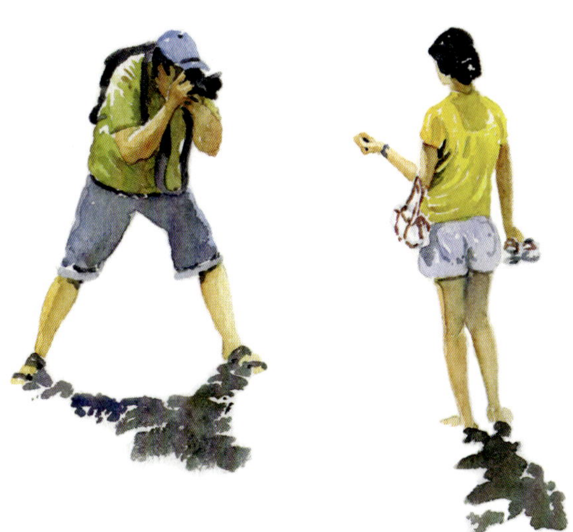

The pleasure-seeking face of Australia: a surf fisherman; tourists on Bondi Beach; a young lifeguard; and, below, Mona Vale Beach in Sydney's northern suburbs. With the exception of partying spots like Bondi, most of the beaches are sparsely peopled stretches of golden sand between massive sandstone headlands.

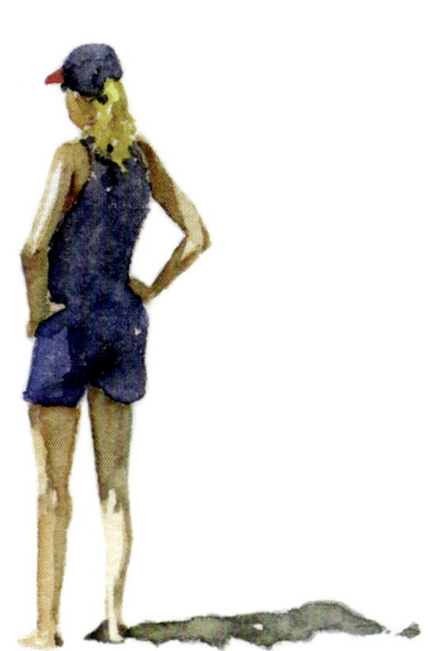

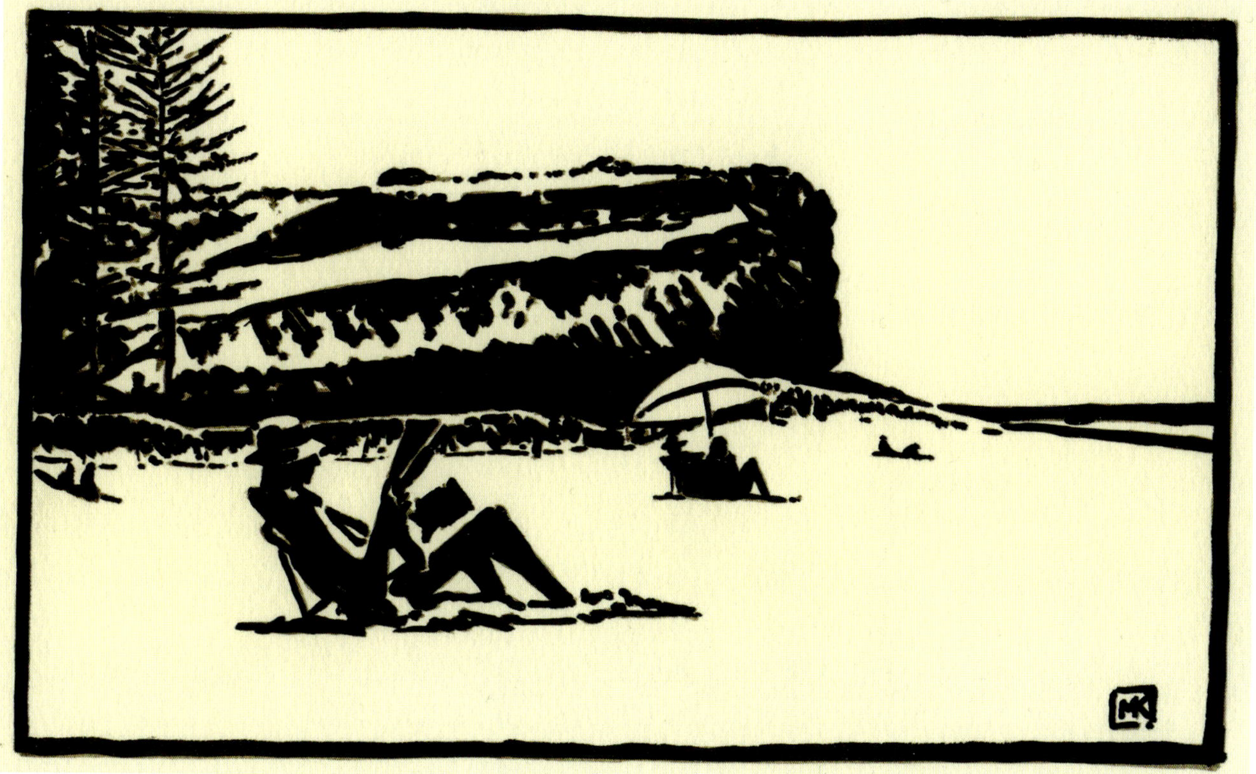

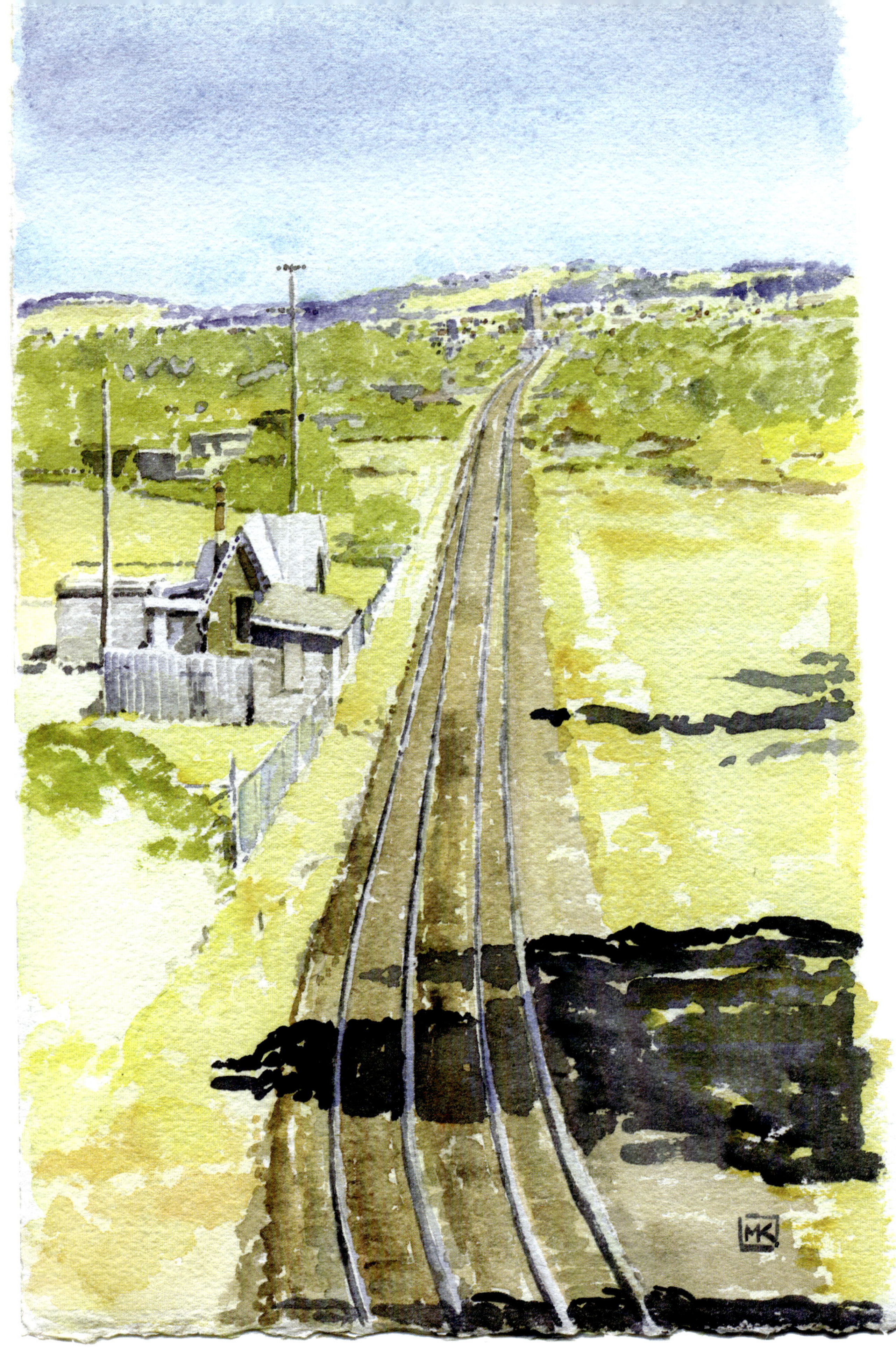

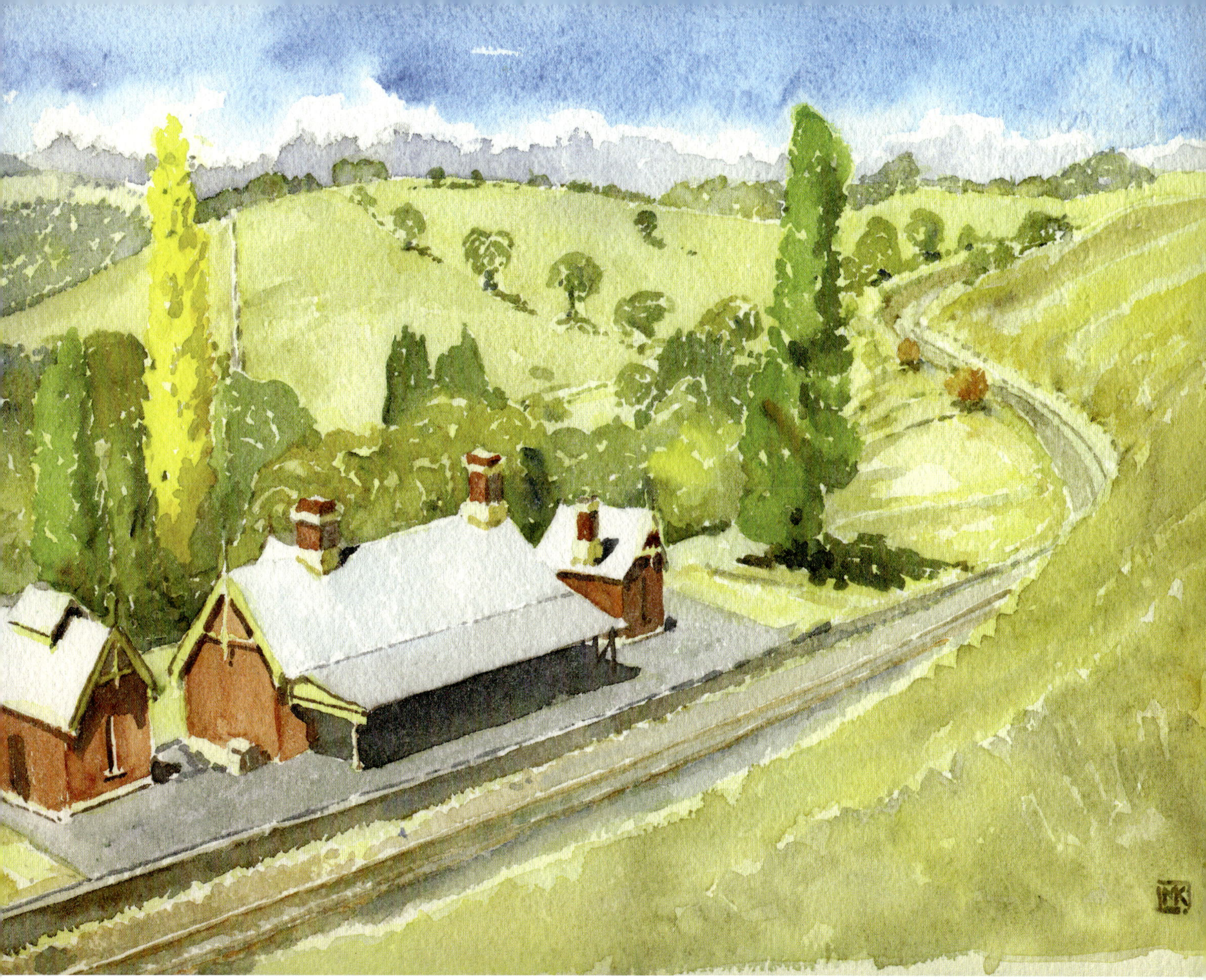

Australia has a pretty easy topography (with the lowest highest mountain of any continent) and lacks the heroic railway-building narratives of Canada. Only a handful of places comes to mind where difficult terrain required complex solutions, such as the zigzag railway descending the western side of the Blue Mountains, now maintained as a tourist attraction.

With federation not occurring until 1901 and the population spread so thinly, the Australian colonies went their own ways, most famously in whether they would accept convicts from Britain, but also in their inability to settle on a common railway gauge. Until 1962 passengers travelling from Sydney to Melbourne, the two biggest Australian cities, had to change trains at Albury on the state border and traverse a station platform about 1,500 feet long.

The country railways still carry both passengers and freight, though not as heavily as in the past. Most goods travel by road. Picturesque Victorian-era stations, many built of sandstone, are beautifully preserved in the dry climate. There are 20 historic stations on the Blue Mountains line, part of the Sydney rail network.

(Above) The pretty brick station with his and hers "dunnies" at Carcoar, a pastoral town of about 200 people in the central plains of New South Wales south of Bathurst, in 2008. In 1863, the town's bank was the first to be robbed anywhere in Australia.

(Previous page) A railway cottage on the edge of Goulburn, a large town southwest of Sydney that was the first inland settlement of the colony of New South Wales. The railway reached Goulburn from Sydney in 1855.

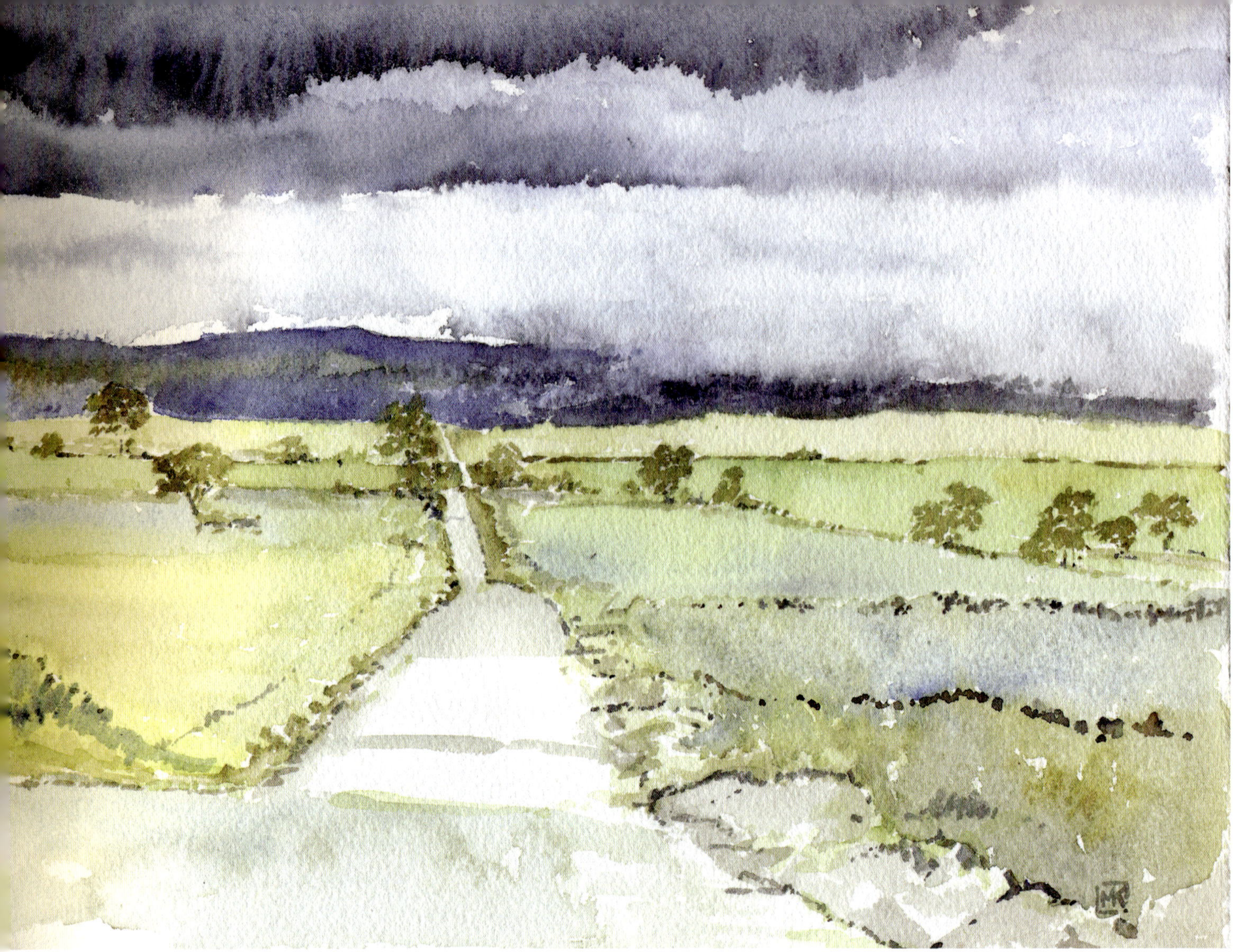

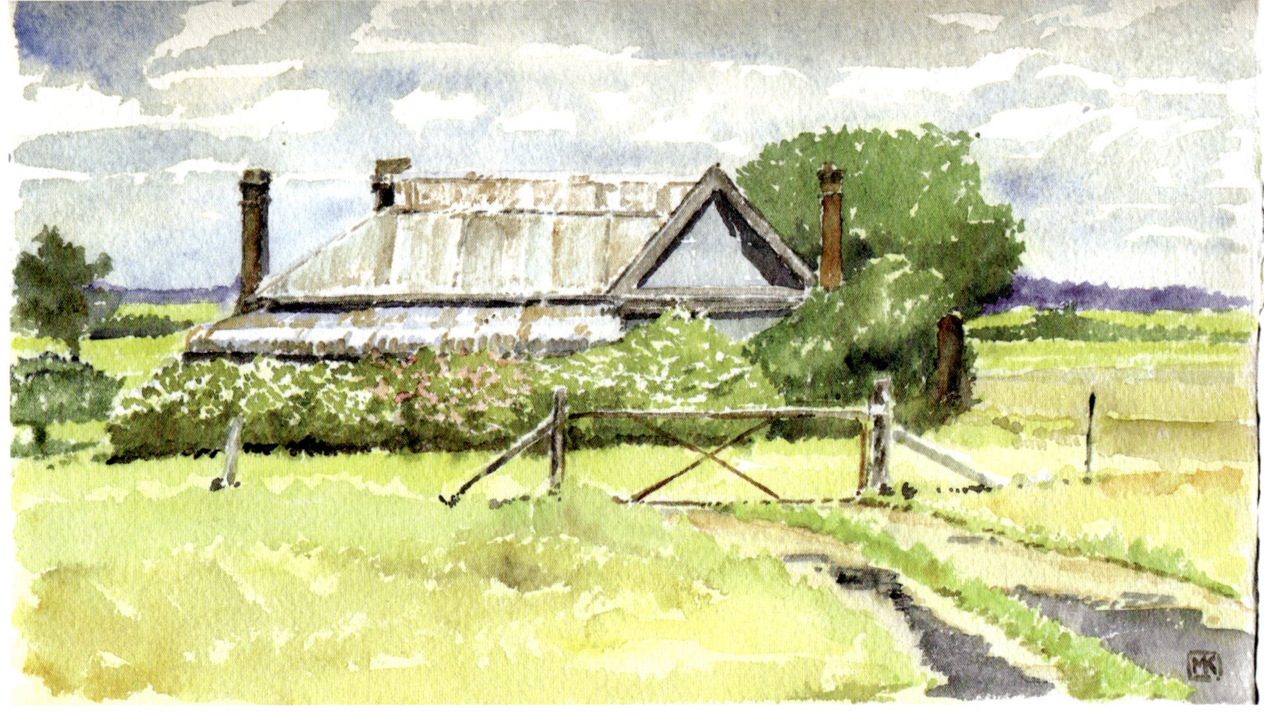

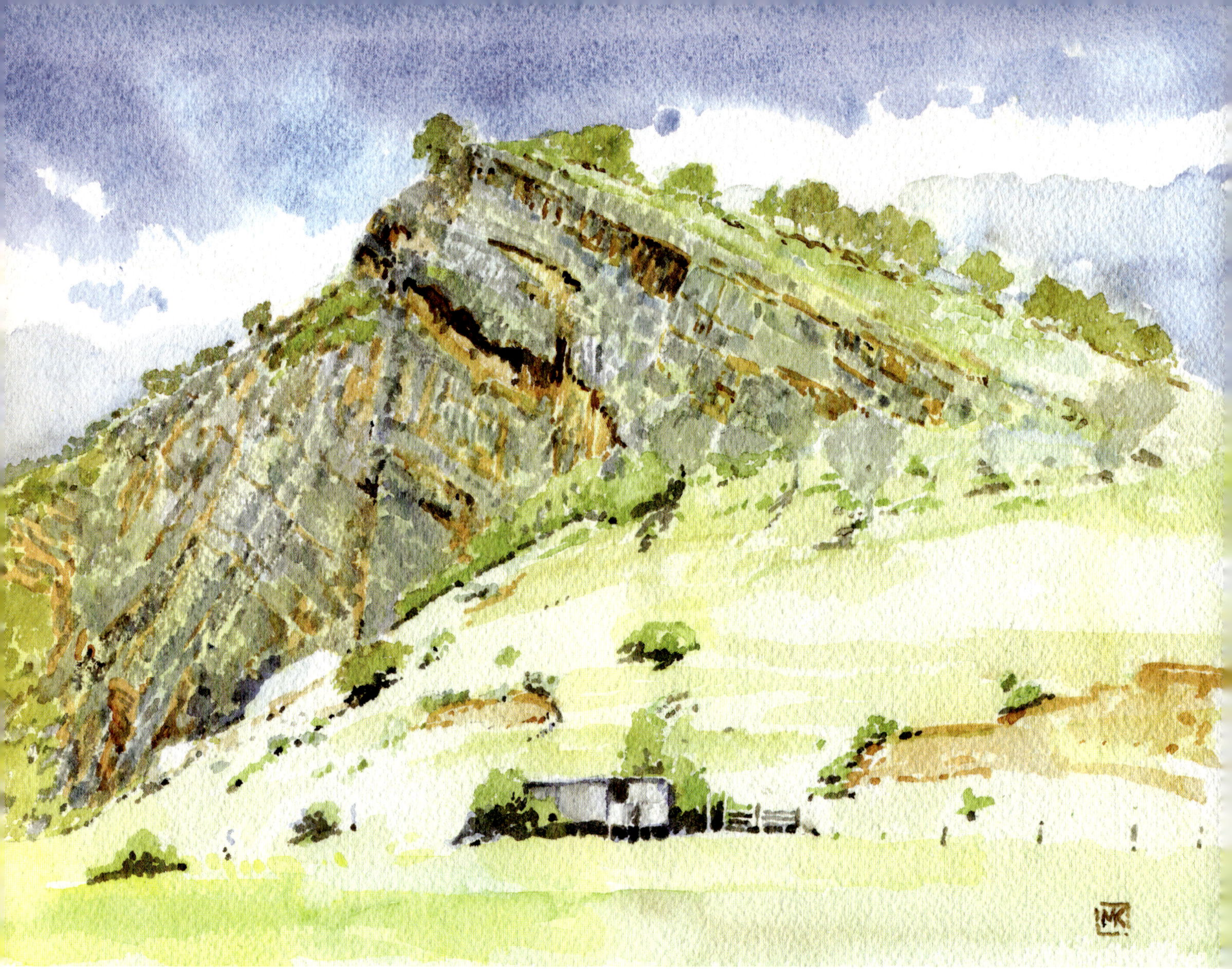

Wanderings with the sketchbook in New South Wales, 2006 to 2009.

The top image across the fold is “the long paddock” – that is, the roadsides that provided emergency grazing for drovers – somewhere near Bathurst, a big country town on the western side of the Blue Mountains about 200 km west of Sydney. The rain clouds are a good example of a definition of watercolour as “the interplay of water and chance” – no matter how much you plan and practise, you can never quite be sure what is going to happen to the pigment as the paper dries. That time it worked.

On the left is a classic Australian country house c. 1900 on the Lue-Mudgee Road, well adapted to the hot climate: a tall hipped roof with a vented triangle at the peak for cooling, rusting galvanized iron roofing, a bullnose (rolled-edge) verandah, a small gabled bay for the parlour, and tall brick chimneys.

Above: Wallaby Rocks along the Turon River near Sofala, a gold rush town made famous by artist Russell Drysdale in the 1940s, before Modernist orthodoxy kept artists in their studios looking inward. There are few barns in the Australian countryside – no need to shelter animals or store winter feed.

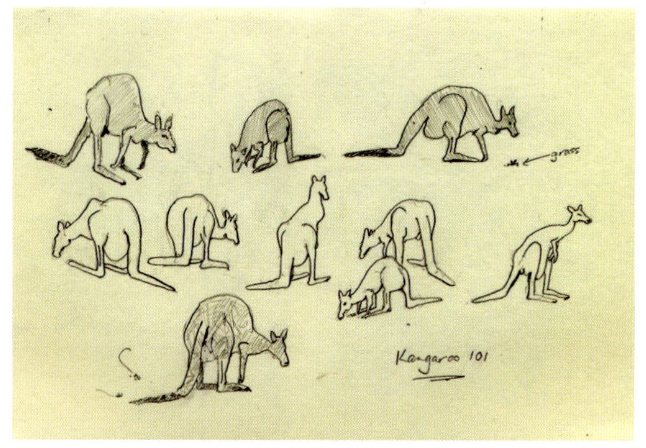

Grazing wallabies in the national park at Pebbly Beach on the NSW South Coast, in 2012. I should have written Wallaby 101 on the sheet.

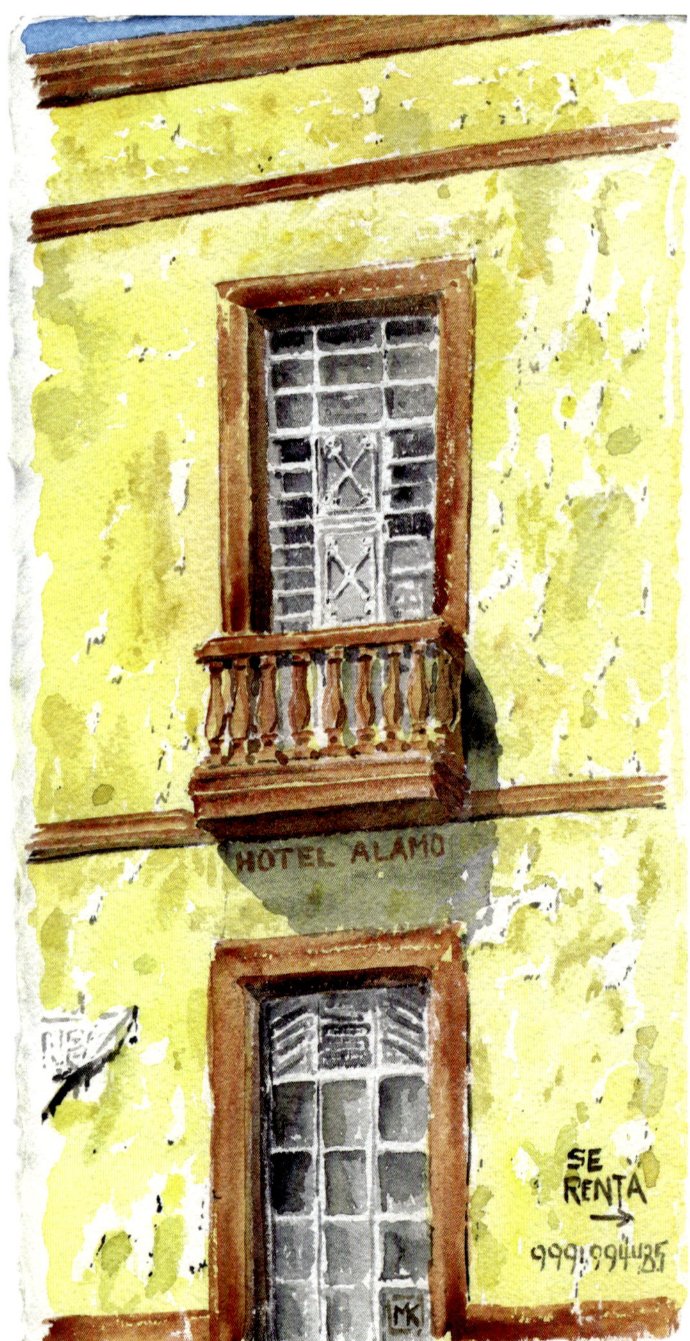

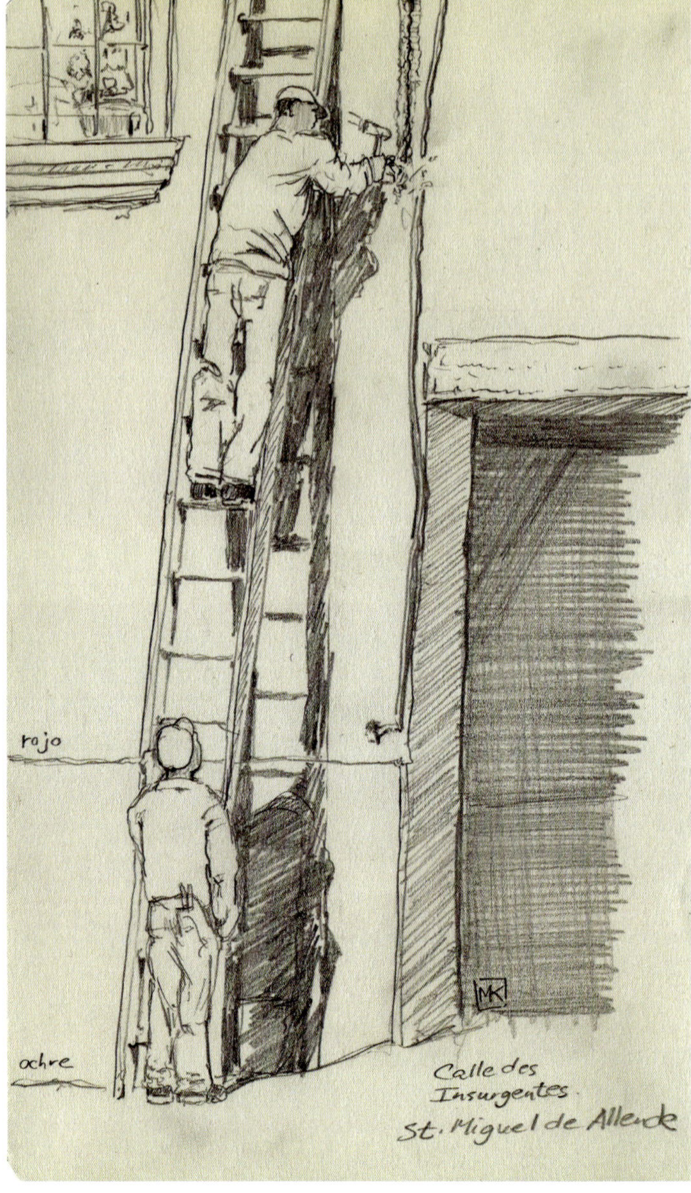

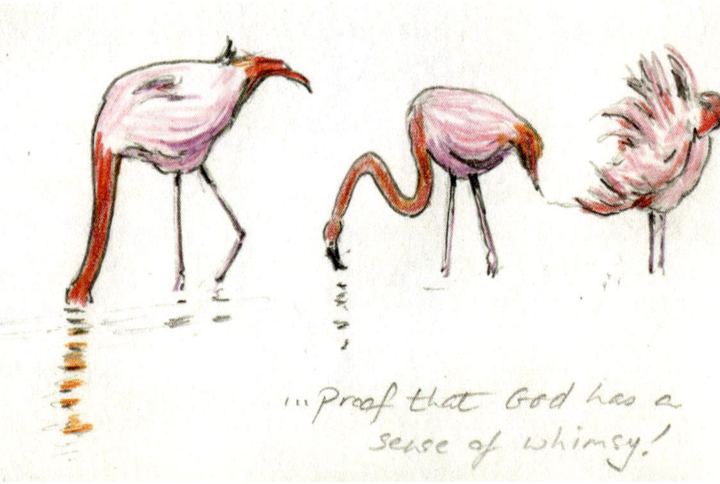

(Left) The Hotel Alamo was a textured wreck between the bus station and the *casa* where we spent a week in Mérida, the charming 400-year-old colonial city in the centre of the Yucatan, in January 2018. Mérida is a world apart from the beach resorts of Cancun on the east side of the peninsula, and a perfect base for day trips by bus to the Mayan ruins at Uxmal and the Celestun Biosphere, where I drew pink flamingoes from a drifting boat.

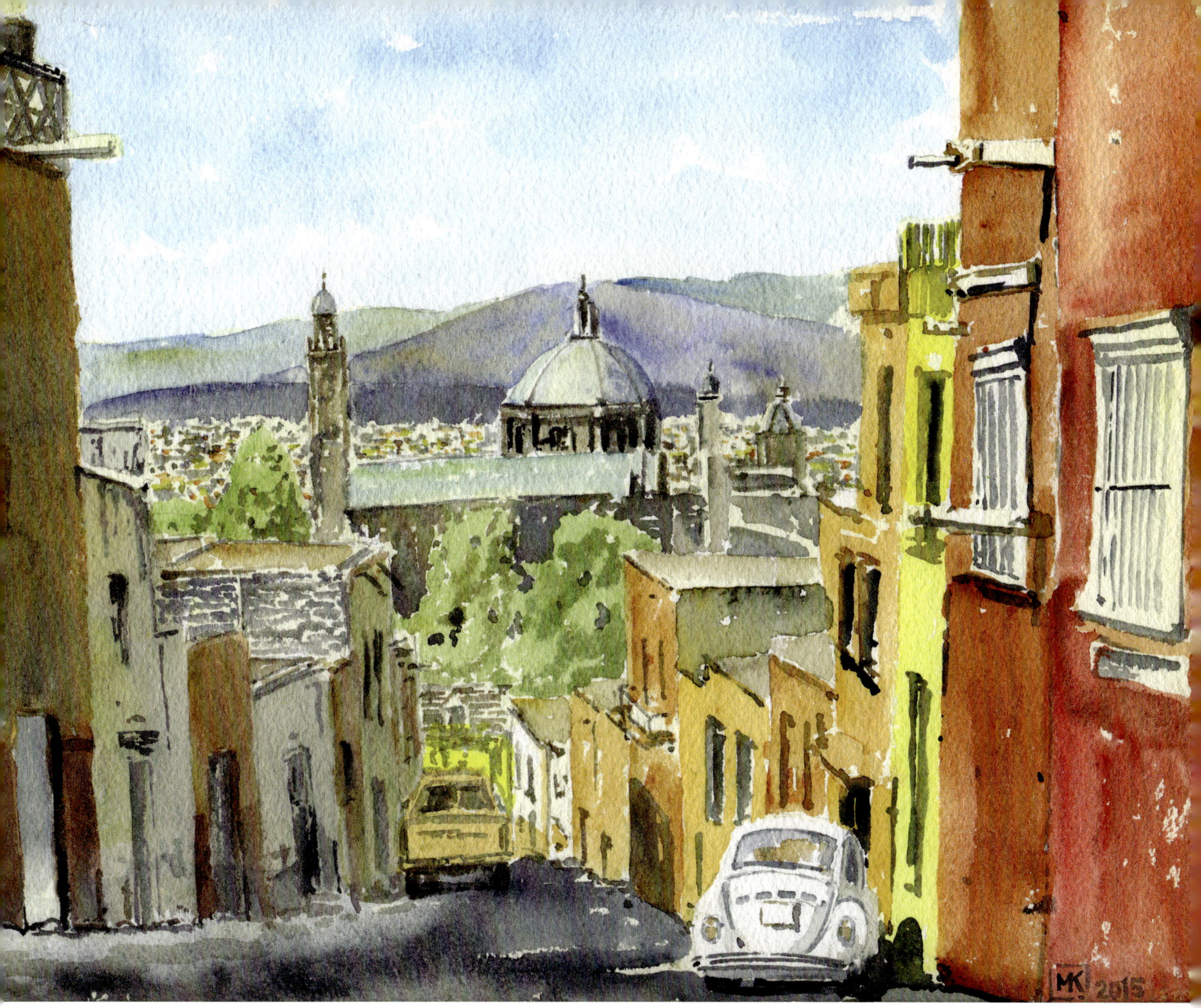

San Miguel de Allende, about four hours by bus north of Mexico City, has been a haven for American and Canadian artists including William Newcombe and Leonard and Reva Brooks since the 1940s. In the winter of 2015, it was a wonderful place to ramble around to draw and paint the mix of colours and views, people, and complex colonial architecture.

Although it is a prosperous city partly due to its expat retiree population, the reality of the Mexican countryside is never far from sight. *Campesinos* come into town, some with loads of firewood to sell, others with all their worldly goods packed on their burros.

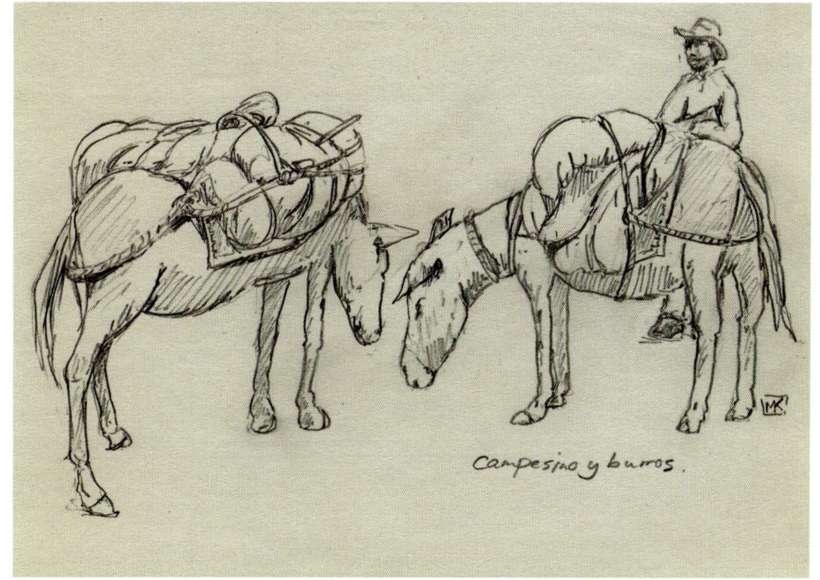

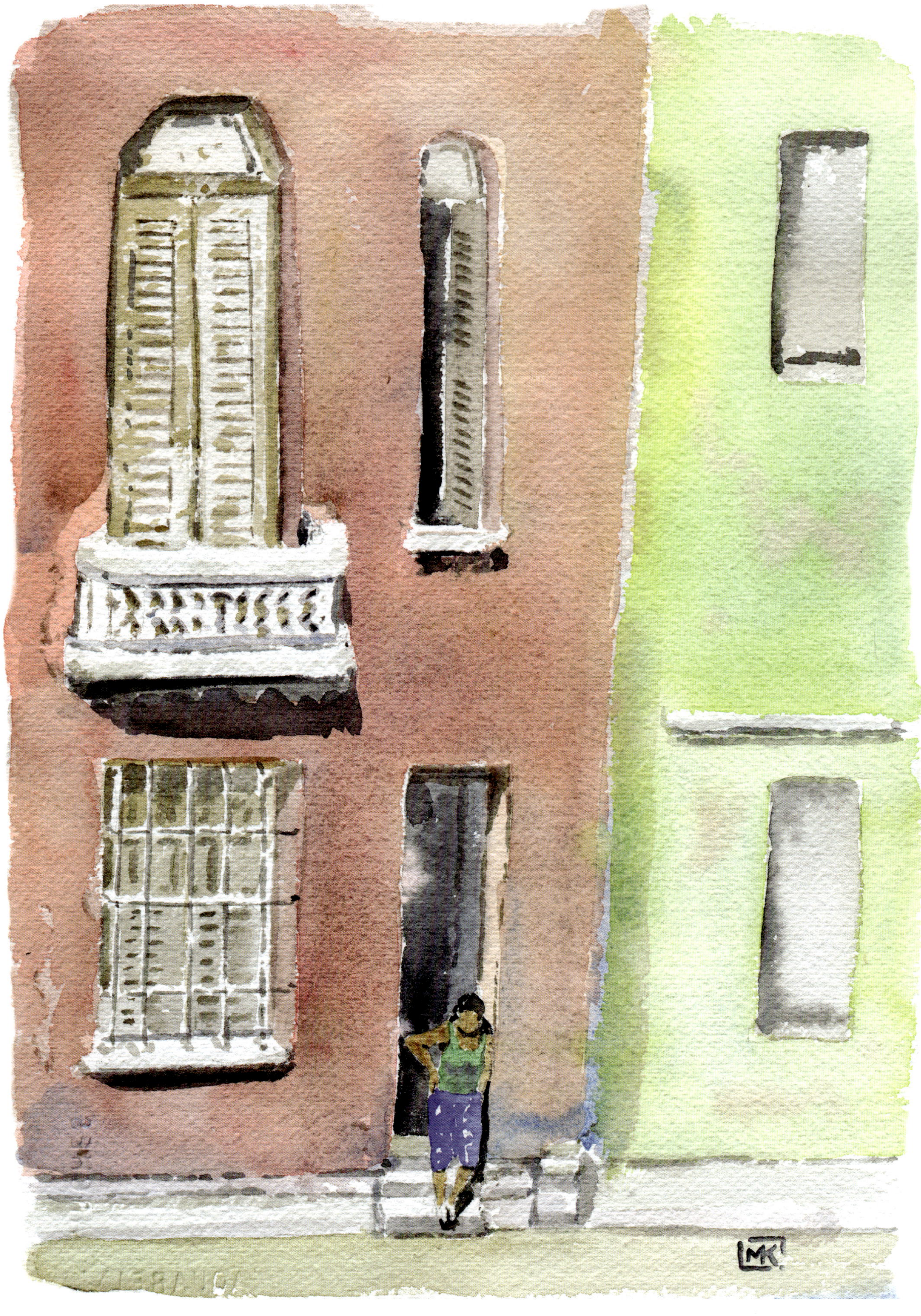

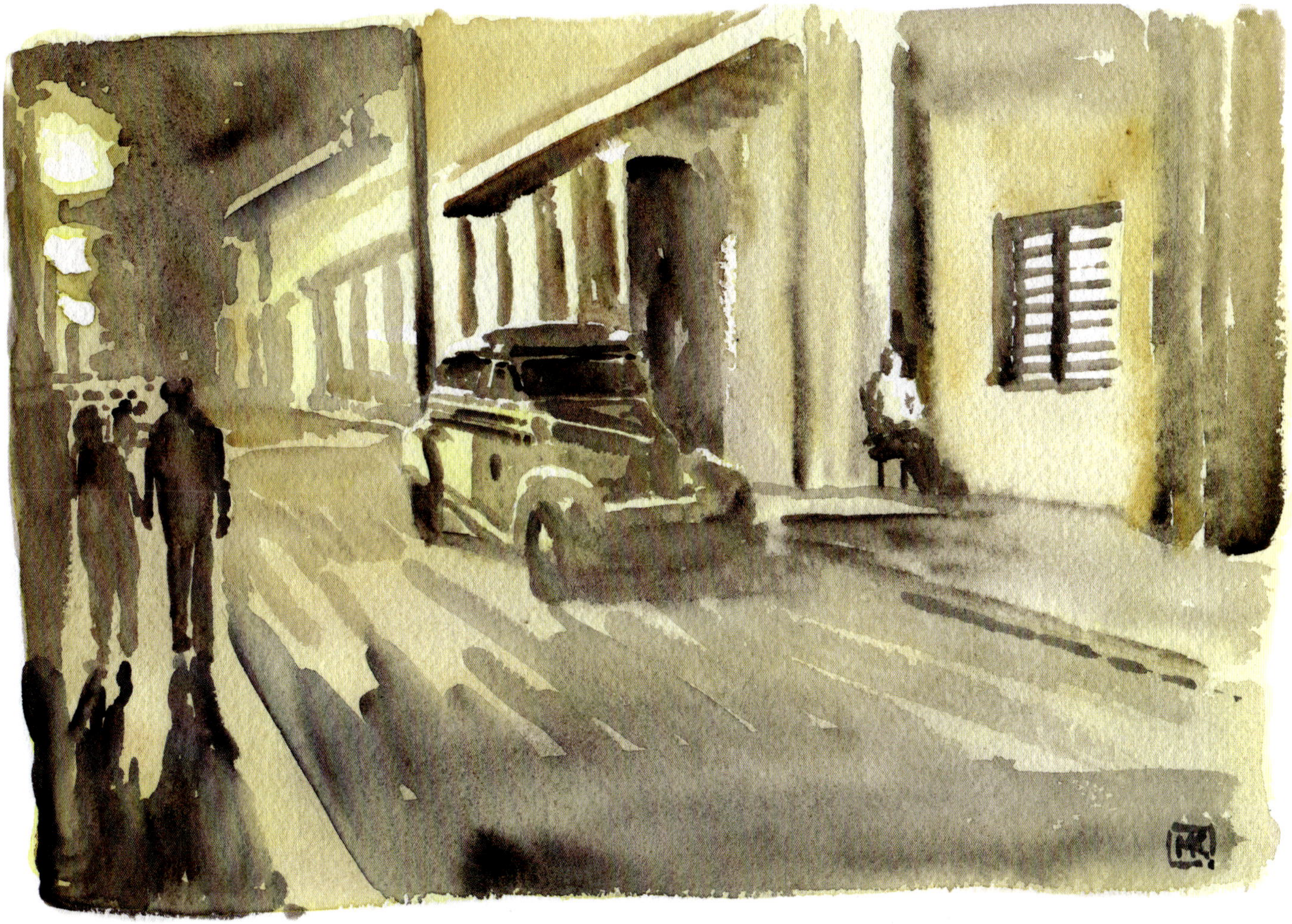

Cuba was a revelation in 2012. There was a kind of managed poverty – extraordinary deteriorated colonial buildings, especially in old Havana (left); the famous Yank tanks, cars kept alive since the pre-revolution 1950s; Santa Clara (above) with a lavish museum to Ché Guevara but horse-drawn carts for public transit; men fishing from inner tubes in a lake near Cienfuegos (right); empty shelves in *mercados;* two currency systems, Cubans wanting to be paid in the tourist's CUC peso pegged to the US dollar but working for the *moneda nacional* worth one twentieth as much. But there was a kind of quiet pride in their country, in its low crime rate and its success at standing up to the giant American bully just over the horizon to the north.

In Havana, we rented a *casa particular* – a bed and breakfast room, one of the baby steps toward a free-enterprise economy in the wake of Fidel Castro's retirement – and when we were ready to move on, the owner phoned a friend in Cienfuegos who rented us a room, and so it went as we moved from town to town.

I wasn't sure whether I was seeing a country stuck in the past or whether I was witnessing the future. The charismatic Ché from the famous 1960 Alberto Korda photo gazed from many billboards, always with a radical, inspirational slogan. I wrote a graphic novel, *2050,* that had its own charismatic autocrat with crazy slogans; it came out just as Donald Trump won election in 2016.

The watercolour on the facing page is from the window of our Havana room on Calle San Lazaro. A neighbour in her doorway watched the buses and cars go by each morning.

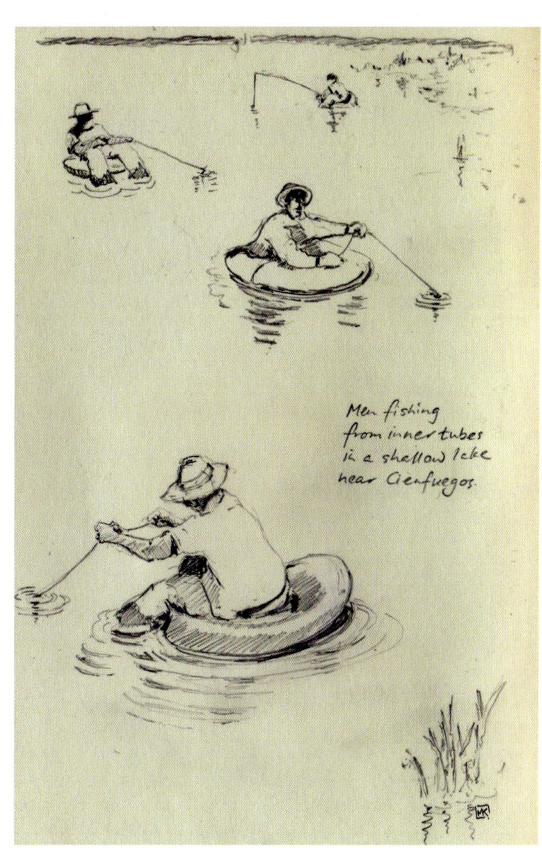

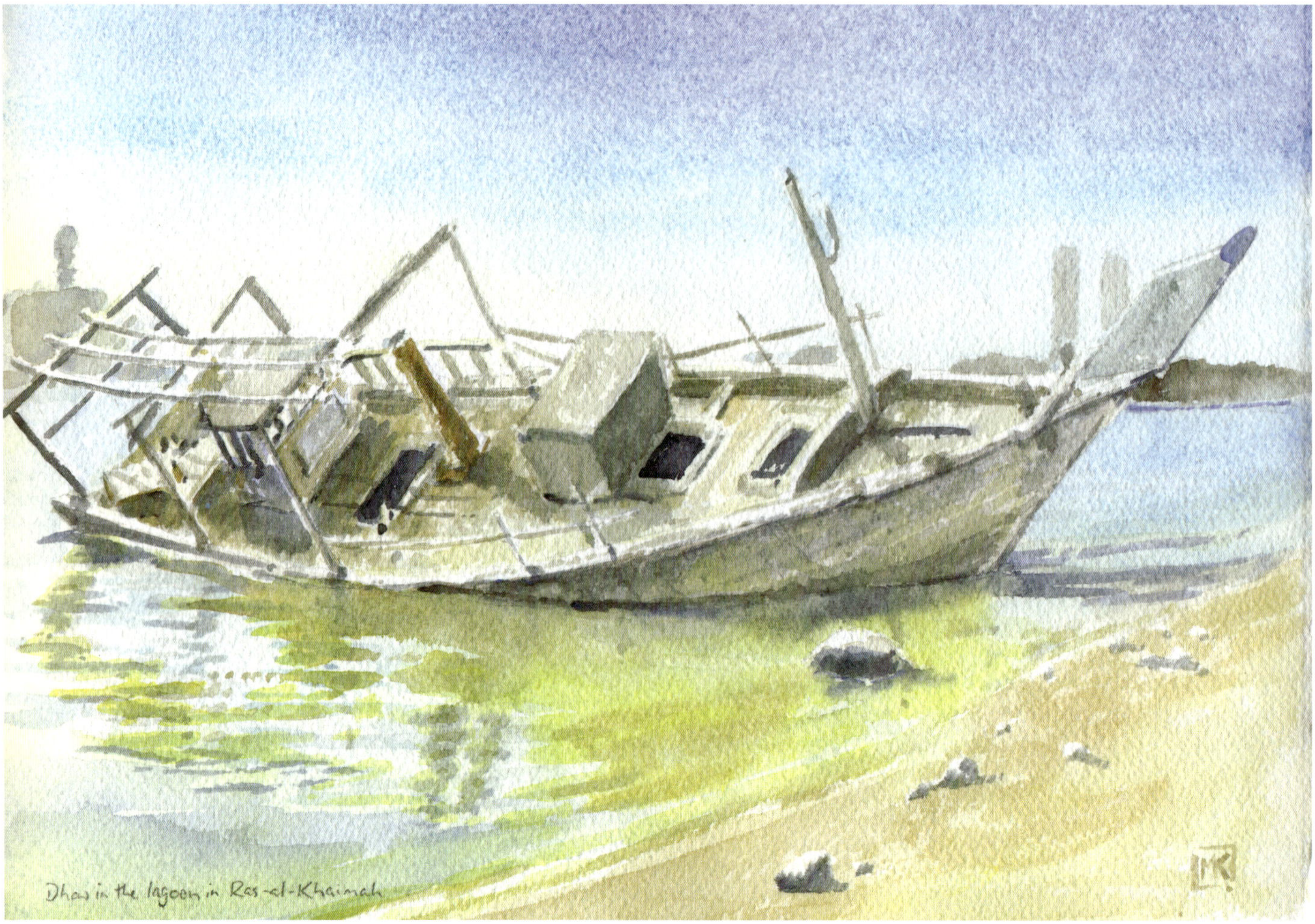

Dhow in the lagoon in Ras-al-Khaimah

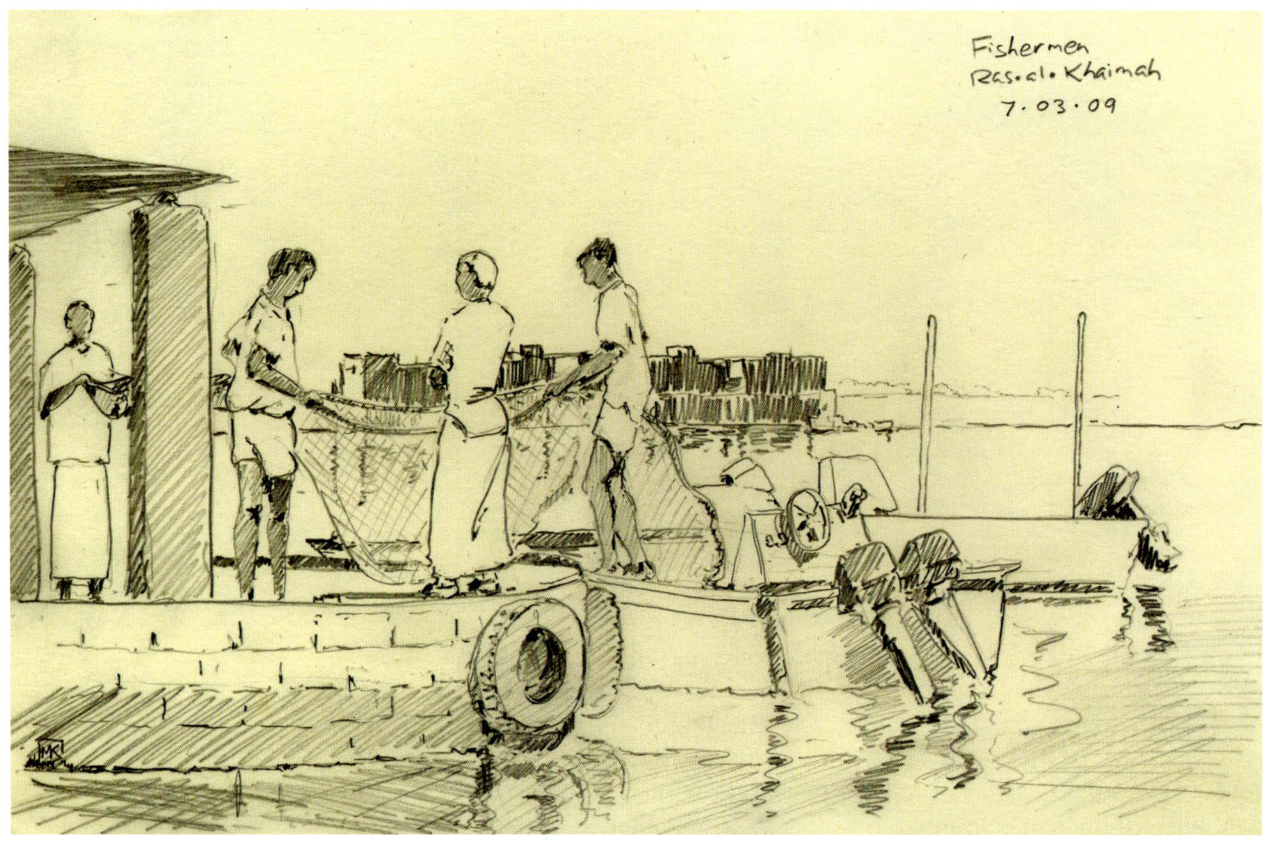

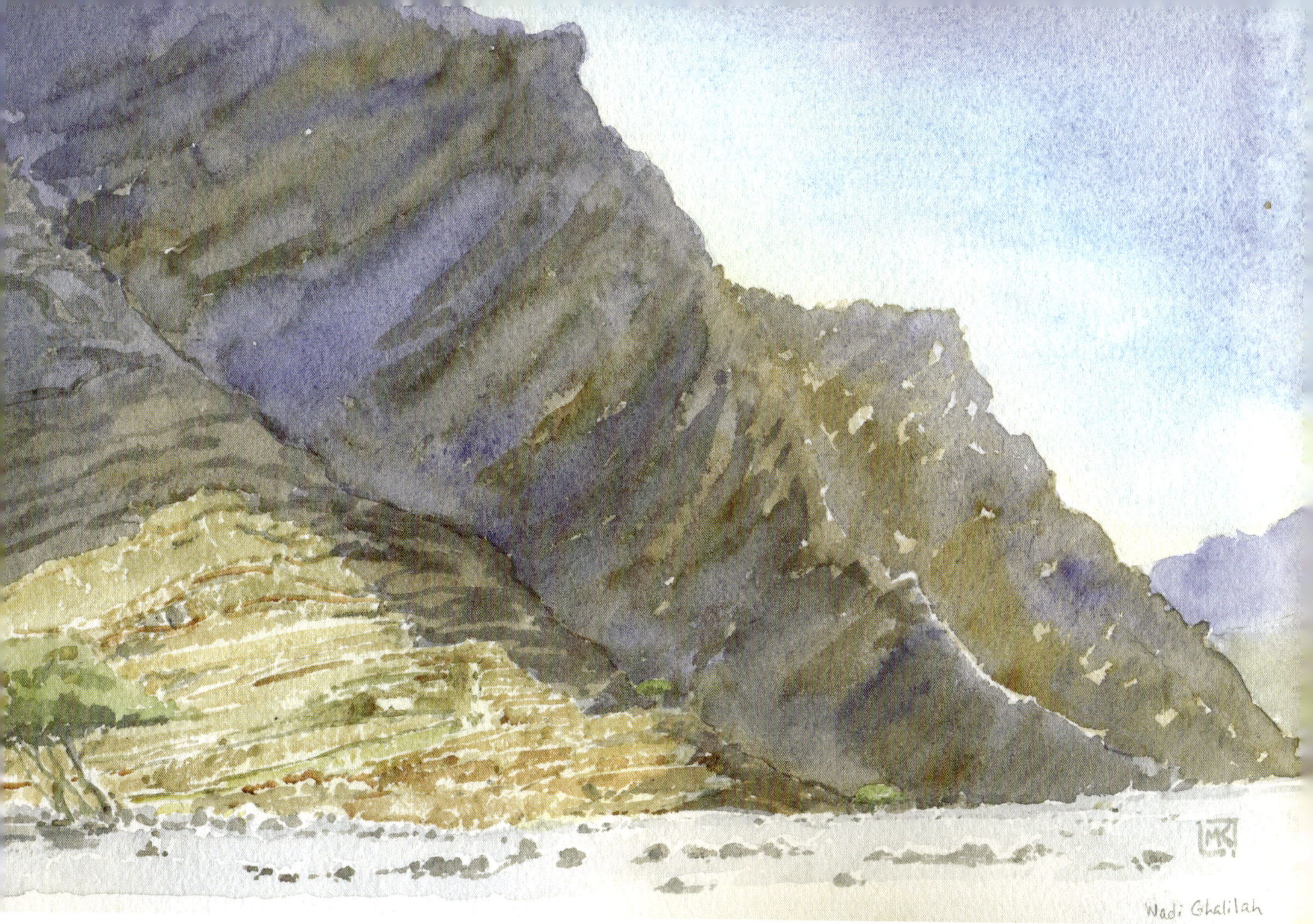

Wadi Ghalilah

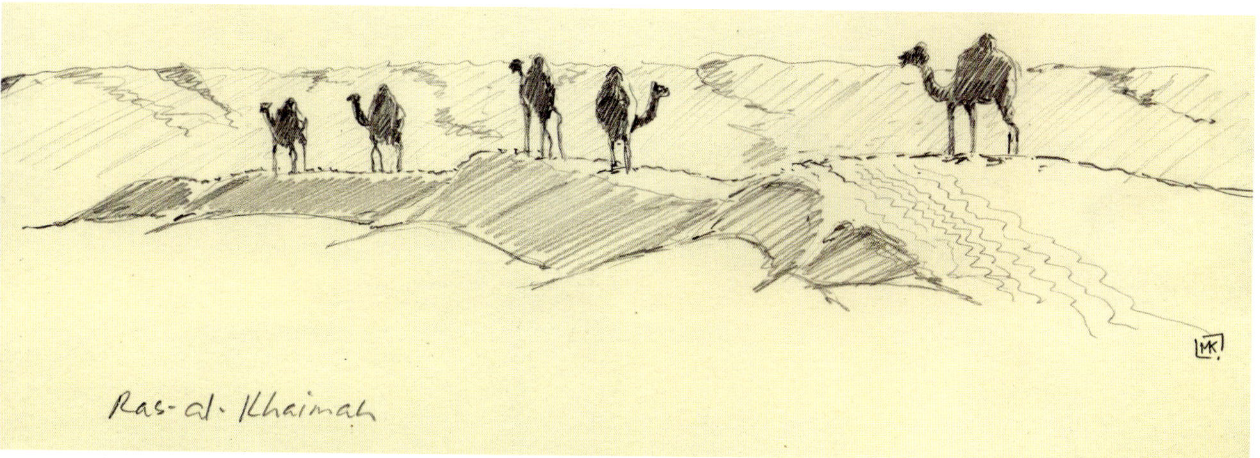

Ras-al-Khaimah is the easternmost of the seven emirates that comprise the United Arab Emirates. Abu Dhabi and Dubai, awash with oil, are the wealthy ones, while RAK is modest by comparison. Our daughter lived there in 2009, teaching at an outpost of an American university. An old *dhow* slept on the shore of its lagoon and a village of Yemeni or Somali fishermen landed their catch in time for the afternoon fish market. The *wadis* are dry valleys that flood in the occasional downpours; Wadi Ghalilah (above) was near the Oman border, and appealed to me because of a goatherder's dwelling, barely visible as it was of the same stone as the hillside, on the sunlit face of the rugged hill – ribbons of coloured stone tossed up and contorted.

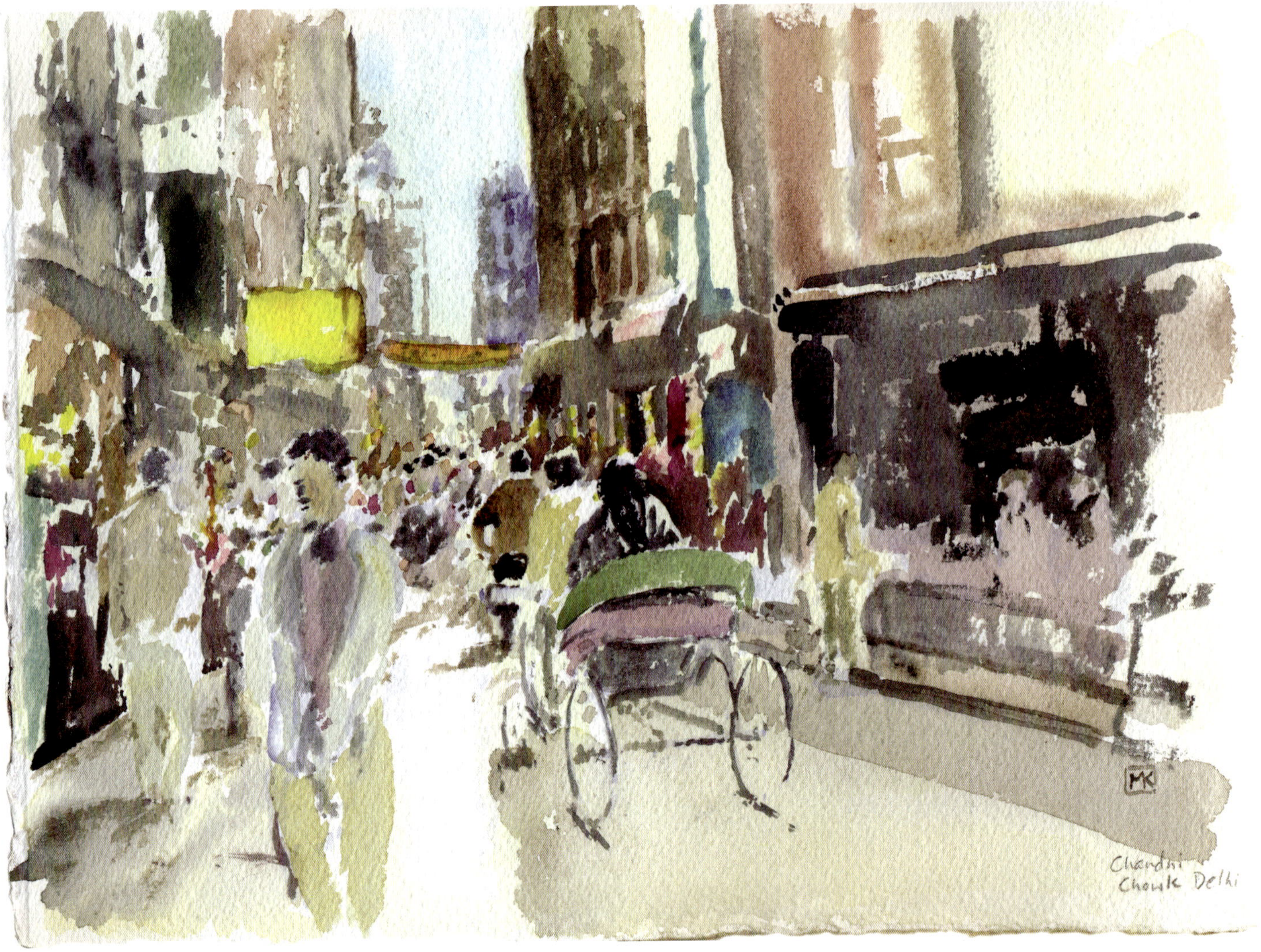

India, 2009. Nothing can prepare you for the vibrant chaos of places like Chandni Chowk, the oldest market in Old Delhi. We took photographs that looked static and unpeopled; I drew it on site and then painted with fractured brushstrokes to try to capture its wild energy.

The crush of people and their friendly curiosity makes painting outside, and even drawing, very difficult. There is no landscape-painting tradition in Indian art. Usually I had about three minutes before a passerby politely asked me, "What are you doing?" He would soon be joined by others who crowded around. A high viewpoint, such as the roof of the Hawa Mahal in Jaipur (next page below) was a better place.

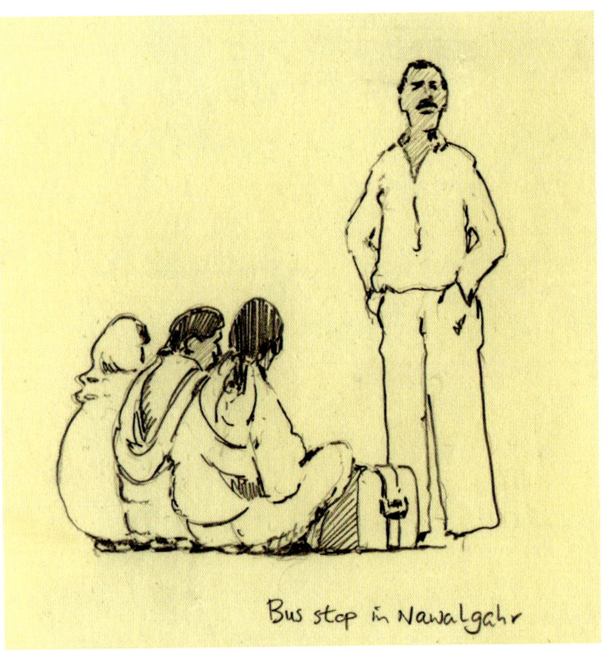

Small towns were much quieter. We hired a driver with an auto rickshaw in Jaipur to take us to Amer, which has a textile cooperative as well as its famous fort, and I found the opportunity to paint two women at the town pump washing clothing (next page above).

Once outside in the cities, there's little opportunity to hide in a café as one would in Europe and in North America or to chill out in a park on a secluded bench; instead, you have to retreat to the calm of a hotel room or, if you're Indian, the sanctuary of your home.

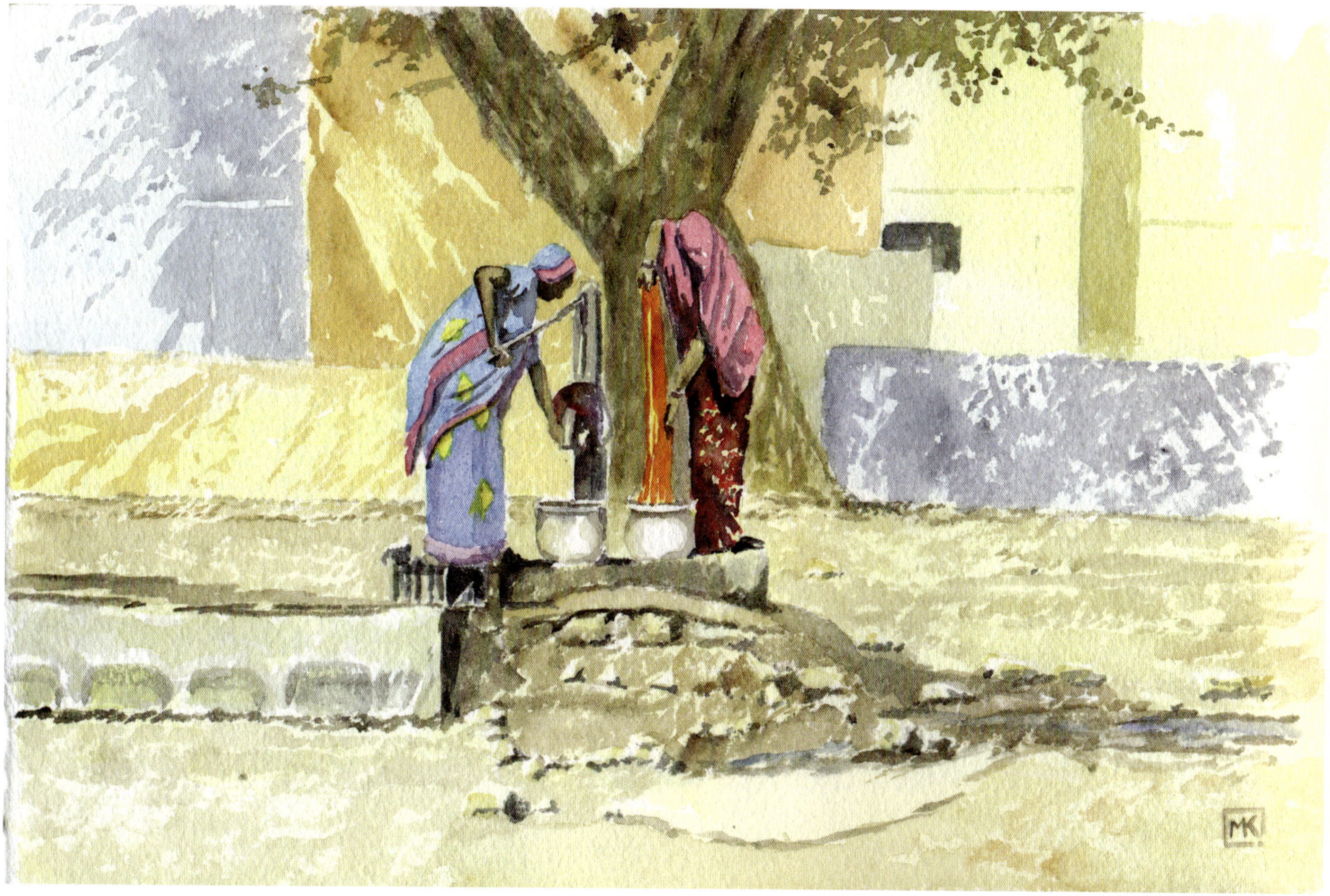

(Above) Washing clothes at the town pump in Amer, Rajasthan, 2009.

(Right) The roof of a *haveli* – a traditional dwelling – in Jaipur. So much of Indian life reflects the extreme contrast between inside and outside, between the "enclosed space" (*haveli*'s meaning in Persian) of the home and the free-for-all of the streets. And for women, many of whom still live in *purdah* (seclusion), their home offers them an opportunity to go about unveiled and – usually – unobserved.

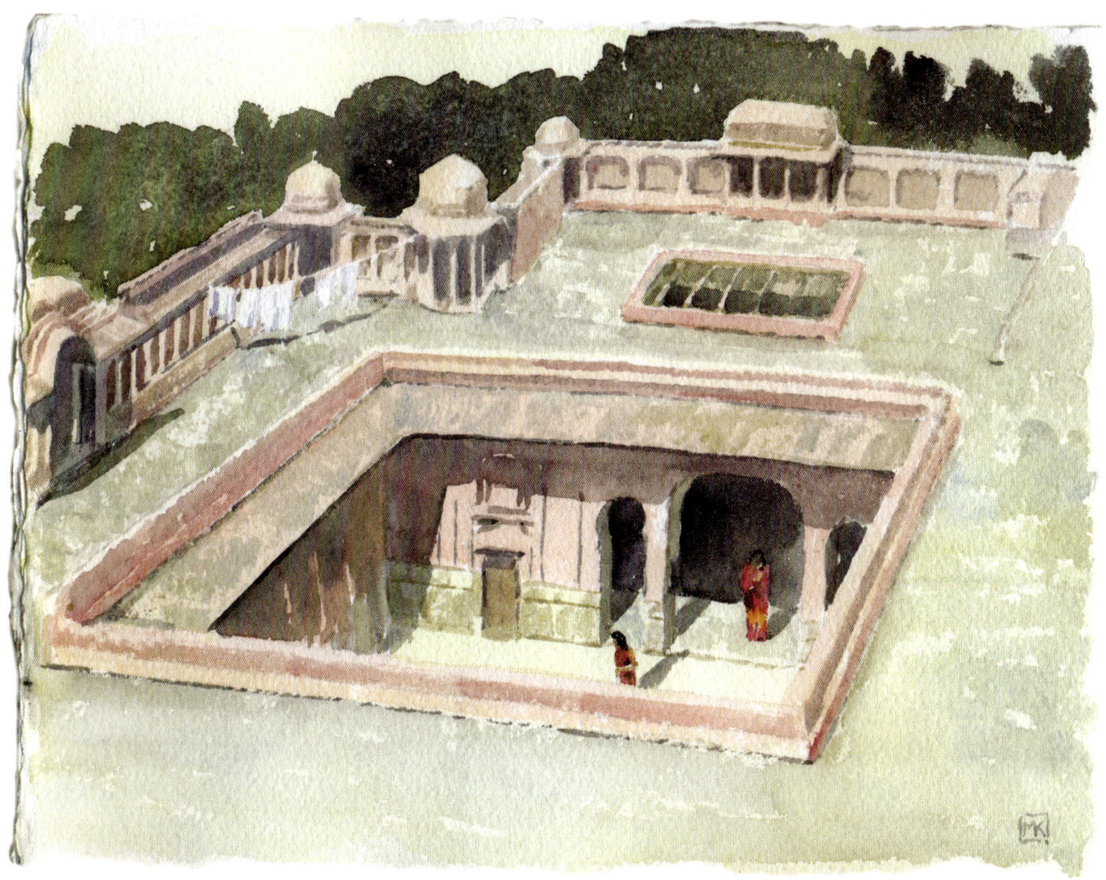

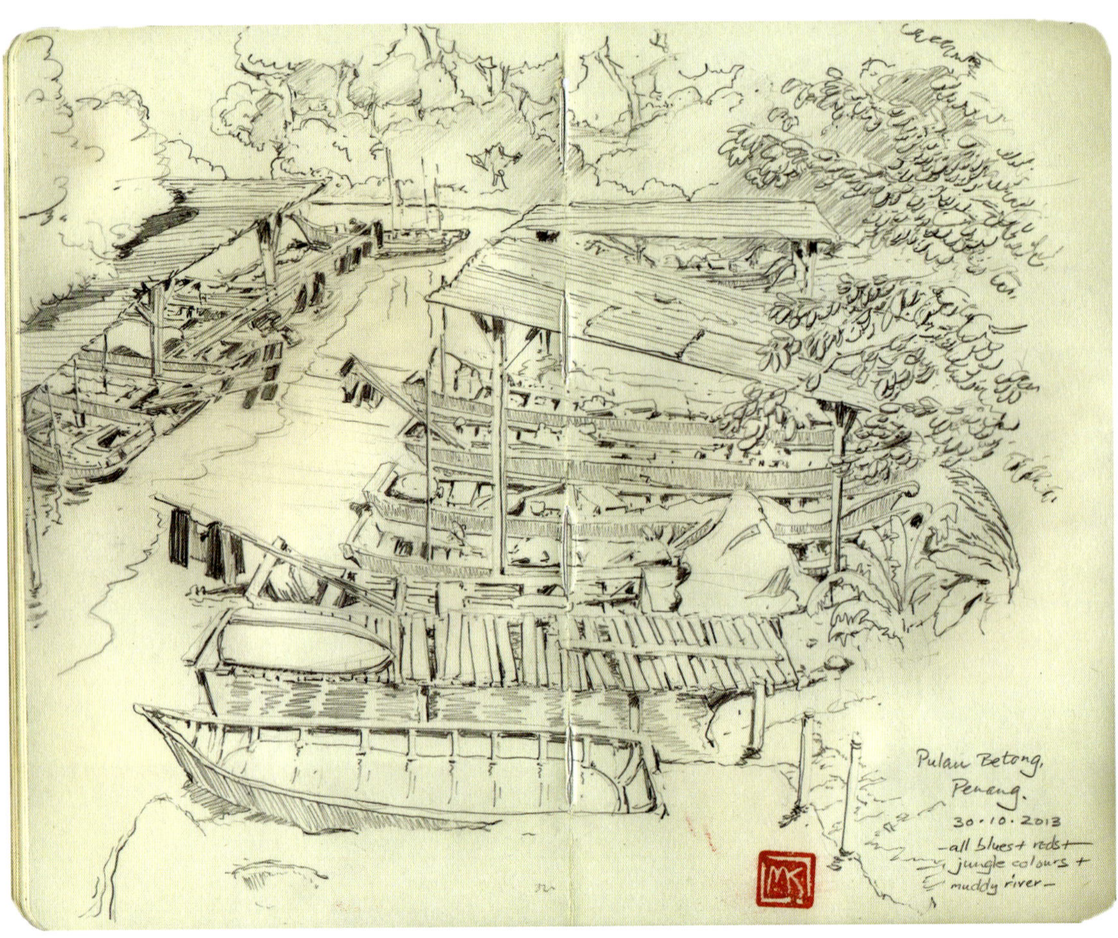

Malaysia, 2013, an extensive trip by local bus and train. One of the highlights was Penang Island and its city, George Town, in the north of the Malayan peninsula near the Thailand border. I avoided a kilo in the luggage this time by leaving the watercolours at home.

Pulau Betong is a *kampung* (village) at the southwest corner of Penang. Blue and red fishing boats docked at the mouth of a muddy tropical river.

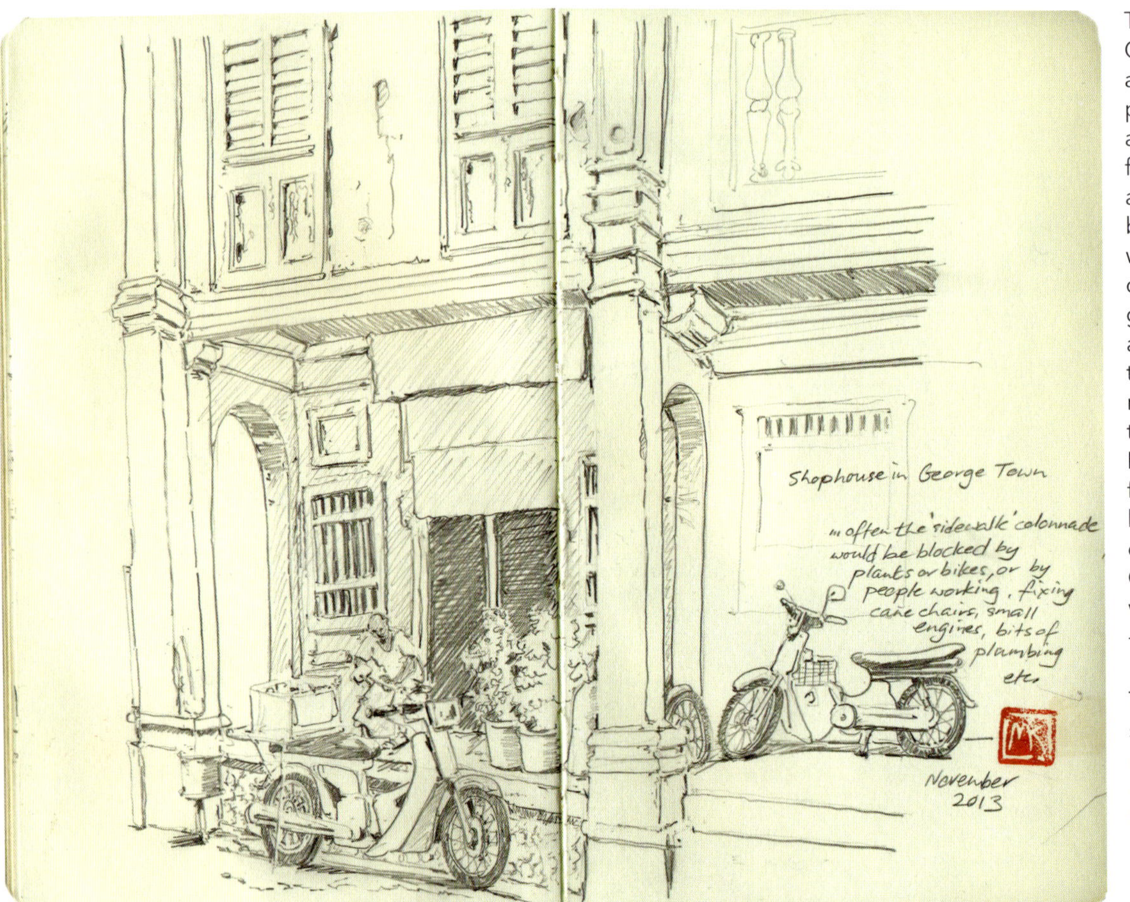

The Peranakan (Straits Chinese) shophouses are the most pleasant, perfectly adapted architecture imaginable for tropical cities. They are two storeys high, between 20 and 25 feet wide and usually very deep, about 200 feet, going back from their arcaded street fronts through a series of rooms and courtyards that are open to the sky. Every type of business from taverns to motorbike repairs is conducted from them. "The Chinese do not settle where there is no trade." – Somerset Maugham.

The red "chop" is a stamp I had engraved in Malacca by a man operating out of a shophouse.

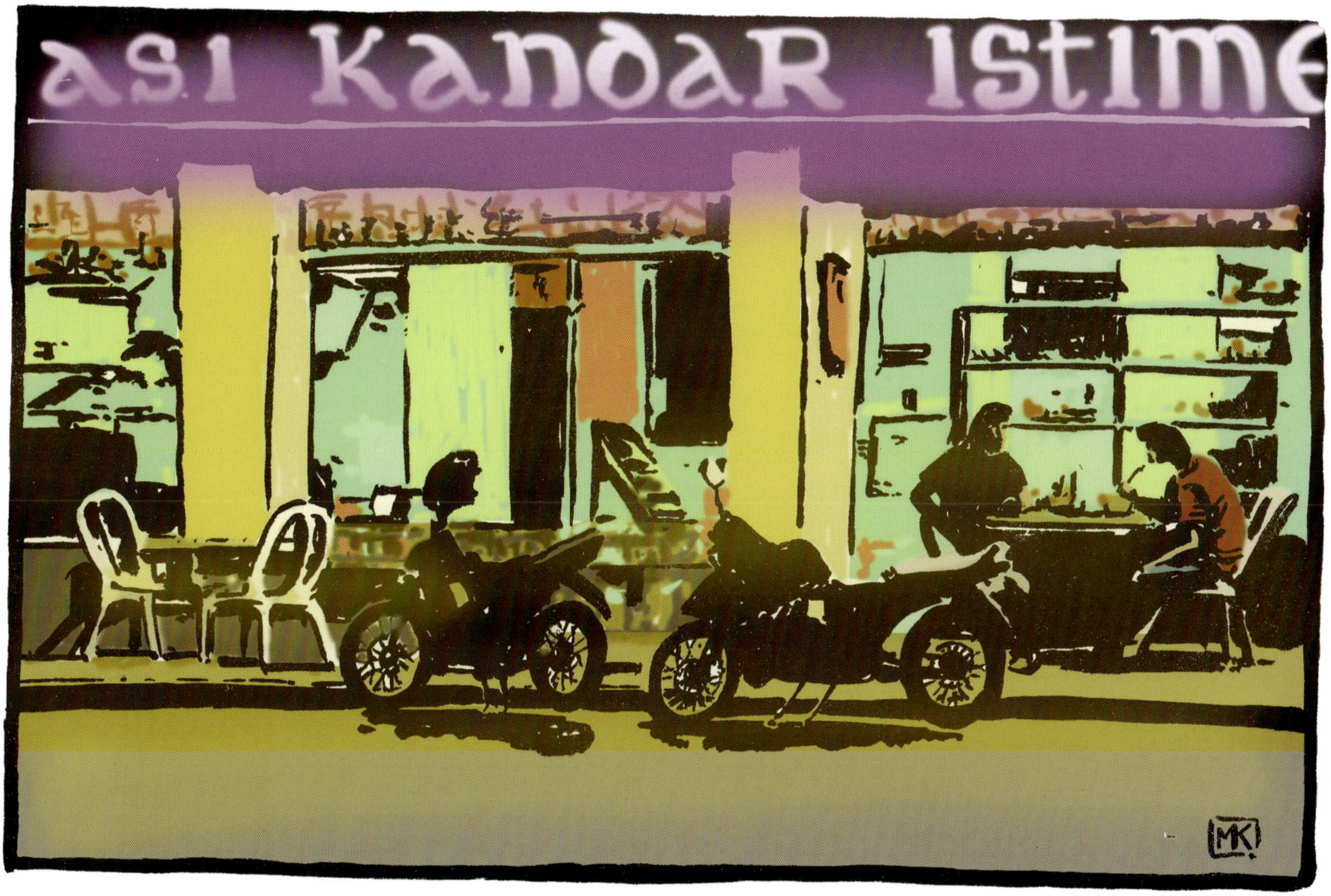

(Above) a restaurant on Jalan Macalister in George Town. This is a drawing that I inked and coloured digitally after the trip. Motorbikes got into almost every drawing, the way cell phones do elsewhere in the world.

(Right) The pleasures of street food and people watching on Chulia Street in George Town. The macaques in the parks are sometimes an attraction, often an aggressive nuisance. As long as you're not eating or drinking they tend to leave you alone – they knew the difference between my drawing pencil and food.

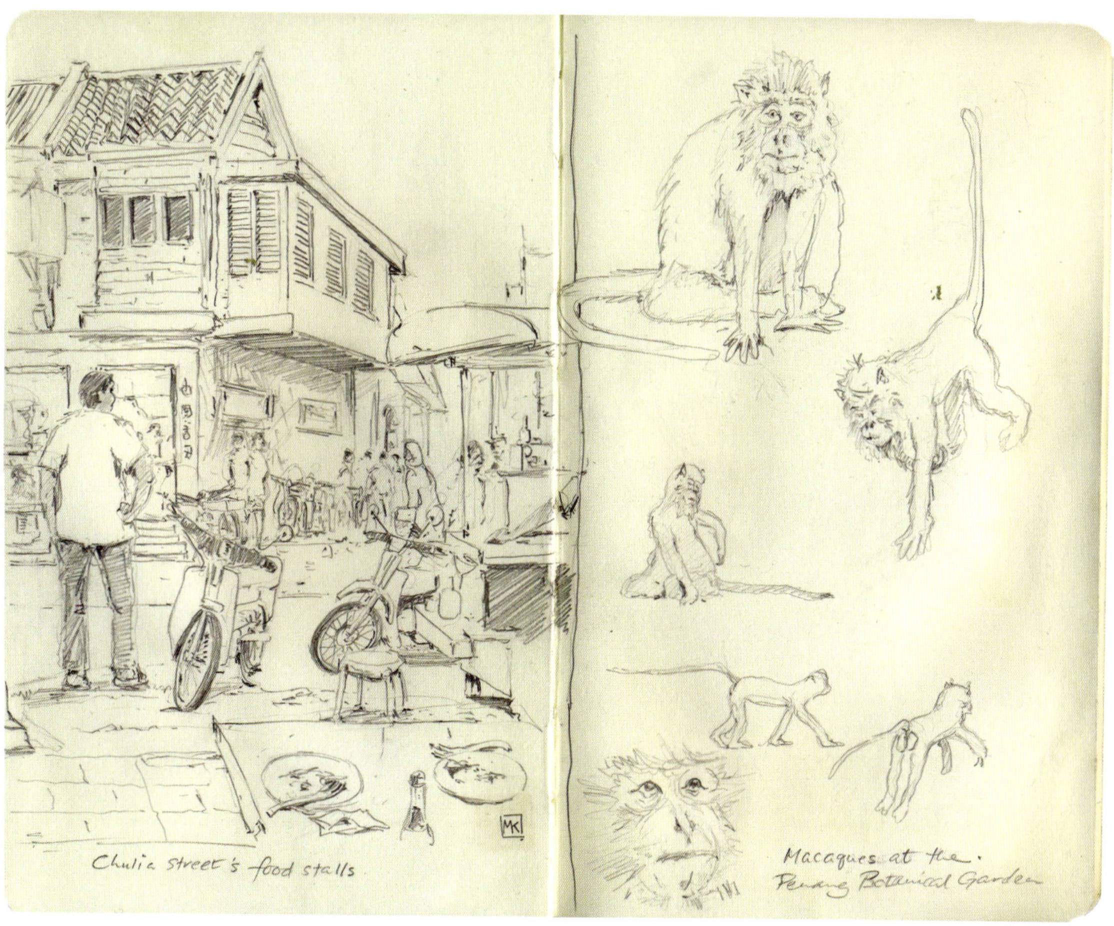

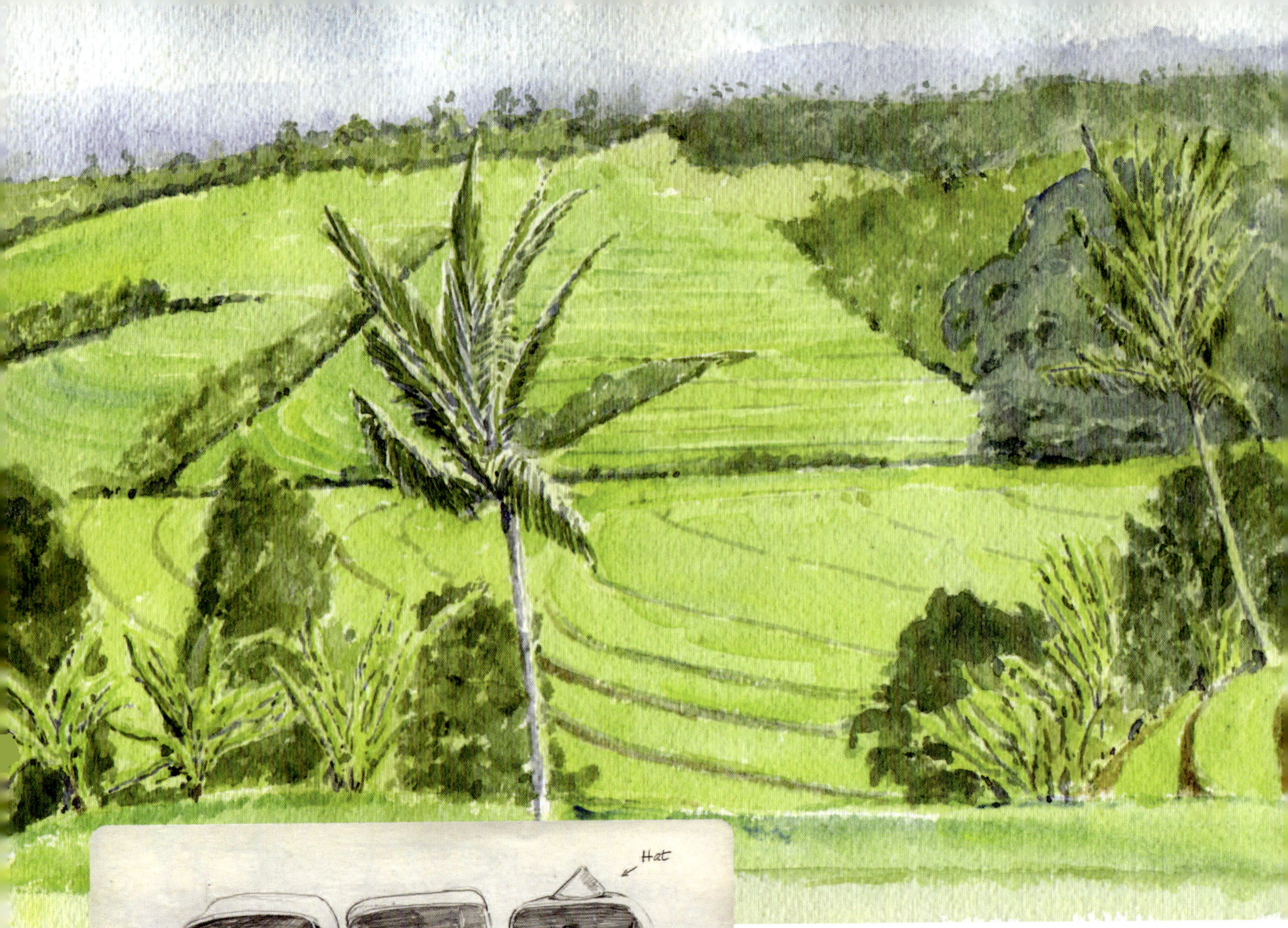

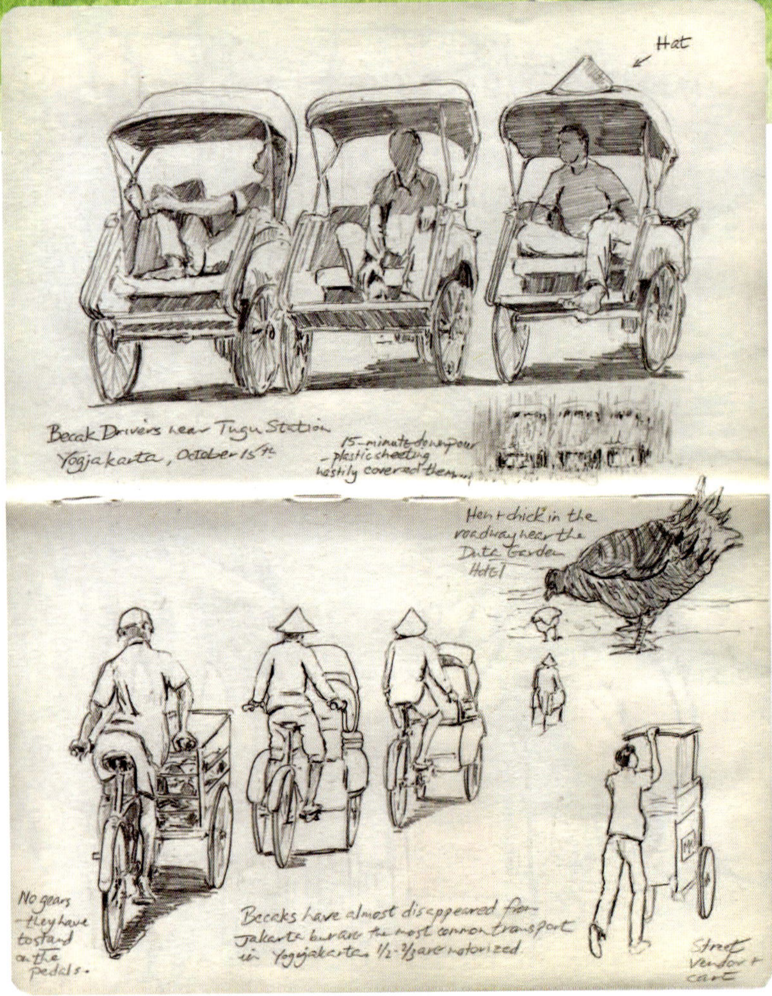

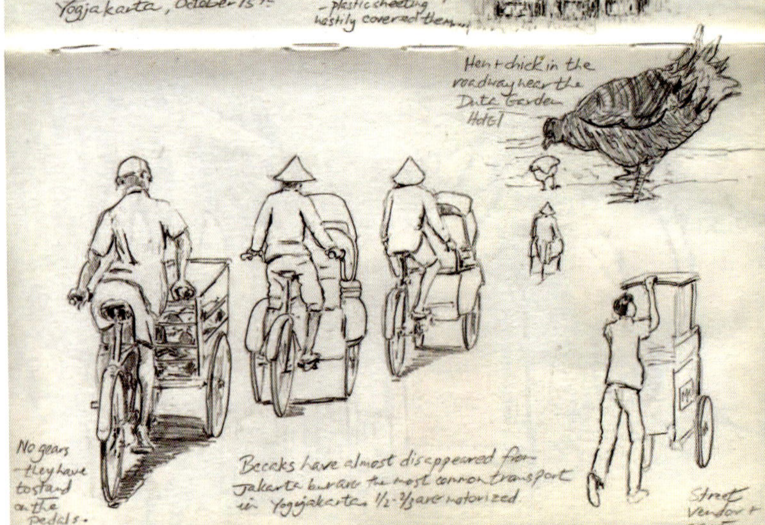
Hat
Becak Drivers near Tugu Station
Yogjakarta, October 15th
15-minute downpour
- plastic sheeting
hastily covered them
Hen + chick in the
roadway near the
Dute Garden
Hotel
No gears
- they have
to stand
on the
pedals.
Becaks have almost disappeared from
Jakarta but are the most common transport
in Yogyakarta. 1/2-2/3 are motorized.
Street
Vendor +
cart

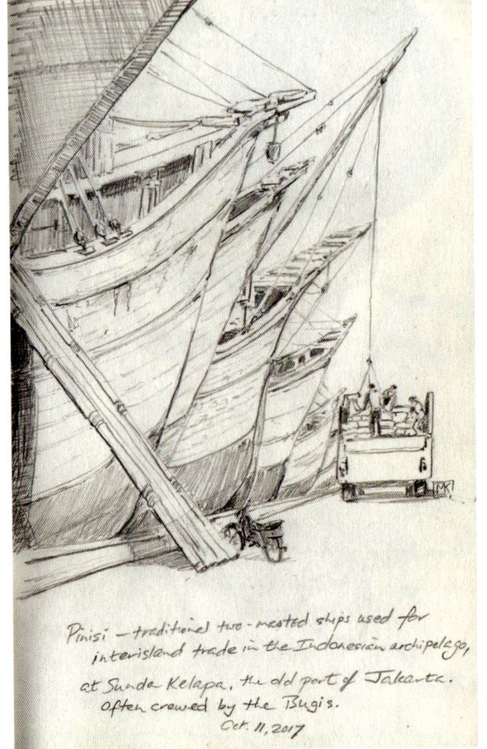
Pinisi – traditional two-masted ships used for
interisland trade in the Indonesian archipelago,
at Sunda Kelapa, the old port of Jakarta.
Often crewed by the Bugis.
Oct. 11, 2017

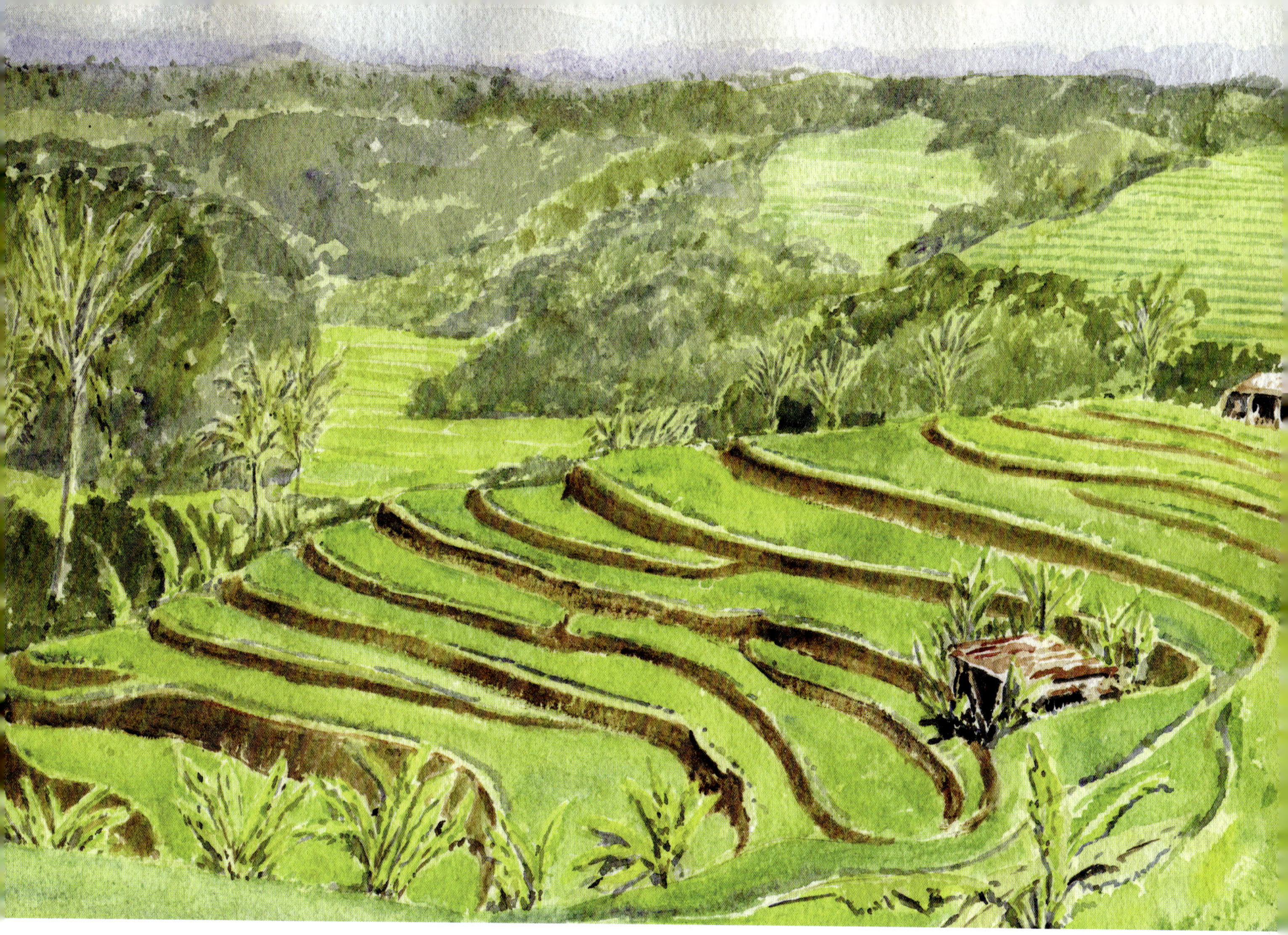

(Above) The marvellous terraced *sawahs* (rice paddies) at Jatiluwah, Bali. I found the combination of saturated colours, especially the greens, with the sun directly overhead and casting no shadows, to be a real challenge as I have developed my art style based on the angled sunlight typical of countries farther away from the equator. The light in Indonesia is an odd combination of bright and dull and the air is somehow "thick" with humidity. Typically, there was at least partial cloud cover that further flattened the light and moderated the tropical heat.

We visited friends in Indonesia's capital Jakarta in 2017 and then took the *kereta api* (carriage of fire = train) across Java to Yogyakarta and thence to Malang. One leg was in *Eksekutif* class, only marginally more comfortable than *Ekonomi* (right).

Java is Muslim and Bali is Hindu, with quite a contrast in cultures. Although Indonesia is home to 260 million people, they are scattered across almost a thousand islands, with unfathomable concentrations such as the 35+ million who live in Jakarta. It is nevertheless amazing how much countryside there is, partly jungle and partly *sawahs* for growing rice.

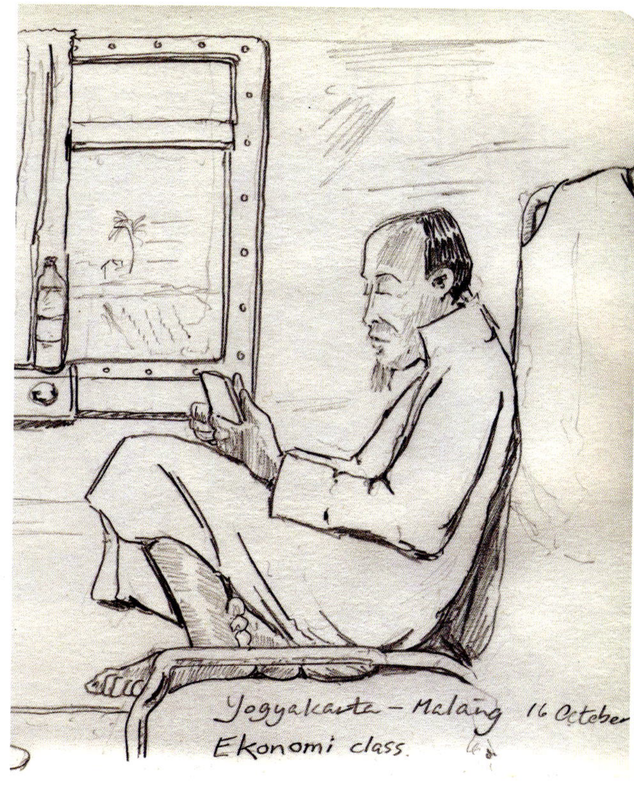

(Previous page) The human-powered *becaks*, cycle rickshaws used as taxis and for freight, are still common in the smaller cities. The huge *pinisi* – two-masted wooden ships – ply the trade routes between the islands.

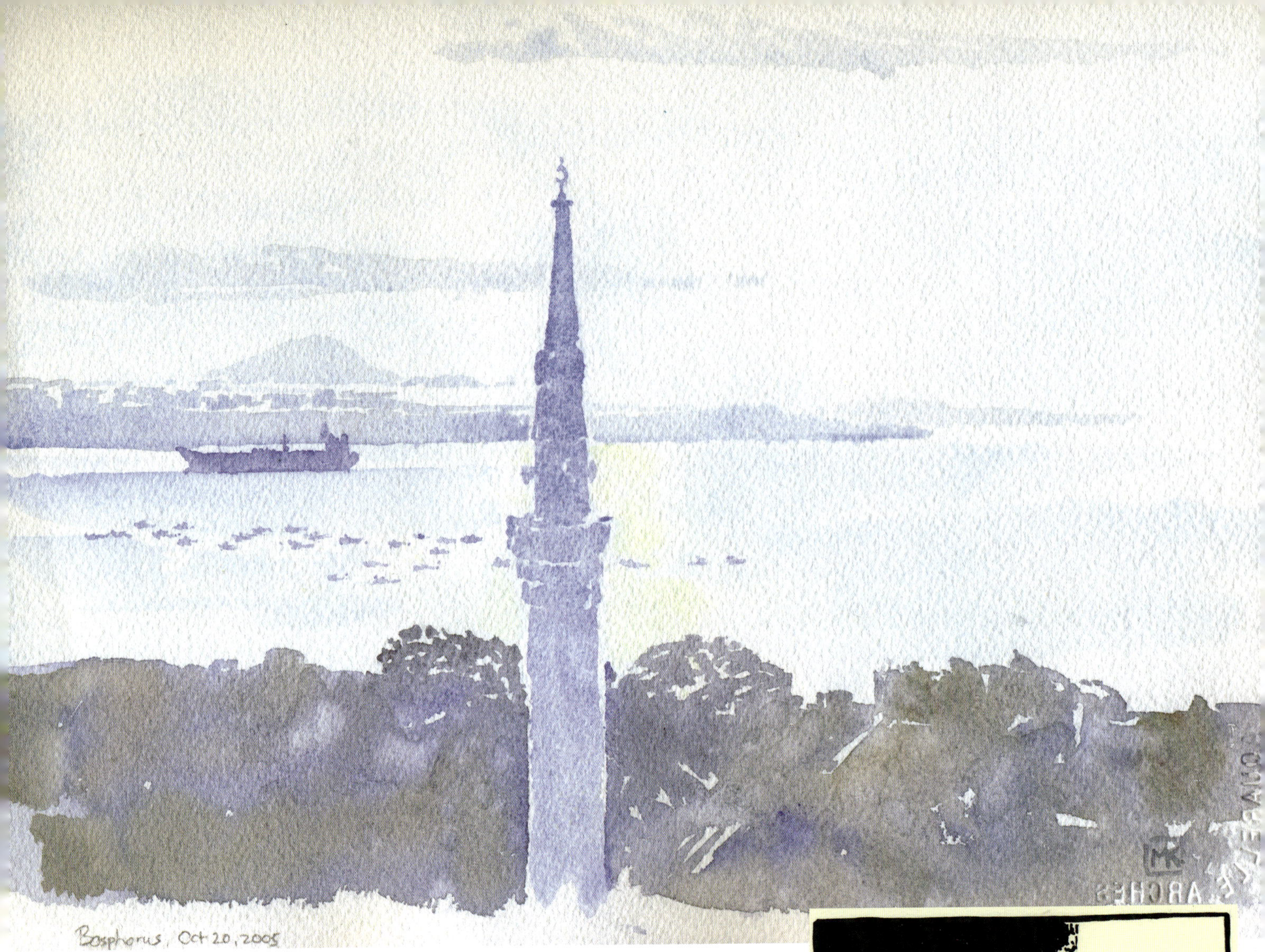

Bosphorus, Oct 20, 2005

Our hotel in Istanbul in October 2005 was in the neighbourhood of Ottoman-era wooden buildings below the Sultan Ahmet (Blue) Mosque – one of the two giant mosques, the other being the Hagia Sophia, that still dominate the skyline.

The little hotel served breakfast on its roof deck at 8 a.m. This view is the other way from the Sultan Ahmet mosque, south over the Bosphorus, the boundary between Europe and Asia, which widens out on the right into the Sea of Marmara. A single minaret, bristling with loudspeakers for the five-times daily prayers, protruded above the modest roofs. The freighter was likely on its way to a port on the Black Sea. Every morning, a few dozen small fish boats positioned themselves between the shore and the main shipping lane.

We wandered down the Turkish coast, ferried to Samos (one of the Dodecanese islands that are part of Greece in spite of being within sight of the Turkish coast), then overnight ferried to Piraeus (the port of Athens) and took a hydrofoil to Crete, where we stayed a week in the curious little house on the next page.

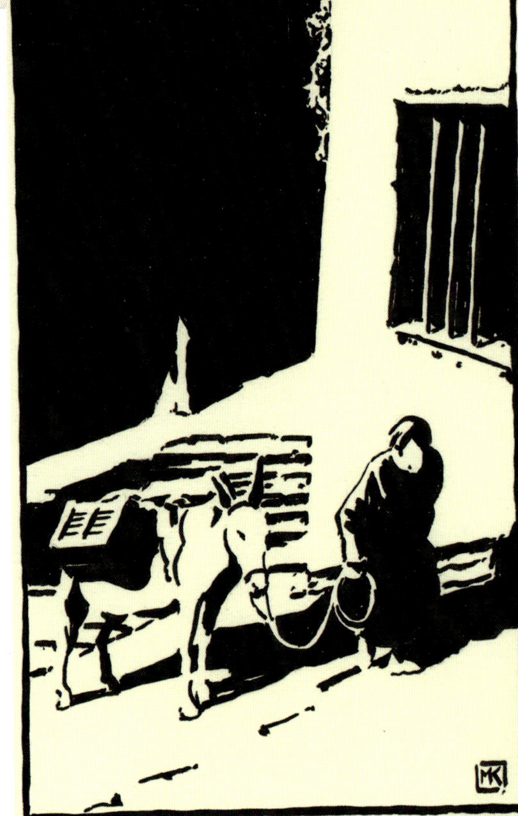

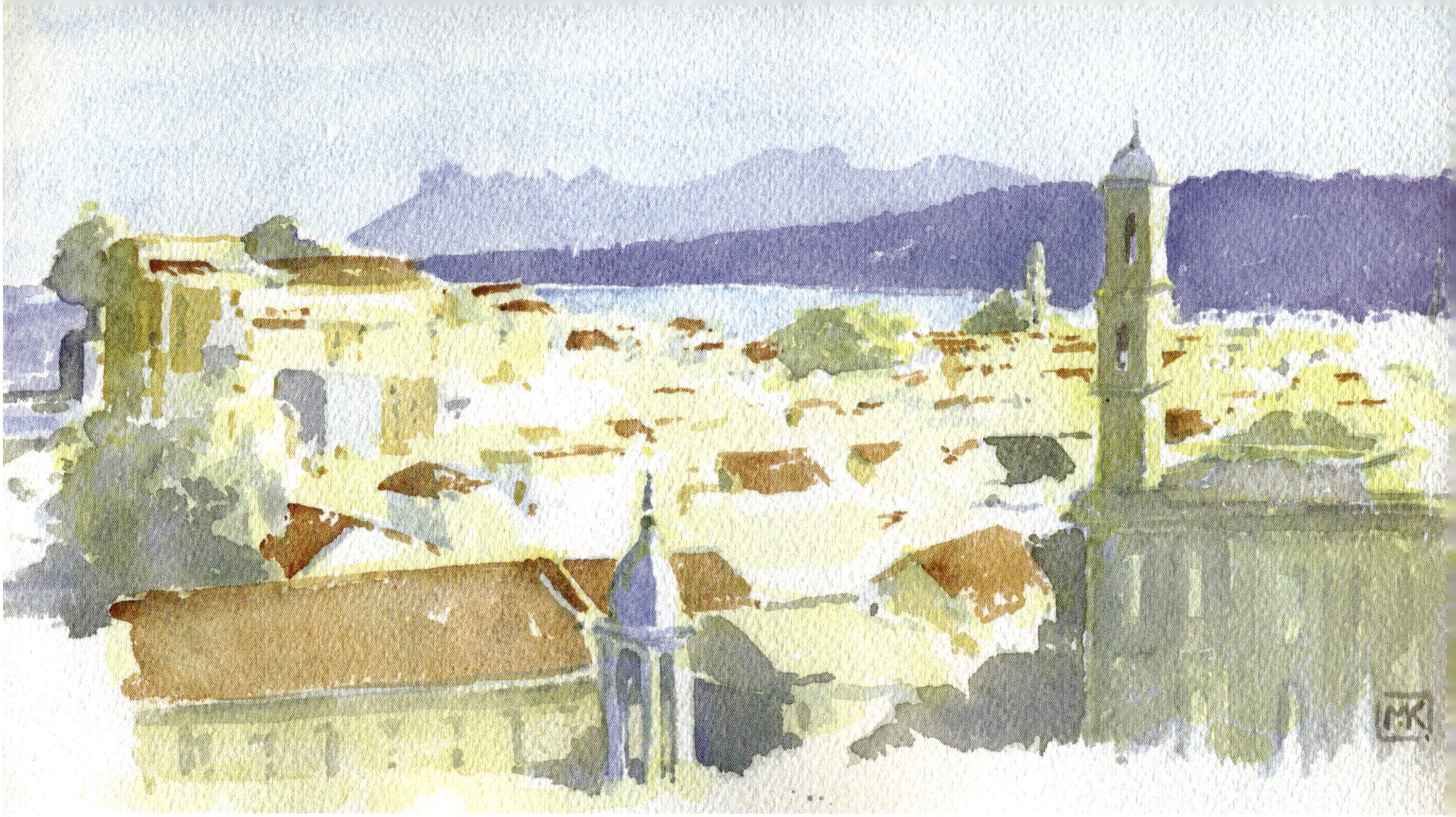

(Above) View of Chania, the second-largest city in Crete, from its old fortification wall early one November morning in 2005. Much of the town was developed by Venetians, then it was taken over by the Ottoman Turks for a time.

(Right) The house in Chania entered off a narrow lane through a side door. Up a steep flight of stairs was a bedroom floor, then up another to the living room, kitchen and bathroom, then up a ladder to a platform, and up another ladder to the roof terrace. We bought a chicken, lemons and rosemary in the market one day and roasted them for dinner. Other evenings we strolled to the waterfront and listened to Cretan folk music in the Lyrakia Café.

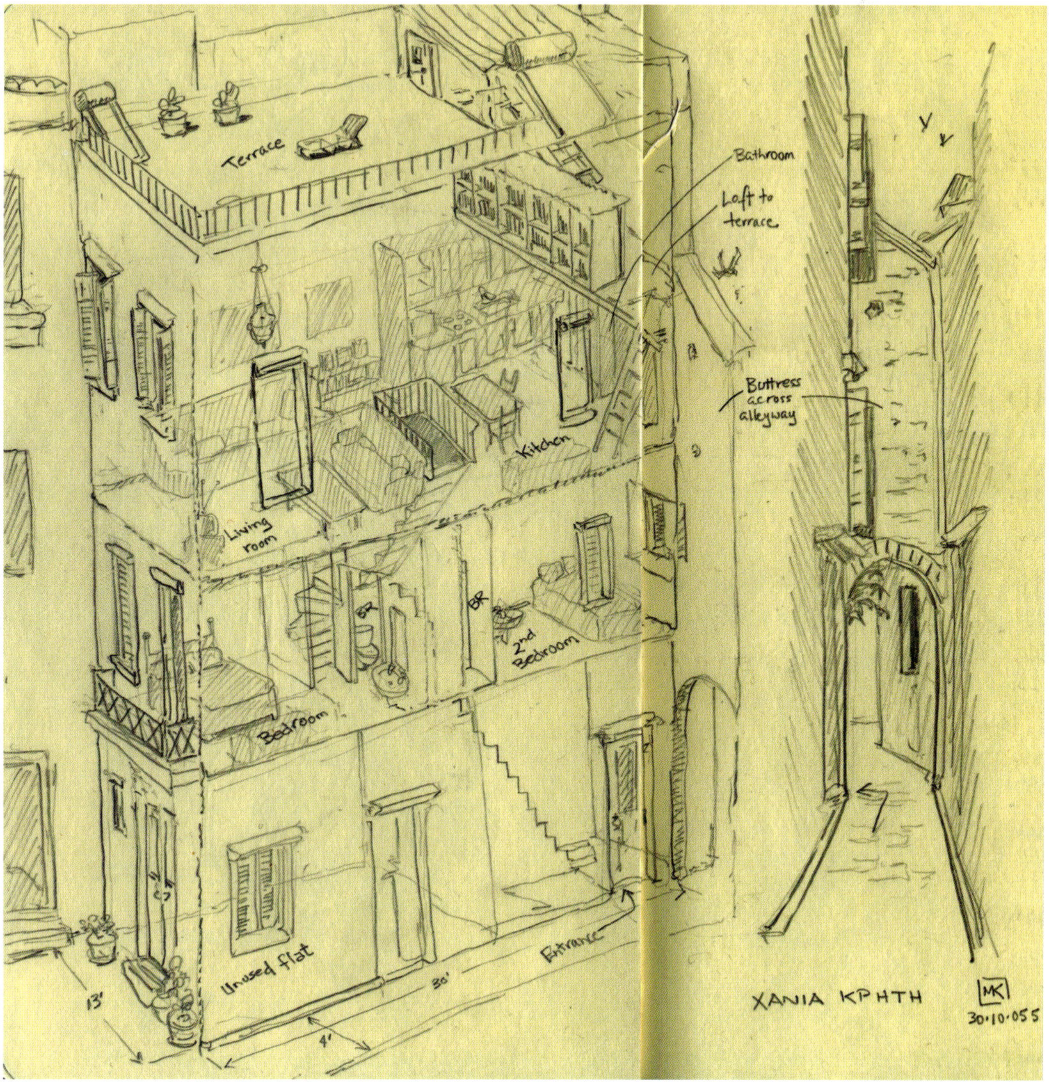

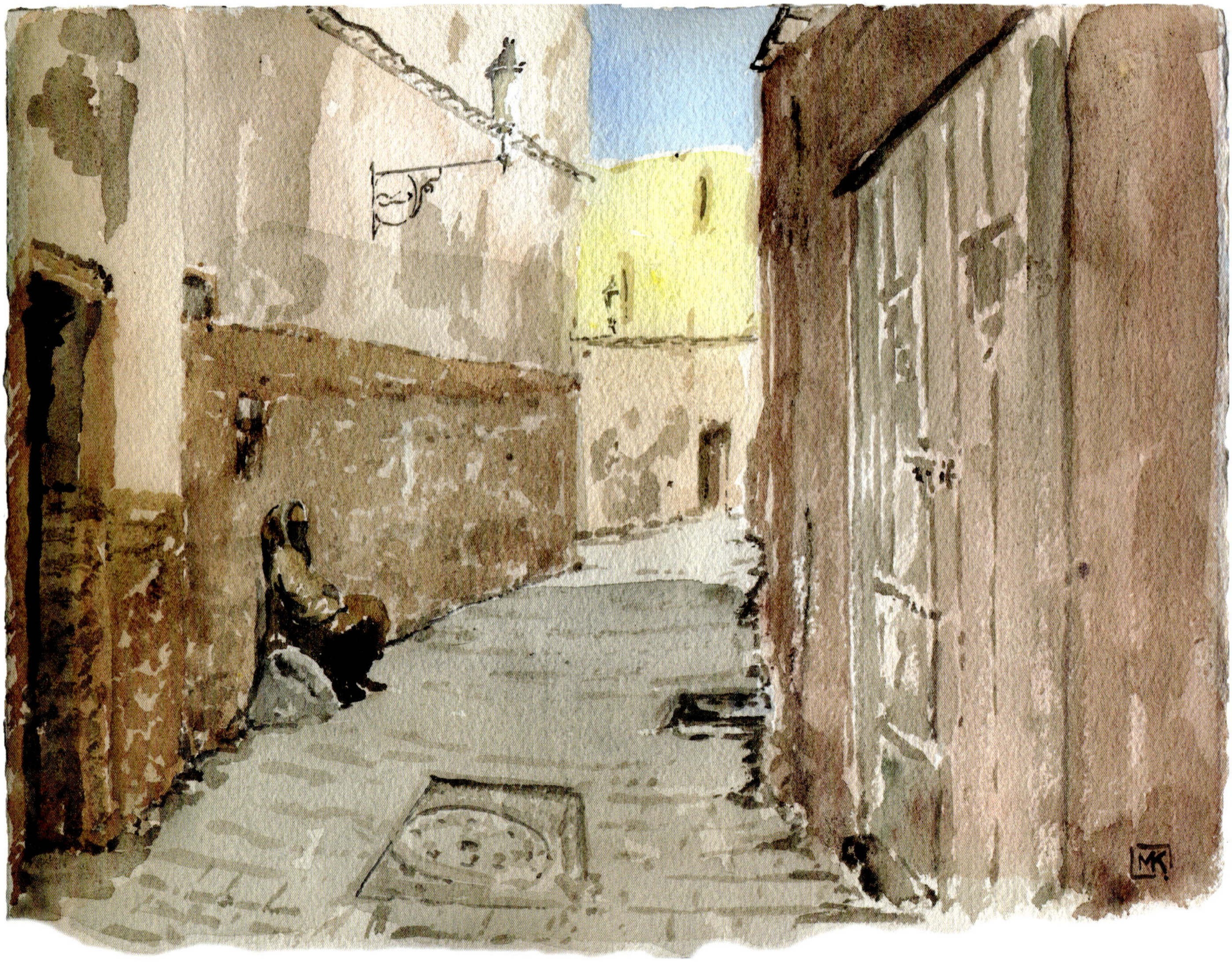

We wandered through the winding, narrow, high-walled *derbs* of Marrakech in January 2015, following my boy scout compass to avoid getting lost between the apartment we'd rented and our various destinations: sometimes one of the *souks* (markets) and, in the evening, the huge "La Place" square where thousands congregated to eat, listen to Berber drummers, buy trinkets and watch performing monkeys and charmed snakes. Every day the beggar woman squatted in a *derb* on our usual route. A boy sometimes sat near her and sold homemade candy when he wasn't elsewhere, presumably at school. There were no landmarks to see above the walls as no building (other than a minaret) could be taller than a palm tree.

Essaouira, the "wind city" on the Atlantic Coast, has more of a formal, French colonial feeling to parts of it, evidenced by the plantings of palms along its major streets (right).

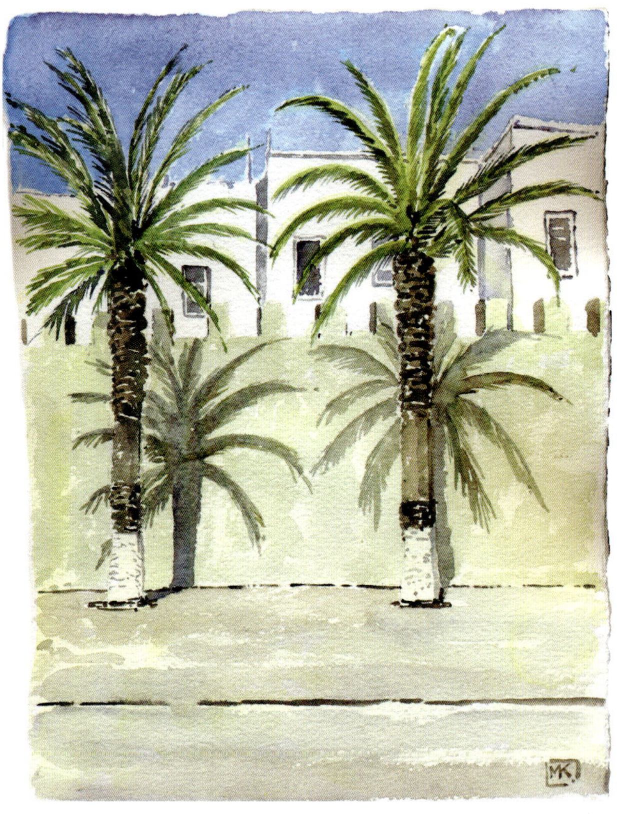

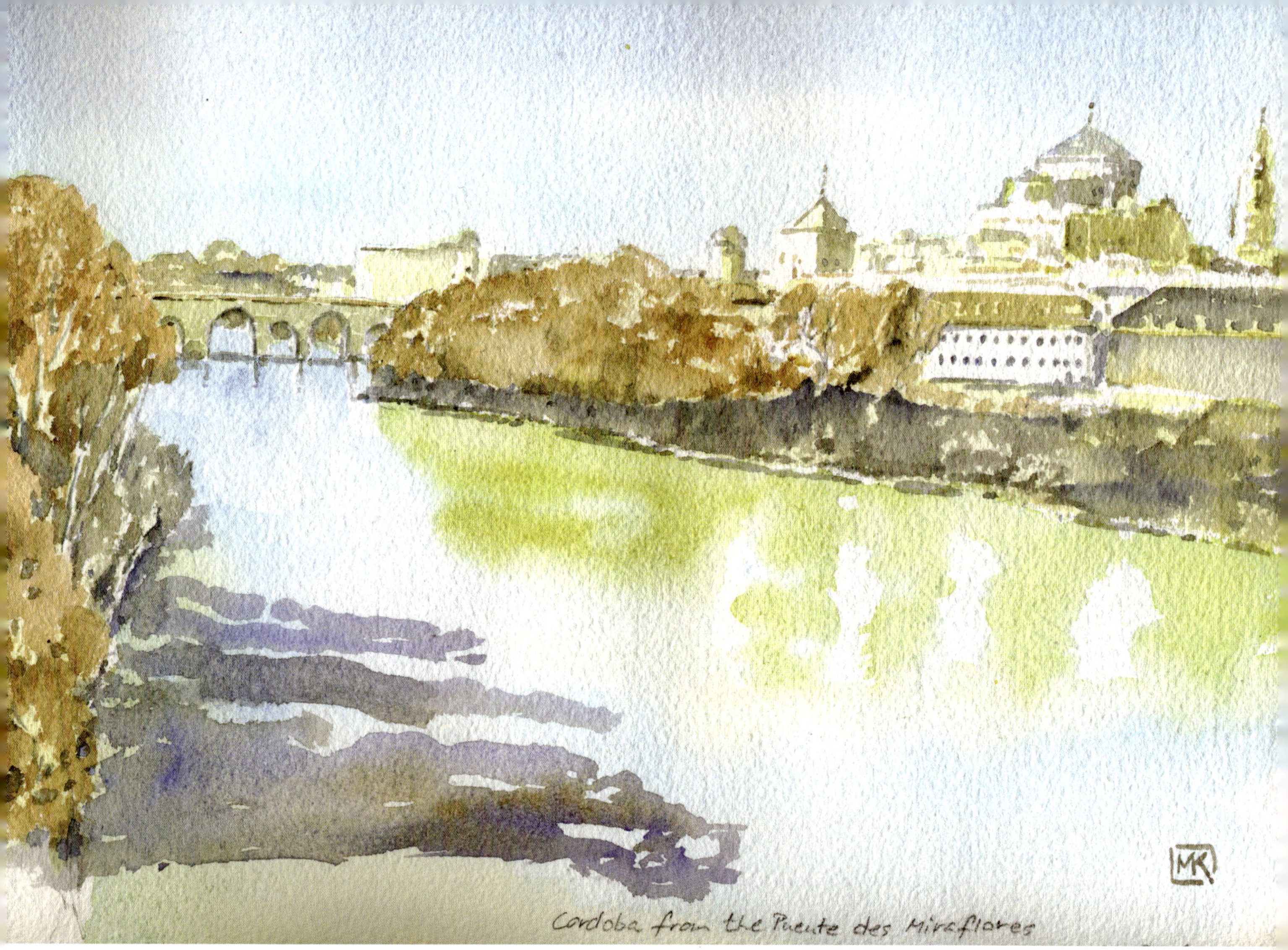

Cordoba from the Puente des Miraflores

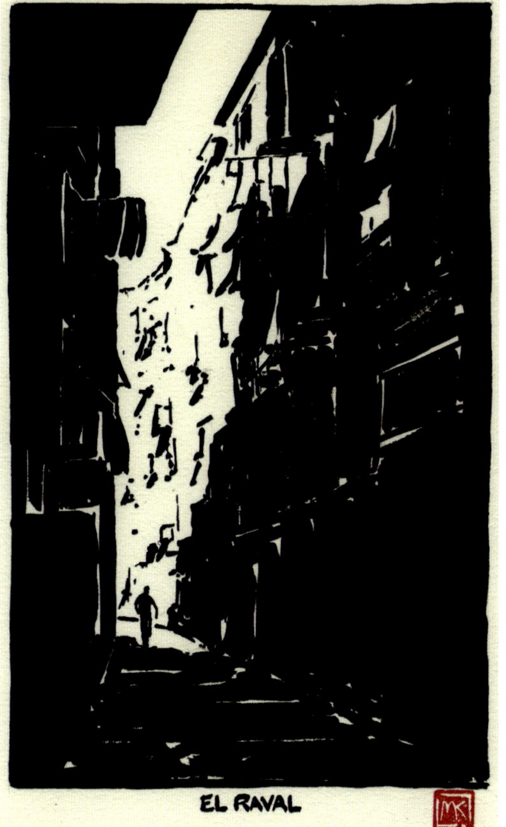
EL RAVAL

On that same trip, we crossed from Tangier to Spain near the Strait of Gibraltar and worked our way northward by bus and train to Córdoba and thence to Barcelona.

The openness of the Córdoba streets was liberating after the confinement of Marrakech's and Tangier's narrow alleys. The landmark is the Grand Mosque-Cathedral, commenced by the Moors in 784 and converted to a Roman Catholic church a few hundred years later. It is the reverse of Hagia Sophia in Istanbul: a church from 537 till 1453, then a mosque until 1931 when it became a museum. Change comes slowly in some parts of the world. The Islamist Erdogan government announced in 2020 that it would revert to a mosque.

In Barcelona, we had an apartment in El Raval, a rough, arty quarter of nightclubs, cafés, an art school and the Contemporary Art Museum; it is on the other side of La Rambla from the Barri Gòtic neighbourhood beloved of cruise ship passengers. The winter sun only penetrated the cold, narrow streets for an hour or so a day.

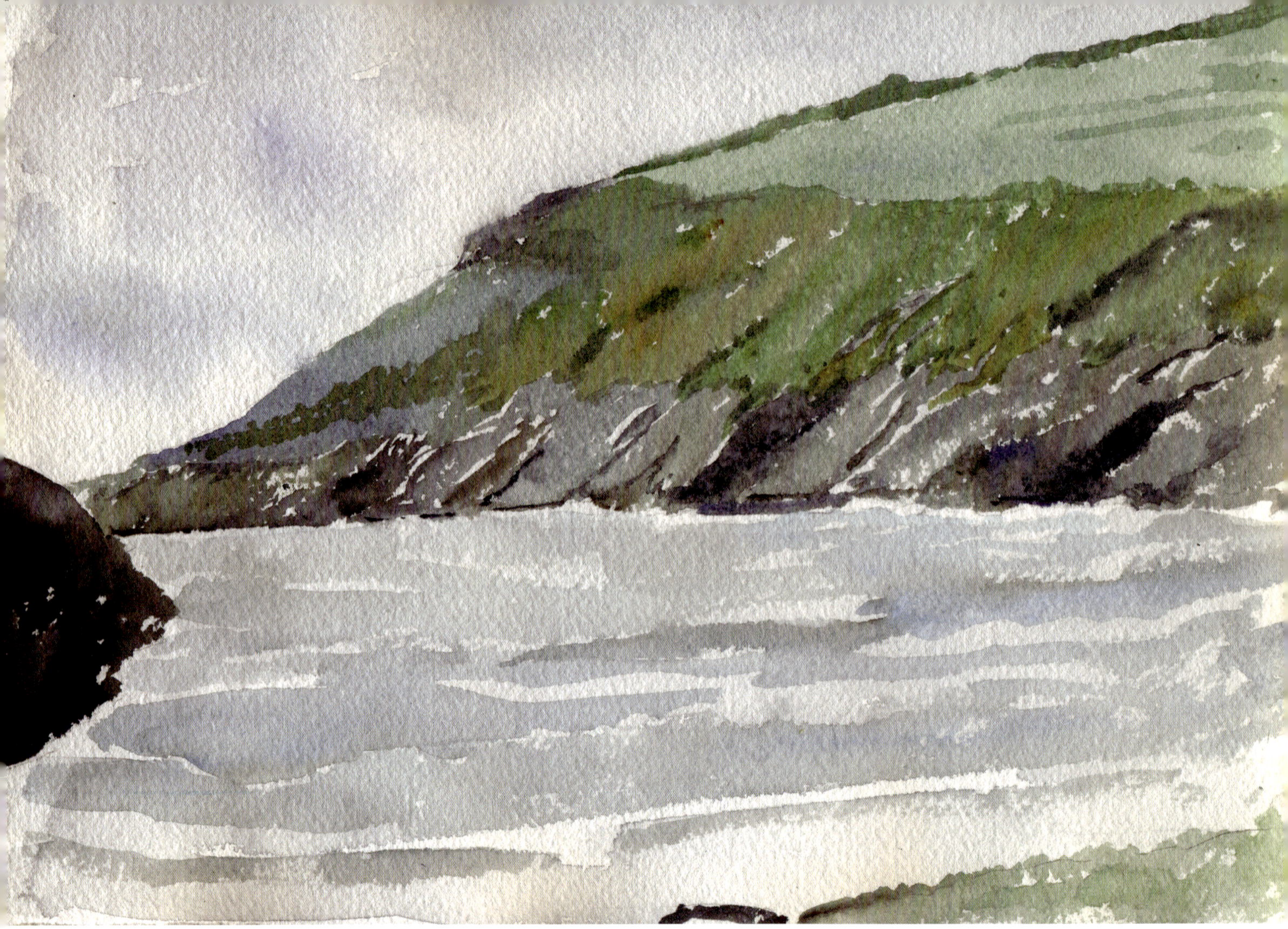

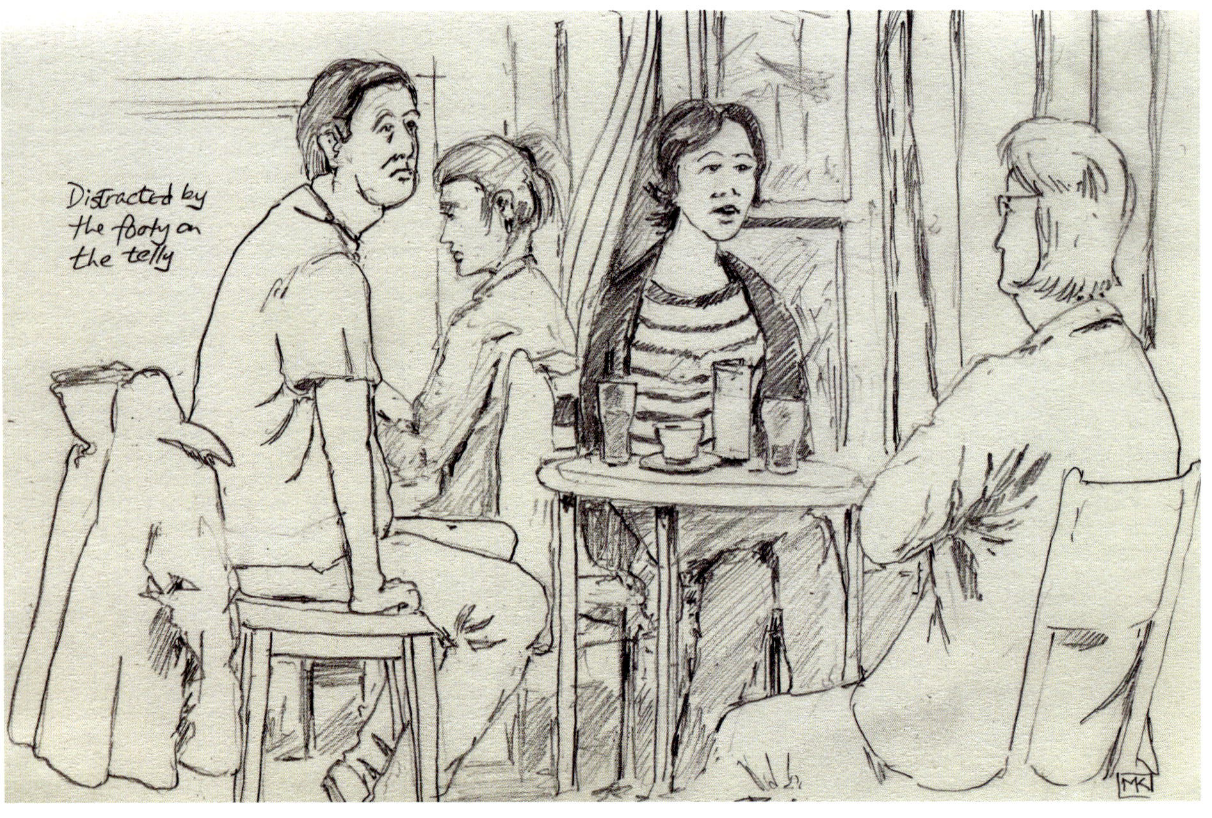
Distracted by
the footy on
the telly
MK

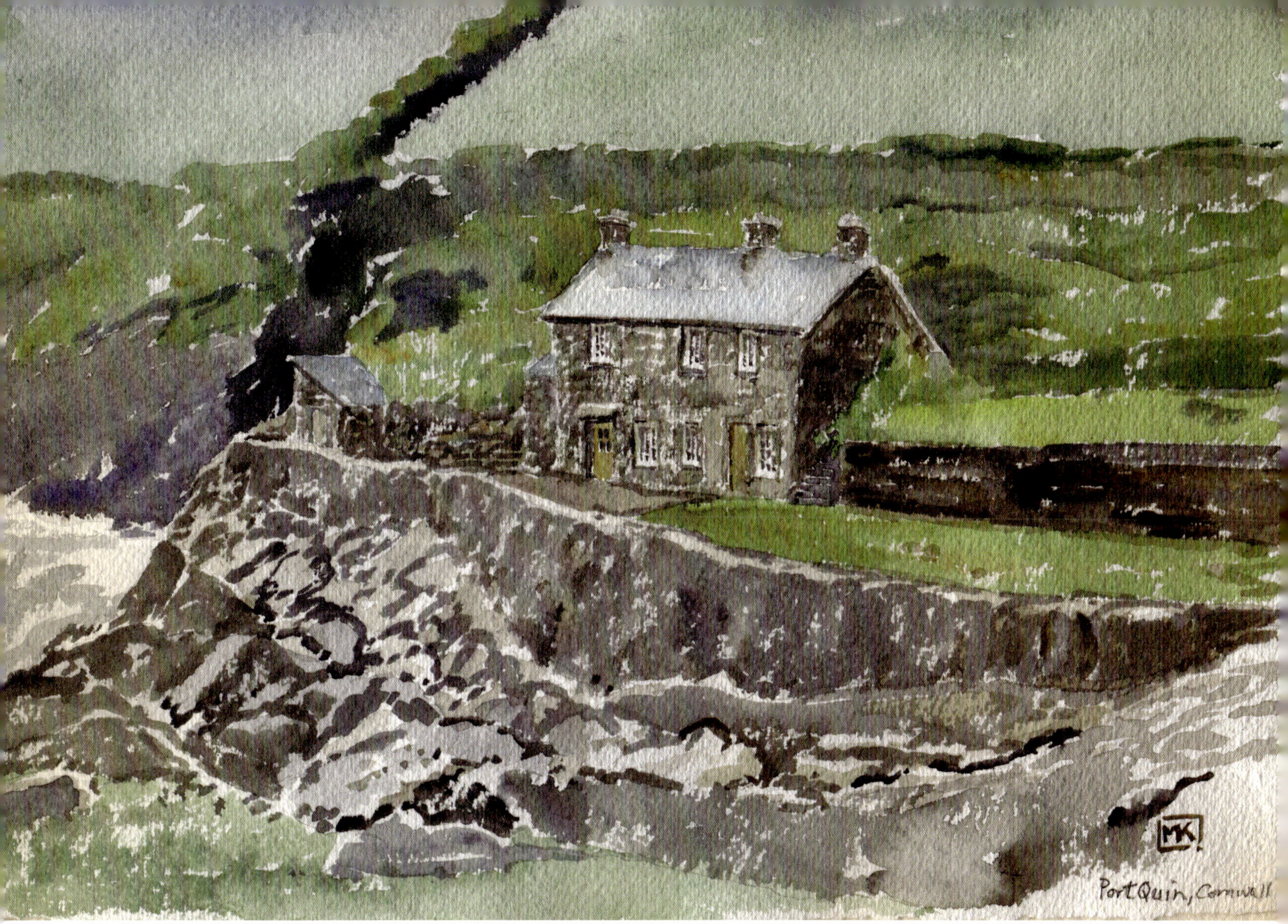

(Above) A dot on the map in Cornwall, UK, called Port Quin, in the blowing drizzle of a May day.

(Right) The picturesque village of Mousehole, Cornwall, between Penzance and Land's End. We sat in the sun on the edge of its little harbour with coffee and flapjacks (Cornish oatcakes) from a local bakery. The harbour's breakwater is on the left with a narrow opening to the sea; boats are chained to rings set in the harbour wall, many of them sitting in the mud at low tide; the village itself is a cluster of grey stone, hipped-roof Georgian-era buildings crowded along narrow streets with a steep hill behind. In relative terms everything is quite new, as the village was burned to the ground by Spaniards in 1595.

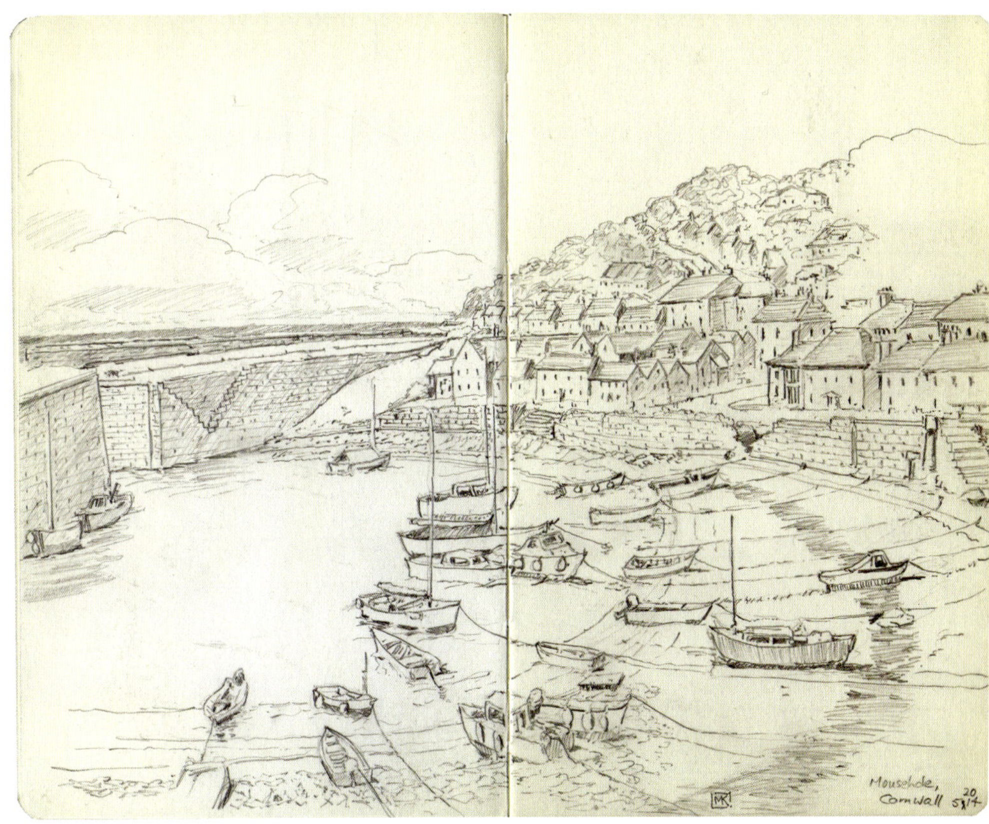

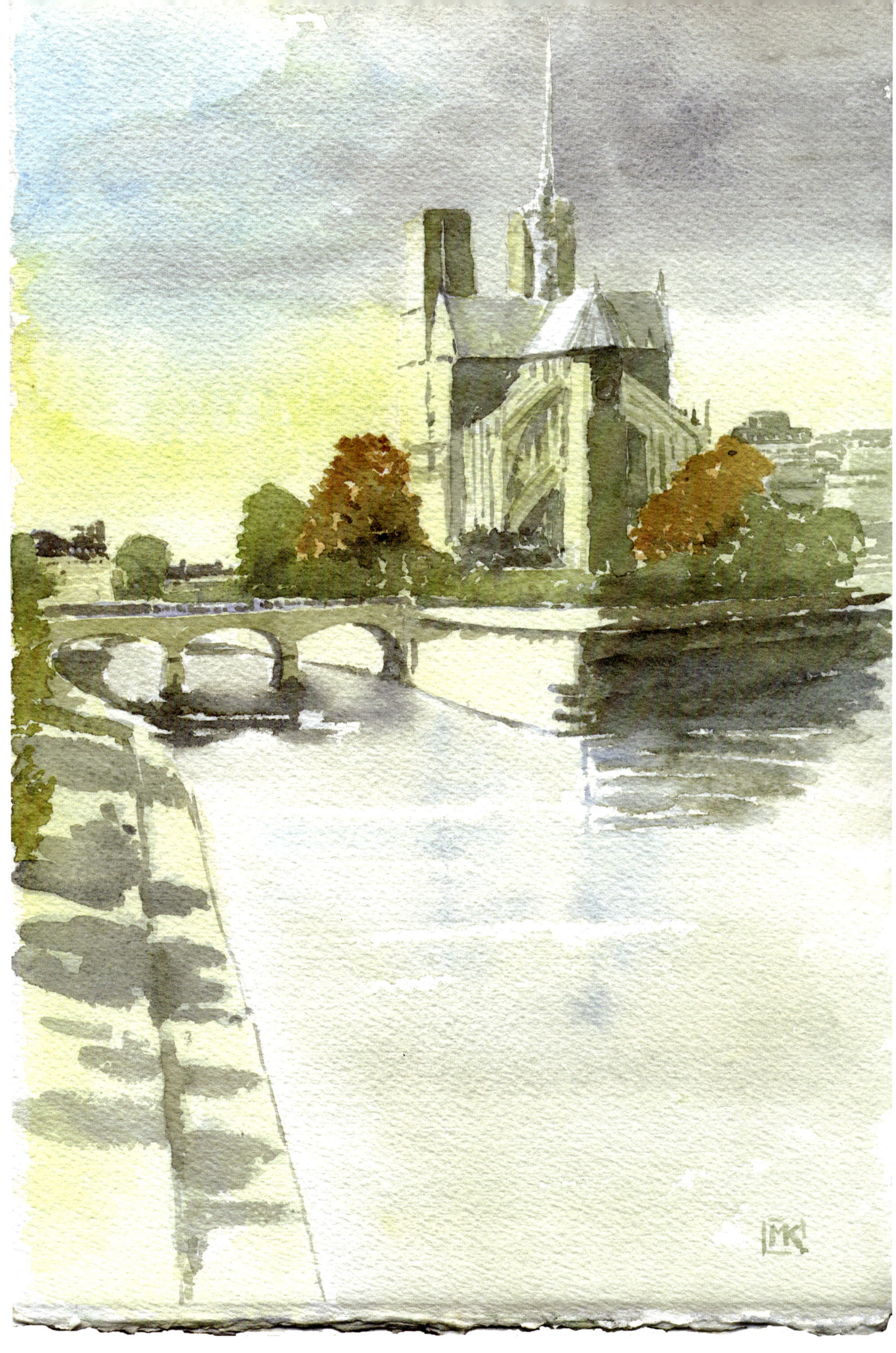

It is probably no surprise that France has been a touchstone for all my travelling and painting days.

I always liked the view of Notre Dame de Paris from upstream at the Pont de la Tournelle where the Seine splits into two channels around Île de la Cité. I decided in the fall of 2008 to paint it, thinking as I did how unchanging French landscapes are and how much their historic buildings are valued and protected. But policy can't trump tragedy, as witnessed by the devastating fire in April 2019. And so it will become like a Japanese temple – unlike in "the West," if a building burns down in Japan it is replaced exactly, and is considered to be the same building. The spirit of a place endures. "Old" is sometimes newer than you think.

On that trip I became slightly obsessed with the filter tips sharing the sidewalks with the dog turds which necessitated the Paris walking technique known as *le slalom sur les crottes*. And in the drawing below, "SDF" means *sans domicile fixe*, that is, homeless.

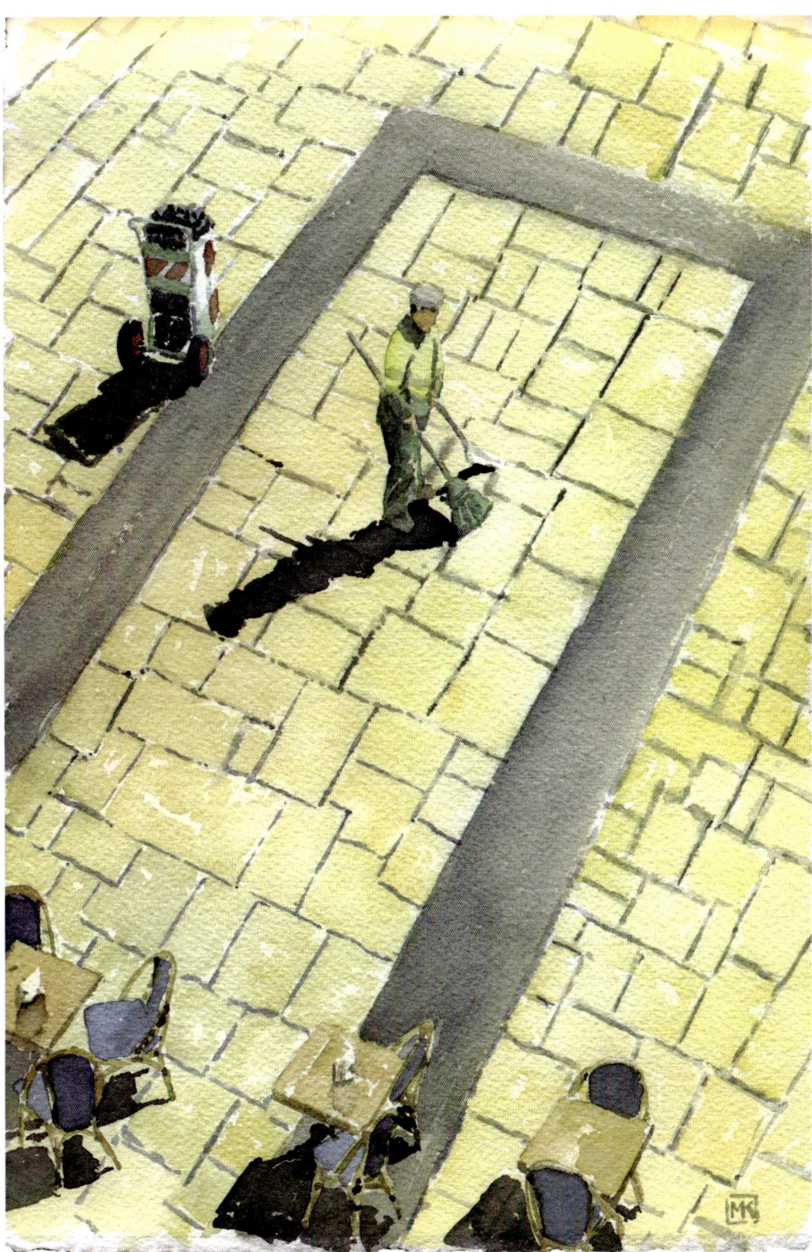

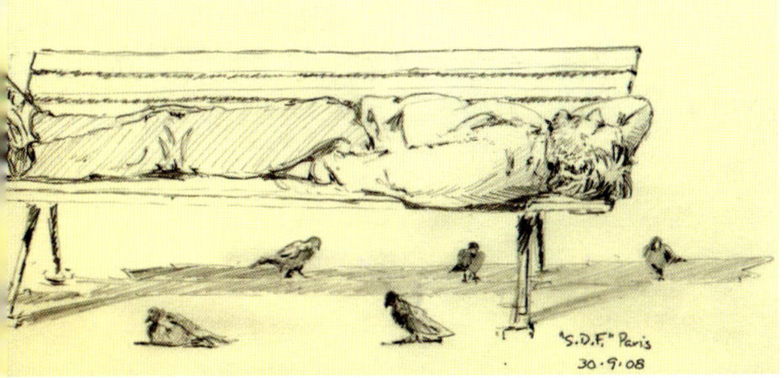

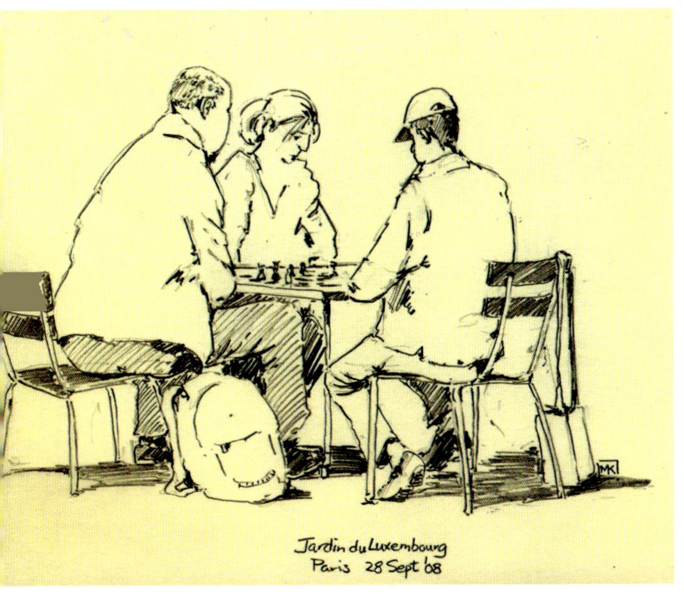

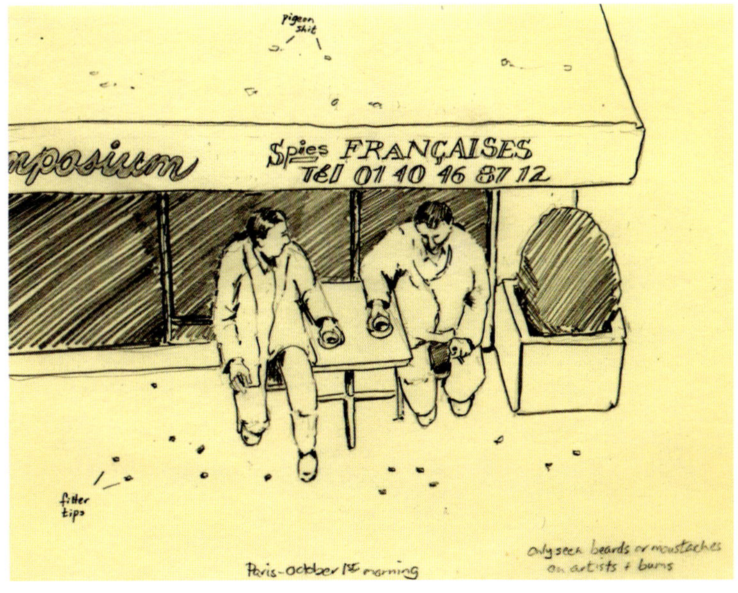

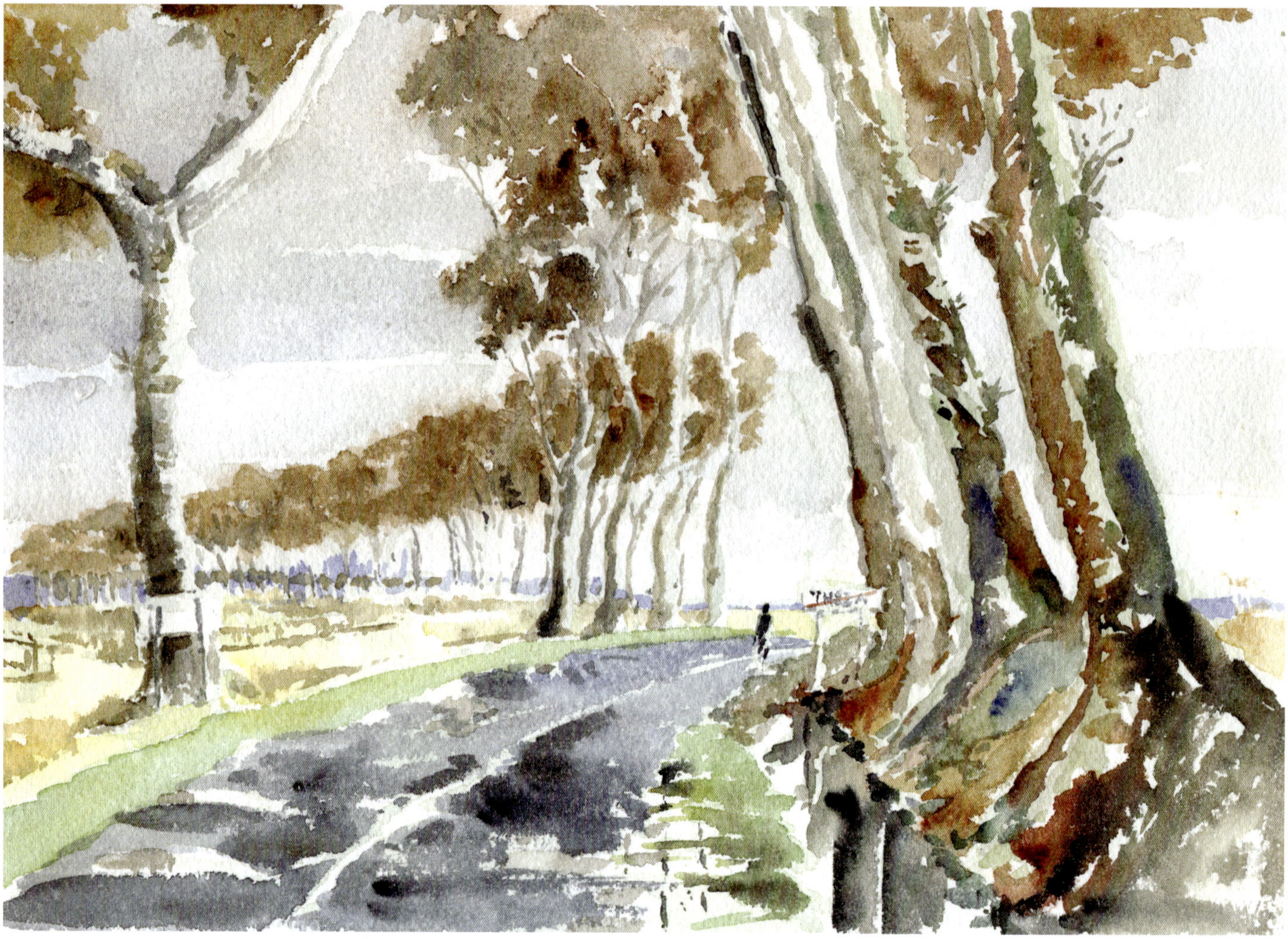

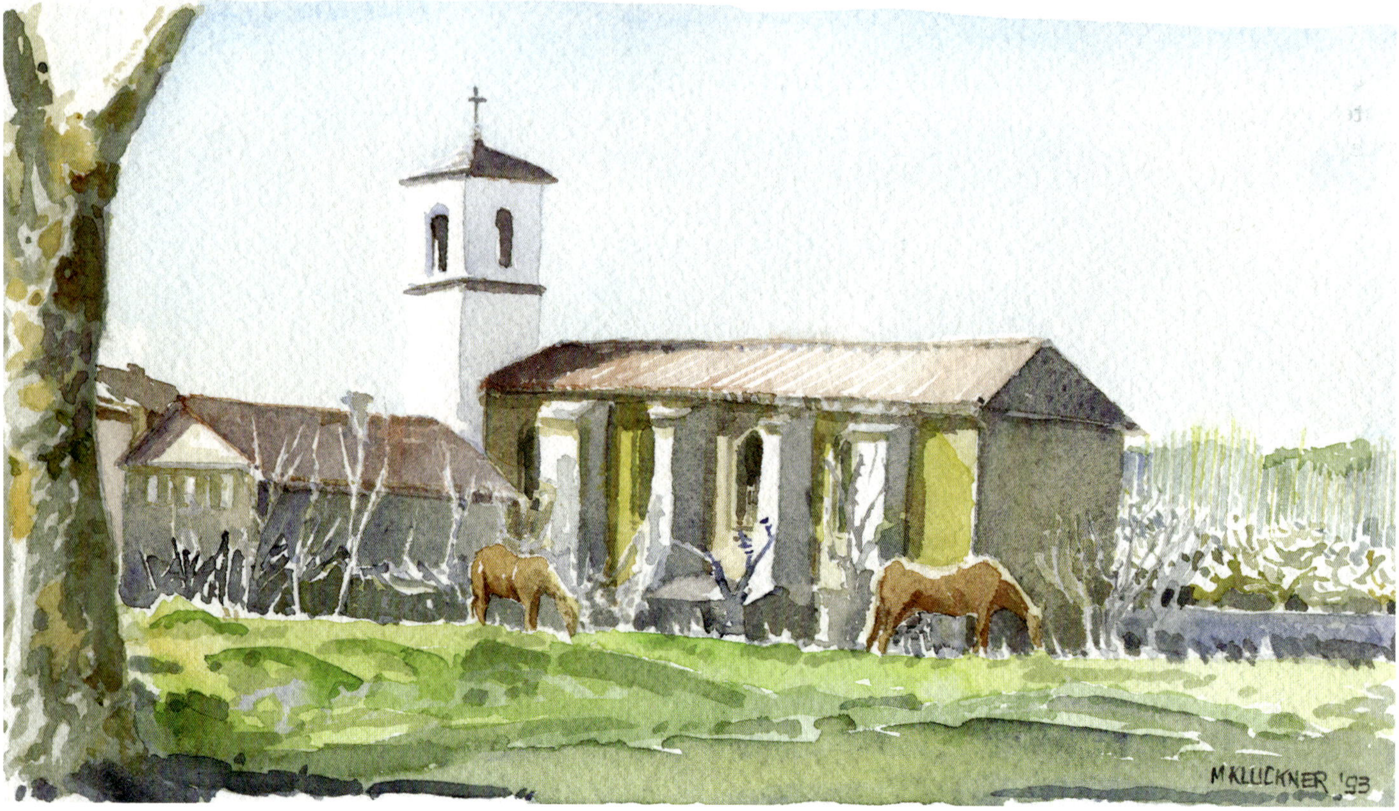

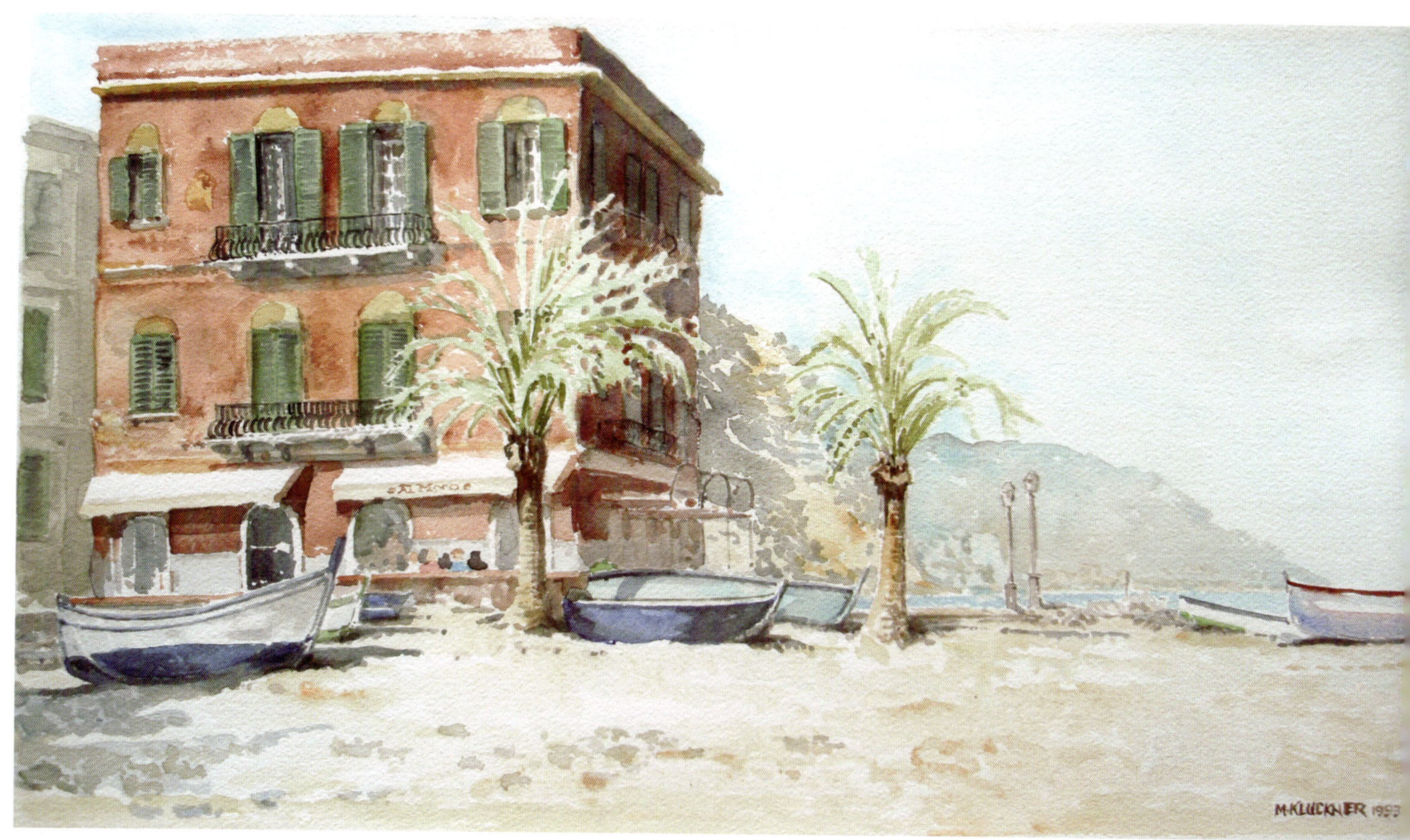

Travelling out of season has huge appeal: the lack of fellow travellers more than compensates for shorter days and the risk of bad weather. In southern France and Italy, it is also like time travel, especially when comparing one's experiences with those of past travellers including literary figures such as Tobias Smollett, Charles Dickens, D.H. Lawrence and especially Robert Louis Stevenson, whose 1879 *Travels with a Donkey* set a standard for a modest journey with his beast of burden, Modestine. The idea of "overwintering" in a place like Nice or Cannes harks back to a period before time zones and quick jet travel to tropical resorts.

Accordingly, we bought a small Renault in Marseilles in December 1992 and spent three months travelling along the Mediterranean coast through Spain, France and Italy, buying vintage postcards in flea markets to compare with the current scene, writing journals and, for me, painting.

(Above) Laiguéglia in February 1993. It is one of the smallest towns on the Italian Riviera between San Remo and Savona, and one of the most attractive because the seashore is not cut off from the town by a railway line. Fishing skiffs spend the winter pulled up on the beach, where they are scraped and painted and await the arrival of spring.

(Previous page above) As everything was closing for Christmas, we rented a cottage in a lettuce field for a week near Perpignan, the last big French town before the Spanish frontier. On December 26th, following a winter storm, the wet trunks of the plane trees that line most French roads glowed under the grey sky.

(Previous page below) Villecroze, a village in the Haut-Var near Barjols, known as "the Tivoli of Provence" for its many fountains, where we rented a cottage for a week in early January.

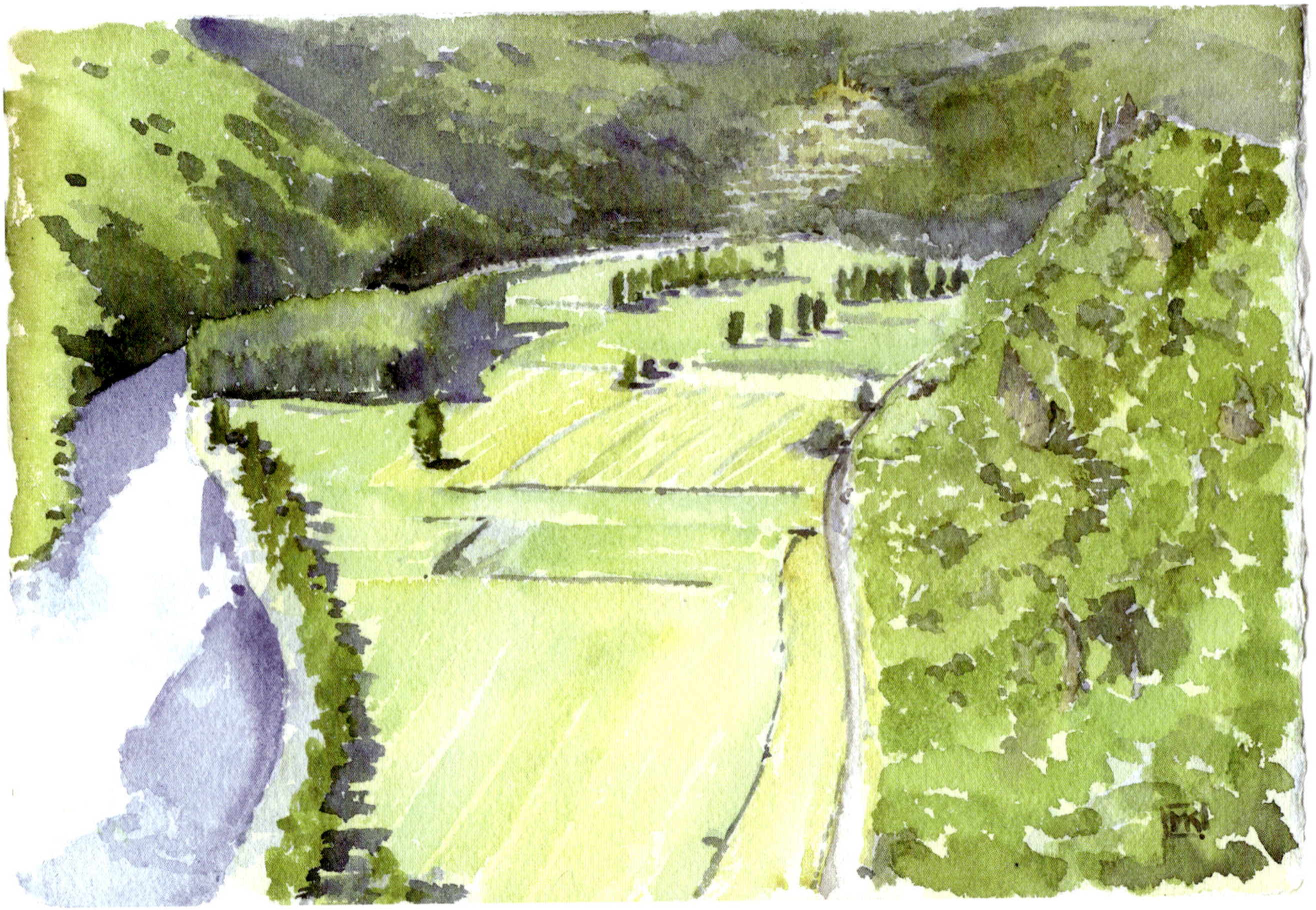

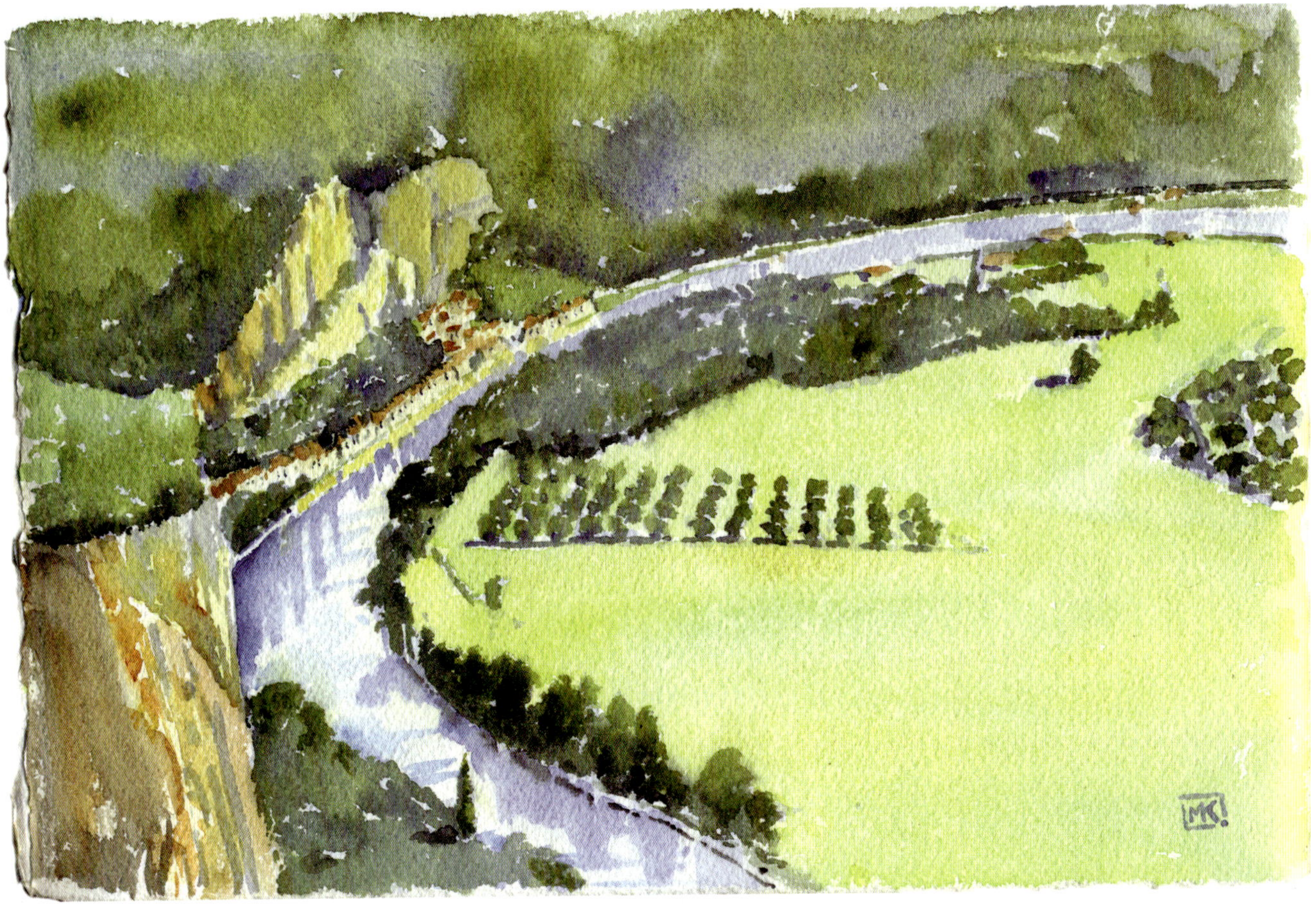

A memorable day's painting in the south of France in October 2008.

(Previous page) Two views of the Dordogne River from a rocky outcropping, part of the hill on which the Château de Marqueyssac sits, in a valley of *châteaux* southwest of Sarlat-la-Canéda. I sat in the sun on a wall on the edge of the cliff and painted, while people visiting the *château*'s garden came by, occasionally glanced or chatted but mostly left me alone. *Anglais*, I heard a couple of them say: people who painted in watercolour *(l'art anglais)*, especially outdoors, were likely English.

(Right) From Bergerac (where Cyrano lived) the D660 runs east through a splendid, picturesque landscape along the Dordogne River, past cornfields and castles. So much corn – more than I ever imagined was grown in France. Perhaps it was grown for force feeding geese to make the region's *spécialité: pâté de fois gras.*

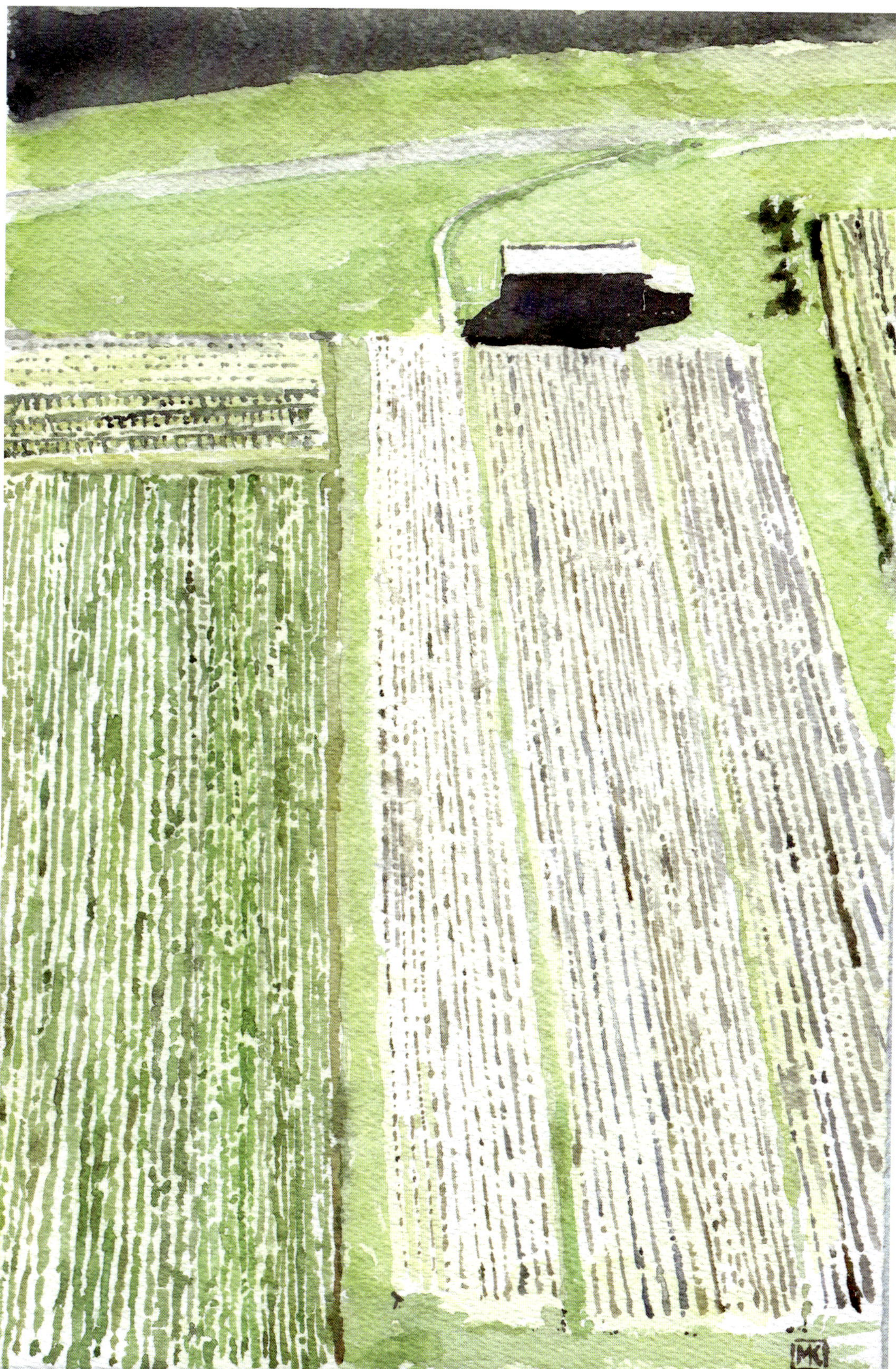

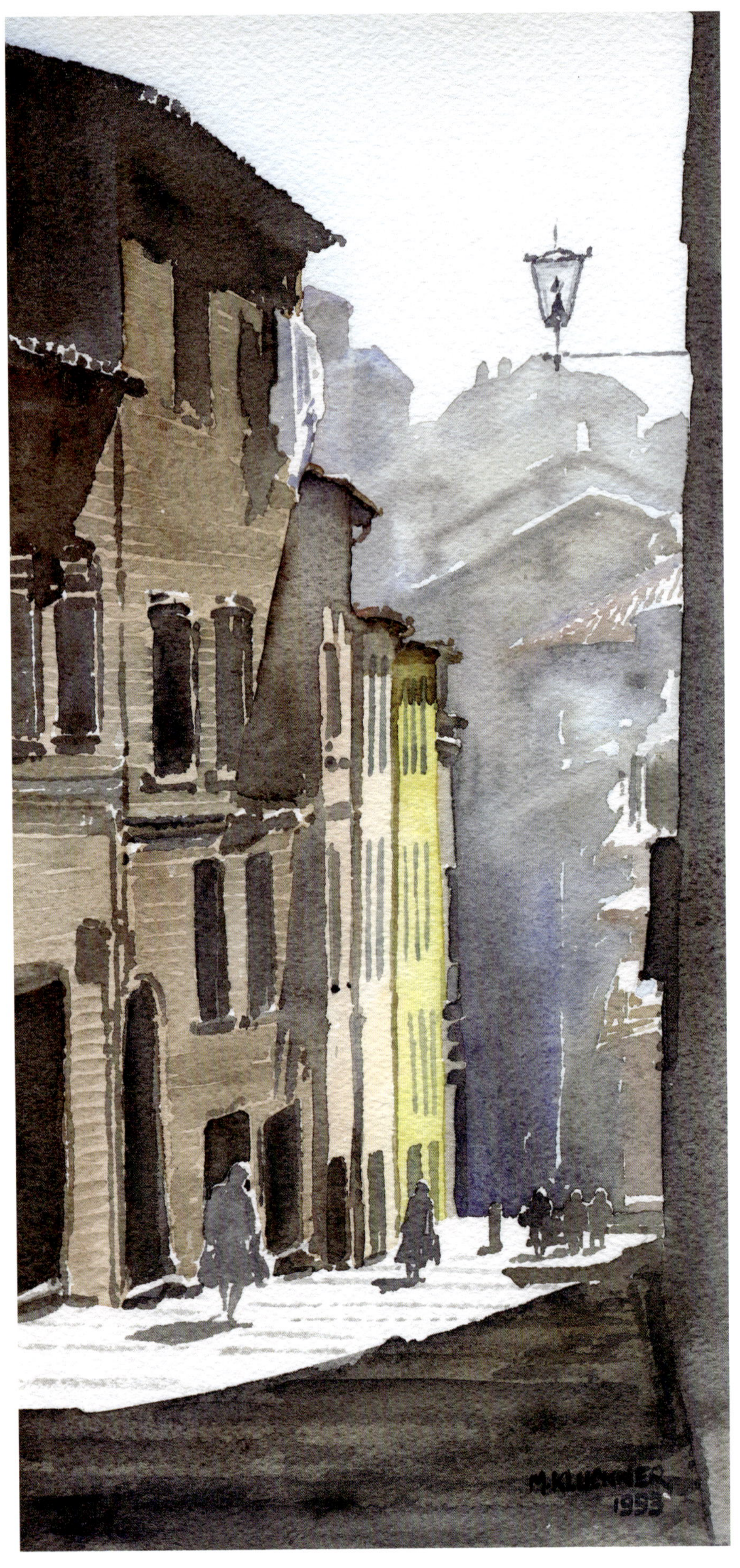

(Left) A street in Sienna, Italy in February 1993. The city was so well built and is so well maintained that it is difficult to come to terms with its great age – its famous Piazza del Campo and surrounding buildings date from the 13th and 14th centuries. Englishman Leigh Hunt wrote in the 1820s: "the first novelty that strikes you … is the singular fairness and new look of houses that have been standing for hundreds of years. This is owing to the dryness of the Italian climate. Antiquity refuses to look ancient in Italy." In-season, in July, the city is overwhelmed by spectators for the Palio – the famous horse race around the piazza.

(Right) Rocamadour is a dramatically sited village in the Lot region of southwestern France. We first visited it in 1986 and ignored the sniffy comments of the author of the *Blue Guide,* who noted that it was "commercialized" and "there are many who would prefer the distant view, the closer merely provoking disillusion. Celebrated in medieval times as a goal of pilgrimage, but for no intelligible reason, it was well promoted and visited by sundry saints and credulous monarchs, as it still is visited, particularly by unsophisticated Bretons, etc." This time, in 2016, I too preferred only the distant view.

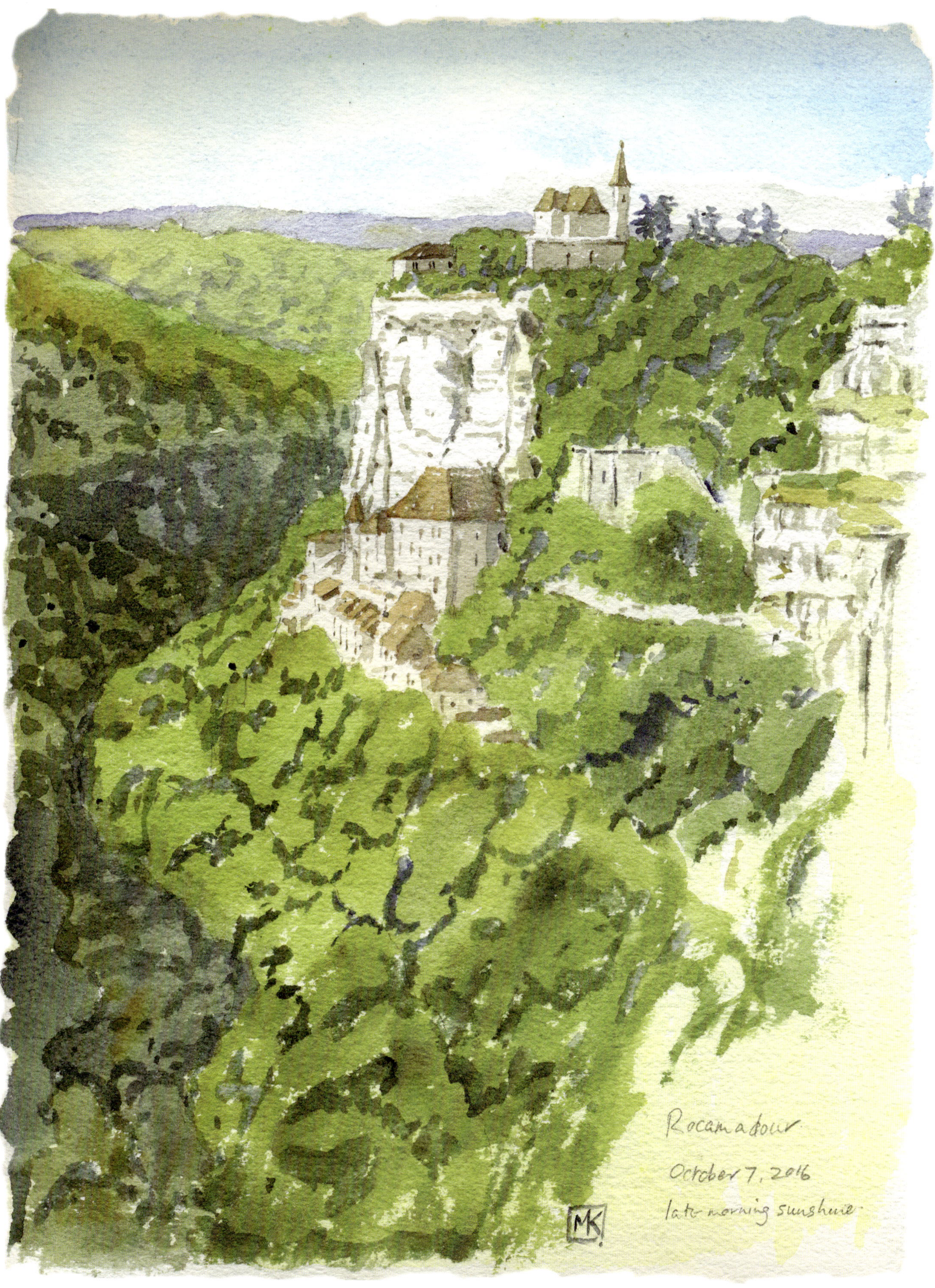
Rocamadour
October 7, 2016
late morning sunshine
MK

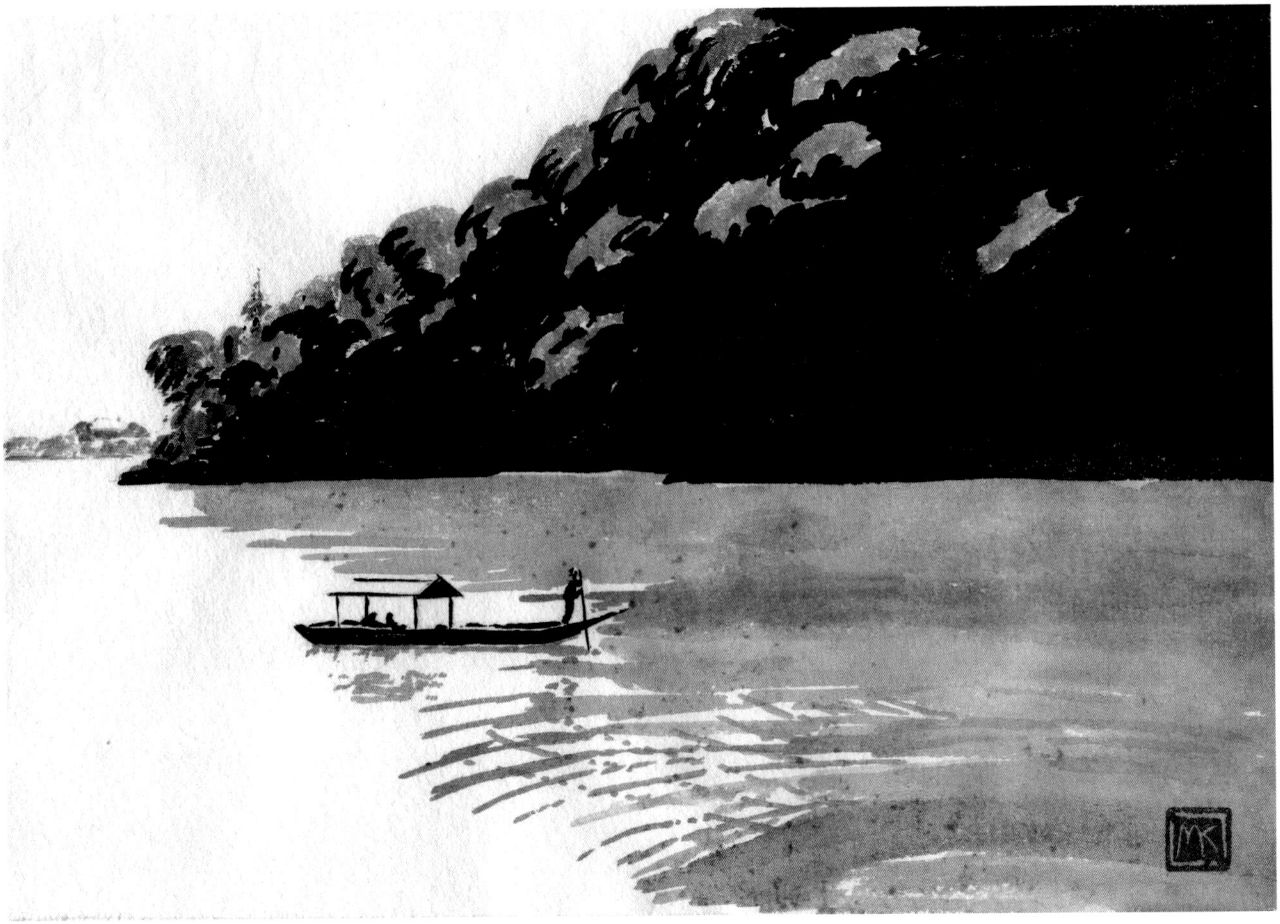

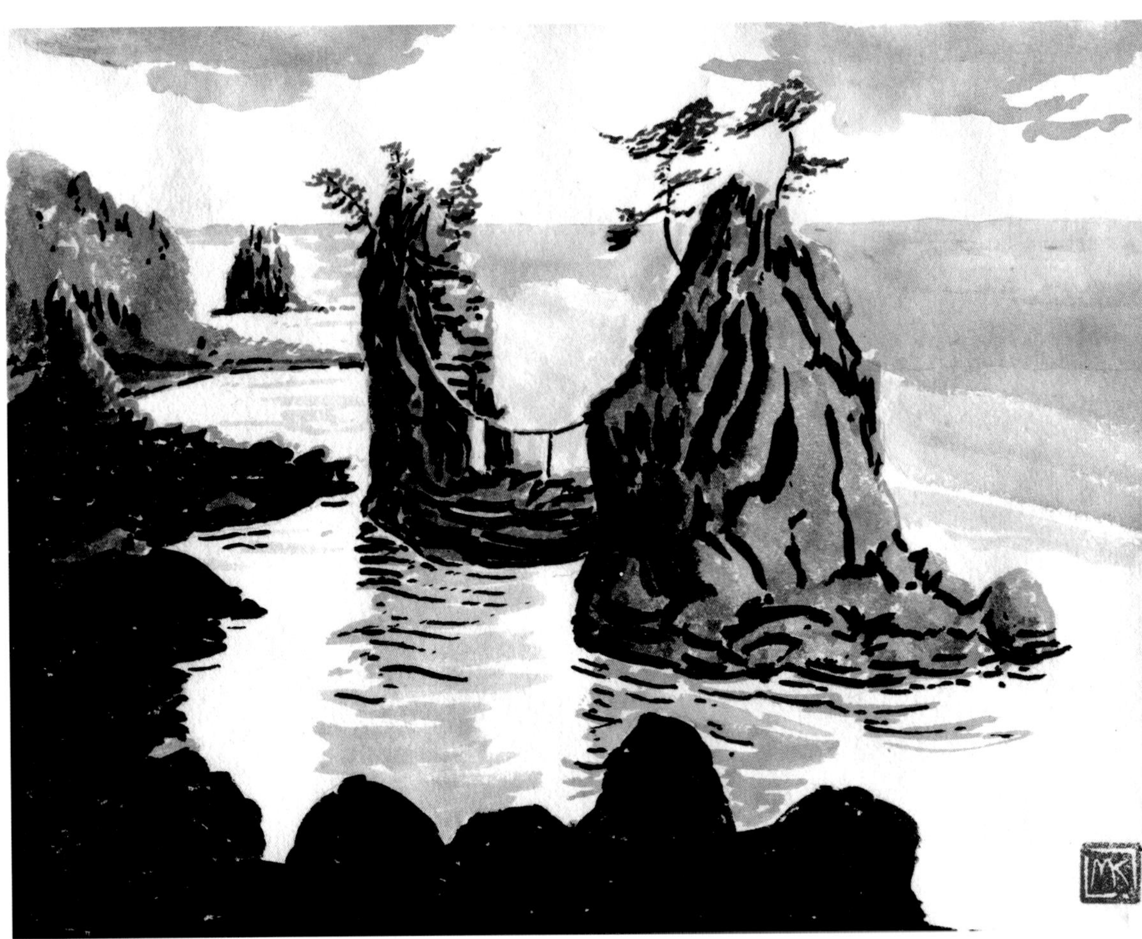

Timeless Japan, in 2019: grinding the *sumi* ink stick in a little water in the *suiboku* technique and painting on *washi* – traditional paper.

(Above) The Katsura-gawa River at Arashi-yama near Kyoto.

(Right) The Noto Peninsula north of Kanazawa on the Sea of Japan: the kind of wild landscape with contorted pines that became a subject for painters and the inspiration for classical Japanese gardens.

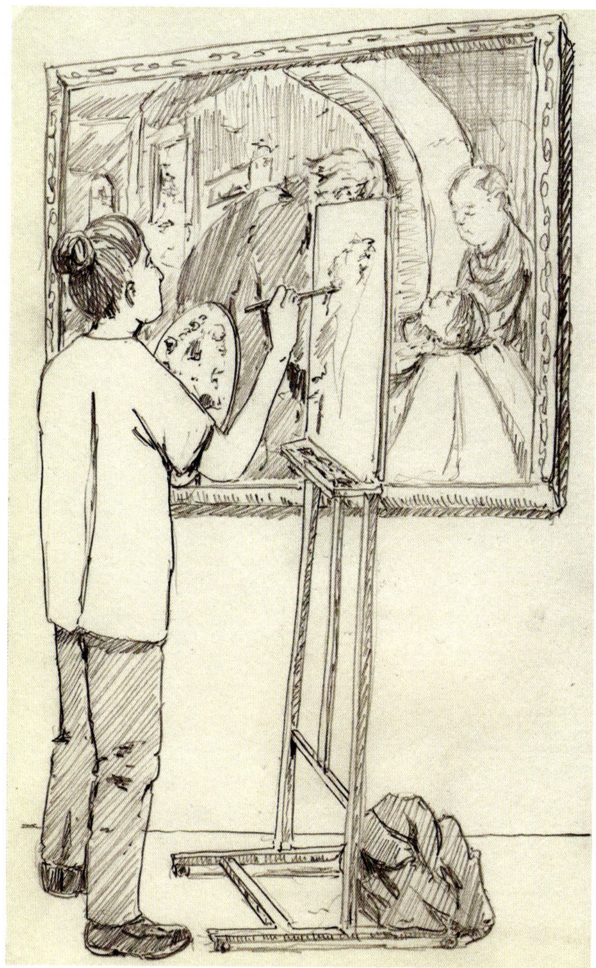

Art student in the Prado, Madrid, 2015, copying an "old master" oil painting and oblivious to me drawing him.

The importance of travel in our lives came into razor-sharp focus when the COVID-19 pandemic of 2020 clipped our wings. "Being gone" from time to time is an essential element of retaining sanity, and faith in humanity, regardless of whether we continue to live in turbocharged Vancouver.

I could have called this book *Home & Away* instead of *Here & Gone*, but so much of here is gone, and much of what is "away" is inaccessible and may remain so for years to come.

The impetus for this little book came when I committed to a show in the gallery at Vancouver's VanDusen Botanical Garden in the Spring of 2021, my first show in four years. I am grateful to Louis Anctil, the steadfast publisher of my recent graphic novels, and dedicate it to my beloved Christine – my constant companion for more than four decades.